"Guitarists and rock fans can rejoice that Eddie Van Halen's story has finally been told, accurately and with insights from those who knew him best. Tolinski and Gill compellingly unravel such details as the development of Ed's two-handed tapping technique and the Frankenstein guitar, and shed new light on every corner of Van Halen's life and prodigious artistry. It's a long-awaited and vital read about the most important and influential guitarist of the modern age."

—Christopher Scapelliti, Editor-in-Chief,
*Guitar Player* magazine

"Few journalists get a front-row seat to witness genius at work the way that Brad Tolinski and Chris Gill did over decades with Eddie Van Halen. In this comprehensive look at the late guitar virtuoso's art and artistry, the pair share everything they learned from the man himself."

—Kory Grow, *Rolling Stone*

ALSO BY BRAD TOLINSKI

*Light & Shade: Conversations with Jimmy Page*

*Play It Loud: An Epic History of the Style, Sound and Revolution of the Electric Guitar* (with Alan di Perna)

ALSO BY CHRIS GILL

*Guitar Legends:
The Definitive Guide to the World's Greatest Guitarists*

# ERUPTION

CONVERSATIONS WITH
## EDDIE VAN HALEN

BRAD TOLINSKI AND CHRIS GILL

hachette
BOOKS   NEW YORK

Hachette Books
Hachette Book Group
1290 Avenue of the Americas
New York, NY 10104
HachetteBooks.com
Twitter.com/HachetteBooks
Instagram.com/HachetteBooks

First Trade Paperback Edition: October 2022

Published by Hachette Books, an imprint of Perseus Books, LLC, a subsidiary of Hachette Book Group, Inc. The Hachette Books name and logo is a trademark of the Hachette Book Group.

The Hachette Speakers Bureau provides a wide range of authors for speaking events. To find out more, go to www.hachettespeakersbureau.com or call (866) 376-6591.

The publisher is not responsible for websites (or their content) that are not owned by the publisher.

Print book interior design by Jeff Williams

Library of Congress Control Number: 2021941651

ISBNs: 978-0-306-82665-8 (hardcover); 978-0-306-82667-2 (ebook), 978-0-306-82666-5 (trade paperback)

Printed in the United States of America

LSC-C

Printing 1, 2022

To Laura, who kept me safe and inspired
while a pandemic swept the land.

—BRAD TOLINSKI


To my wife, Jennifer, for her patience while I
was away in Hollywood, Atlanta, Bethel Woods,
and other parts of the US talking with Ed.

—CHRIS GILL

# CONTENTS

# CONTENTS

# CONTENTS

# OVERTURE

F OR THREE DECADES, starting in the late 1980s, Chris Gill
and I frequently found ourselves driving up the twisting roads
of the Hollywood Hills to Edward Van Halen's spectacularly
unspectacular 5150 recording studio, located just a short uphill jog from
his house. From the outside, the building looked more like an industrial
tool and die shop than a sexy rock and roll hideaway, but that no doubt
appealed to Ed's grungy, homemade aesthetic sensibility. It was his own
private hit factory—a place where he could be found every day, playing
guitar and composing tunes, some of which, he hoped, would one day
appear on Gold and Platinum discs.

When we'd pull into his driveway, we were greeted by the sight of Ed
waiting for us in his backyard, often chatting with his brother, Alex, or his
studio manager, Matt Bruck. Invariably, he would flash his famous smile
and wave us inside the studio.

Though not quite messy, 5150 definitely felt comfortably lived in,
with an array of banged-up guitars strewn about the floor and resting
on couches, disembodied guitar necks hanging on a wall, and stacks
of recording tape and CDs filled with snippets of ideas and song fragments spilling off shelves throughout. And there'd usually be an ashtray

overflowing with cigarette butts teetering on the edge of his recording console.

On occasion, Ed would sniff the air, rub his hands in eager anticipation, and in his distinctive, nicotine-stained rasp say, "Hmmm, smells like work in here." It was always a joke, and it was always true.

Because work is what he did—often for hours on end—writing songs, recording ideas, or futzing around endlessly with his guitars. As much as he was a musician Ed was also a revolutionary guitar designer and technician, and his workbench was forever crowded with parts on their way to being incorporated into his next great "Frankenstein" or tossed onto a scrap heap.

As a teenager growing up in Pasadena, California, Eddie spent much of his time in his bedroom, putting in the ten thousand hours of intensive practice that *Outliers* author Malcolm Gladwell insists is the key to success in any field. As an adult, his enormous artistic and commercial success notwithstanding, he remained that driven, curious teenager, spending those ten thousand hours and many more at 5150, which ultimately was just an infinitely more sophisticated version of the bedroom where he became Eddie Van Halen, once-in-a-generation guitar player and designer.

Both his childhood room and the studio were far more than places where he could work, practice, write, experiment. They were sanctuaries to which he could repair when the outside world annoyed him, angered him, or sometimes became too painful for him to deal with. At 5150, he was happy and in complete control. And it was his favorite hangout, the place where he spent the lion's share of his time with Van Halen.

It was in this laboratory—this land of loud amplifiers, misfit guitars, and where he recorded albums like *1984* and *OU812*—that I or my coauthor, Chris Gill, would shoot the breeze with Eddie. As players and veteran guitar journalists, we spoke his language, and he knew that we'd have a clear understanding of who he was as a musician and a human being.

So, it's hardly surprising that the first thing that flashed through our minds when, on October 6, 2020, we heard the terrible news that he had died of cancer was Ed playing guitar and recording at the studio, as vital as a man could be. It wasn't possible that such a force of nature was gone. Yet he was.

WHEN EDWARD VAN HALEN WAS alive, several books about him had already been published. Some were both informative and flattering; others, not so much on either score. A couple focused on Eddie, the young, inventive genius who early in his career seemed as if he could do no wrong. Others saw him as a star who was as emotionally fragile as he was confident onstage. Bandmate Sammy Hagar's account of their time together painted a darker picture of Ed, whom Hagar saw as gifted, brilliant, but also erratic and duplicitous.

But each of the books missed the bigger picture while at the same time neglecting to convey who Ed was at his core or to capture his essence.

Our intention with *Eruption: Conversations with Eddie Van Halen* is to present for the first time a panoramic view of the man considered to be the most inventive guitarist since Jimi Hendrix and perhaps the greatest rock player of all time. He was a unique phenomenon in the annals of pop music, a nonsinging instrumentalist whose enormous talents and charisma made him the dominant force in a band that sold more than eighty million records worldwide. He also singlehandedly changed the course of music for much of the eighties and nineties by reviving guitar-oriented music, whose primacy had been threatened by the synthesizer in New Wave and the sleek orchestrations of disco.

But Ed was more than "just" a guitarist whose radical approach to the instrument was so exciting—so *other*—that it bordered on the magical. He was also a brilliant songwriter and a world-class inventor. And in his personal life, few things were more important than his parents, brother, wife, and son.

Sadly, maybe inevitably, this smiling artist also struggled with his share of personal demons throughout much of his life and career. As a youngster, he was an immigrant child who, because he spoke no English, was the target of bullies. It was not difficult to see that this harrowing time was responsible for his lifelong debilitating social anxieties and insecurities. He was also the son of an alcoholic, and Ed struggled his entire life to tame his own addictions to alcohol, cocaine, and cigarettes.

For more than six decades, both sides of Eddie Van Halen—the light and the shade—wrestled each other, creating an often-unbearable amount of pressure that fueled his obsession with attaining greatness . . . and caused him to periodically self-destruct.

In this book, my coauthor and I strive to illuminate how these contradictory sides of the man came together to create one of the greatest musical minds of the twentieth century. How could a person who projected so much warmth and confidence onstage be beset by such demons? How could a man so totally disciplined from childhood, always brimming with creativity, throw so much of his life away on soul-crushing dependencies?

We had our theories, but we didn't really need them—because during our hours with him Ed always told the truth about himself. This was a man who was all too familiar with his soaring strengths and destructive weaknesses—destructive not only of himself but also of the people he loved most, those who always supported him.

In the following pages, we will take you on a tour of the dramatic arc of his complex and, ultimately, all-too-short life. This is the story of the remarkable rise of a great American artist, his excruciating fall, and his extraordinary redemption. It is also the story of his death, the pain of which was felt by the millions of fans around the world whose devotion to him and his art never wavered.

So, what we have here, what you'll find in this book, is the true essence of Eddie Van Halen. He knew exactly what it was. "We're musicians," Ed once said of himself and his band. "We make music for a living. It's that simple. Nothing else matters."

—BRAD TOLINSKI & CHRIS GILL

# 1

# CALIFORNIA
# DREAMING

*Edward Lodewijk Van Halen moved to Pasadena,
California, from his native Nijmegen, Holland, when
he was seven, along with his parents and his older
brother, Alex. When they arrived in 1962, they had
"fifty dollars and a piano."*

" We were like a kid freak show. "

I N 1982, VAN Halen was one of the largest rock bands in the world.
Starting with their 1978 debut on Warner Bros., each of their first
five albums went Platinum and peaked as high or higher on the
Billboard 200 Albums chart than its immediate predecessor. *Diver Down*,
released in 1982, produced their biggest Billboard Hot 100 hit, "(Oh)
Pretty Woman," thanks in large part to heavy airplay of its surprisingly
quirky video on MTV, the experimental cable music channel launched
just a few months earlier in 1981.

In the video, the band members appeared dressed as a samurai (bassist Michael Anthony), Tarzan (drummer Alex Van Halen), a cowboy

gunslinger (guitarist Eddie Van Halen), and Napoleon (singer David Lee Roth). They are called upon by a hunchback to rescue a girl (played by transgender entertainer International Chrysis) held captive by a pair of dwarves, who fondle her against her will. Falling somewhere between a wacky episode of *The Monkees* and a perverse John Waters arthouse film, the video carefully gave equal time to each member of Van Halen, establishing their individual personas while depicting the band's affability, chemistry, and off-the-wall humor.

The clip was ultimately banned from MTV for its depiction of two little people molesting a woman (actually a drag queen), but millions of fans saw it and loved it, as did hipsters who enjoyed the unexpectedly weird and edgy content. One thing was certain: Van Halen understood the promotional possibilities offered by the nascent MTV far better than most of their contemporaries. The "(Oh) Pretty Woman" video helped sell boatloads of records and placed the band at the vanguard of popular culture.

By the time Van Halen finished recording their next album two years later, their instincts about the cable channel had proved to be prophetic: MTV had become arguably the biggest driving force in the music industry.

Robert Lombard, who directed the "(Oh) Pretty Woman" video, remembered, "Once Van Halen got into MTV mode, they got into it. David Lee Roth was glued to the television. He threw something through his TV set one night because they'd dropped in rotation on MTV . . . they were obsessed. It was like a new drug."[1]

When it came time to film their next video to promote their new single "Jump," there was some disagreement about its content. Singer Roth wanted to create another surreal, larger-than-life fantasy similar to the "(Oh) Pretty Woman" video. And why not? It worked once . . .

However, director Robert Lombard and Pete Angelus, the band's road manager and lighting designer, had something different in mind. They wanted to buck the trend of big-budget videos produced at the time by artists like Madonna, Duran Duran, and Michael Jackson, envisioning something "more personal." Perhaps a simple performance clip showing what the guys did best: play music in their charming, knockabout fashion.

There was something joyous and life-affirming—Beatles-like—about Van Halen. Their chummy stage chemistry and rainbow-colored clothing made people feel good. From the unbridled way Alex Van Halen attacked his drum kit, to Michael Anthony's rowdy, everyman approach to playing bass, to David Lee Roth's breathtaking jump splits and gregarious stage patter, there was no other band in the world that projected such excitement and good-natured bonhomie. That went double for their virtuoso guitarist, Eddie Van Halen, whose shaggy exuberance recalled the joy of a Labrador retriever chasing a Frisbee.

Lombard and Angelus understood the power of the group's appeal perhaps better than Van Halen themselves, and they were determined to capture it in a simple performance video without any little people or clutter. But there was one thing they agreed would be essential: getting Eddie to smile.

Smiling was something Ed did naturally—and often—to great effect. Though he was unquestionably the most dynamic and innovative electric guitarist since Jimi Hendrix or Led Zeppelin's Jimmy Page, Edward's boyish grin was one of the things that distinguished Van Halen from other huge rock bands at the time, such as the menacing Judas Priest, Black Sabbath, and AC/DC. Unlike most guitar heroes who affected an anguished look during their solos, Ed performed his spellbindingly complex guitar parts while flashing that smile augmented with a hint of "gee whiz" bashfulness that made girls' hearts melt and guys want to be his best friend.

Even one of rock's most important guitarists and thoughtful observers, The Who's Pete Townshend, commented on Eddie's beatific countenance on more than a couple of occasions. "His smile was just classic," he said. "A man in his rightful place, so happy to be doing what he did. The Great American Guitar Player. I was hoping he might be president one day."

Released in January 1984, the music video for "Jump," directed by Angelus and Lombard, was exactly what they'd envisioned—a brilliant song, performed by a charismatic band, with no special effects (except for the guitarist's irresistible grin). "Jump" leaped up the charts and became Van Halen's most successful single, reaching number one on the US Billboard Hot 100, while the album *1984* went on to sell over ten million copies.

An irony: genuine and heartwarming though Ed's smile was, behind its brilliance lay a complicated life that was anything but joyous. You would never know it from watching his effervescent performance on

"Jump," but in the early eighties Ed was unhappy with many things, and because of this the band that appeared so brilliantly footloose before the cameras was actually dangling by a thread.

Yes, Ed was smiling through his problems. Then again, he was used to it—he'd been doing it for most of his life.

ALEX VAN HALEN WAS EIGHT years old and younger brother Eddie was seven when their father Jan announced that they were leaving their native Holland for California. The family had been struggling to make ends meet, and the boys' mother, Eugenia, thought it would be a good idea to leave their home in the town of Nijmegen to join her relatives in "the land of opportunity." But there were other reasons for their move to America.

Eugenia, who was of mixed Dutch and Southeast Asian ancestry, was considered a "half-breed" in the Netherlands, as were her children, and the prejudice against people of mixed descent was so strong that the Van Halens decided it would be better for their sons to leave the country and start fresh somewhere else.

It wasn't the first time prejudice and discrimination would impact the Van Halen family, and it wouldn't be the last.

JAN VAN HALEN WAS BORN in the Netherlands (informally, Holland) in 1920 and became obsessed with music at an early age. By the time he turned eighteen, he was playing saxophone and clarinet at a professional level and performing in jazz bands and orchestras throughout Europe. When World War II erupted in 1939, he enlisted in the Dutch Air Force and was assigned to play ceremonial and marching music in a military band.

However, when Germany invaded Holland in 1940, it conquered the small country in just five days and all Dutch soldiers were conscripted to fight for Germany. Those who resisted were shot on the spot. Jan was reassigned to play propaganda music for the Third Reich, which he detested, but it was preferable to taking a bullet in the head or fighting in the trenches for Hitler.

After the war ended, instead of returning home he traveled to Indonesia, a large Southeast Asian island nation that had been under Dutch colonial rule since 1815. Work for musicians was relatively plentiful there, and it was where he met and, on August 11, 1950, married Eugenia van Beers.

The couple attempted to make a home there, but once again geopolitics intervened. After World War II, the Netherlands attempted to reestablish colonial rule in Indonesia, but a bitter armed struggle ensued, ending in December 1949 when, in the face of international pressure, the Dutch formally recognized Indonesian independence.

Indonesians subsequently became increasingly hostile to any Dutch residents, which made it difficult for Jan to find work. He decided it was best for him and the pregnant Eugenia to return to Holland, and on March 4, 1953, they left for Amsterdam. Two months later, on May 8, Alexander Arthur (Alex) was born, followed by his brother, Edward Lodewijk (Eddie), on January 26, 1955.

But just as the family was regarded with great suspicion by Indonesian nationals for being Dutch, Eugenia felt the brutal sting of discrimination in Holland for being half Asian, and she worried that her young boys would be victimized by what she described as the same "horrifying" treatment. So, on March 9, 1962, despite knowing almost no English, the family packed their bags and moved to America on a jammed steamship, sleeping in the lowest, cheapest quarters.

In their possession were a few suitcases, seventy-five Dutch guilders (the equivalent of about fifteen dollars at the time), and a piano made by the Dutch-owned Rippen Company. Given their circumstances, it seems odd that they dragged a piano halfway around the world, but both Edward and Alexander had been taking lessons from the time each was six, and their parents had dreams that they would grow up to become respected classical musicians. So, the family made the difficult decision to bring the piano with them.

It was a nine-day boat ride, and to help pay their fare, Jan, Edward, and Alexander, the boys on piano, provided the ship's musical entertainment. It would be nice to imagine their experience as something out of a quaint 1930s musical, but the Van Halens' financial situation was dire, and Jan and the kids were busking for their very survival.

"We were like a kid freak show," Eddie remembered. "Dad would pass the hat, and we'd make an extra twenty dollars."

Once in New York, the family took a four-day train ride across the country to Pasadena, California, to be near relatives who'd emigrated before them. With the money they earned on the ship, Jan and Eugenia were able to afford a cramped house they shared with two other families until they could get on their feet.

Pasadena, located eleven miles northeast of Downtown Los Angeles, is perhaps best known for its Tournament of Roses Parade, an annual event that marks the start of the Rose Bowl college football game held on New Year's Day. But when the Van Halens arrived, the city was also a major West Coast industrial hub after its transformation during World War II into a research and manufacturing center for scientific and electronic precision instruments, and by the time the fifties rolled around, almost four hundred such firms were headquartered in the city. Add the Arroyo Seco Parkway, which provided a fast and direct route to Los Angeles, and Pasadena was an inexpensive and attractive place to live for people who worked in LA.

During the postwar boom, newcomers flocked to the city in droves, and Pasadena saw a steady influx of African Americans from Texas and Louisiana, as well as a large immigrant community, particularly people from China, Japan, Indonesia, and other Southeast Asian countries.

But despite the opportunities afforded by what was a boomtown, work was difficult to come by for Jan and Eugenia, who barely spoke English. While Jan desperately searched for jobs as a musician, he often had to make do with janitorial work and washing dishes.

"My dad didn't know the language and was unable to drive a car, because in Holland you rode bicycles," said Ed. "He often had to walk six miles to work, because in the beginning we couldn't even afford a bicycle."

Whereas things were tough for their parents, Ed and Alex's early days in America were almost as grim. "It was beyond frightening," said Eddie. "We had to go to school, and Al and I didn't know anything about anything. We were two outcasts, so we became best friends and learned to stick together."

The first school the boys attended was segregated, with students of color relegated to one side of the playground and white kids on the other. Since they spoke no English, the Van Halens were grouped in with the black and brown kids.

As Ed confided in a 2004 interview, "My first friends in America were black. It was actually the white kids that bullied me. They would tear up my homework and papers, make me eat playground sand, all those things. The black kids stood up for me."

Alex, the more extroverted of the two boys, made the best of a bad situation and worked hard to fit in. But his extremely sensitive younger brother retreated into his own world—the world of music. While words often failed him, as a child Edward expressed himself through the piano, which he studied with a strict Russian-born instructor, maintaining a rigorous practice schedule under the watchful eye of his mother. That discipline and the obvious fact that he'd inherited his father's musical gifts led Eddie, at the age of nine, to defeat thousands of other kids in local classical music competitions.

A few short years later, at the age of twelve, he would apply the same diligence to learning the electric guitar, spending countless hours locked in his bedroom developing the technique that would help him become one of the greatest players in the world.

For all Ed's later incredible success, the pain of those early years never left him, especially his discomfort in social situations and his fear of ridicule. But the things that helped him deal with his childhood difficulties—his unyielding determination, his belief in the power of family, and his unique ability to channel his emotions in his playing—also remained with him. Music and his family, said Ed, "saved us." During this time, an inextricable bond with his brother also formed. "Our struggle to make it in America made us stronger, because you had to be."

And though he had been traumatized in his youth, Ed learned to smile through it all. Perhaps David Lee Roth was thinking of the Van Halen brothers when he wrote "You got to roll with the punches to get to what's real" in the buoyant "Jump." It was certainly something Alex and Eddie could identify with, and it was that vibe the cameras captured in the song's iconic video.

**You started off on piano.**
Alex and I both started playing at age six. We had to learn to play piano because that was the "respectable" instrument to play. It was my mom's dream that if we were going to be musicians, at least be respectable. We were seriously being trained to be concert pianists, like Vladimir Horowitz, that type of deal.

When we moved to the States, my parents did their best to find a really happening concert pianist teacher. They found this older guy, Stasys Kalvaitis, who had studied at one of the top conservatories in Russia [the Imperial Conservatory in Saint Petersburg]. He didn't speak a word of English, and he would just sit there with a ruler ready to smack us if we made a mistake. He would have us practice all year for this contest they had at Long Beach City College. I actually won first place three years in a row, but I *hated* it. I never learned how to read. I always fooled the teacher. He'd play the song for me first and I'd watch his fingers and learn the piece by ear. I could read a little, but never like Al.

**So, you won the competitions by "faking it"?**

Yeah, I guess I was blessed with good enough ears to pull it off. I won first prize out of two thousand kids, and the judges would make remarks like, "Hmm, very interesting interpretation of Mozart." And I'd think, "Oh, shit, I thought I was playing it right!" But I guess they got off on the fact that I put myself into it.

**An important part of playing classical music is the performer's interpretation.**

Oh, exactly. That's why my favorite pianist was always Horowitz. He had such a great sense of humor in his playing—he always put his own spin on Bach or Chopin or whatever he was performing. Segovia was the same way. He created his own interpretations of the classics for guitar, and people who just copy his transcriptions note for note miss the point. You're supposed to find your own voice.

I think that's why when I found the guitar, I refused to take lessons. I was going to do my own thing and find my personal emotional release, and I didn't want to be told how to approach the instrument.

**What about the guitar appealed to you? Is it because on the guitar you can bend the strings and get in between those tempered notes found on the piano?**

Absolutely. With a guitar you can bend or use vibrato to reach all those microtonal notes and those feelings that fall between the cracks on the piano. The same is true of any fretless stringed instrument, like the violin and the cello—just listen to Yo-Yo Ma play the Bach cello suites.

Actually, I've been playing a lot of cello lately—you'll probably hear some on one of our albums in the future. And at this point, I'm finding it a little too easy to fall through those cracks—a lot more than I want to! (*laughs*)

But back to your point, the guitar is such an expressive instrument because, like being with a woman, your touch is everything. You can play it angry or you can massage it sexy—how it responds depends on your touch. There's a touch involved in piano, but you're not actually touching the strings. So, there's an agent in between you and the strings—a middleman. On the other hand, I'm not sure I'd really want to hear somebody bend the strings on a piano, but it'd be fun to watch them try!

**You also played violin.**

Yeah, for about three years. Al did, too. That was at the end of elementary school and the beginning of junior high. It was school-based stuff. Al actually made All City Orchestra on violin. I never did. I didn't like the music they made me play, so I just started messing around with it and lost interest.

**You did smuggle a bit of Kreutzer's famous *Etude No. 2* for the violin into your solo in "Eruption."**

(*laughs*) It was a bit of a joke.

**Music was an important part of your family.**

Playing music is what *saved* our family. My father, mother, brother, and I came here with fifty dollars and a piano. In the beginning, we lived in one room, shared a bathroom with two other families, but we were able to get our own place because my dad made extra money by playing gigs on weekends.

**How long did you study piano?**

My interest in playing the piano didn't hold water for long after we went to the United States, although I kept playing until I was twelve.

**Is that when the guitar and the idea of playing rock and roll come into the picture?**

Yeah. It's really funny because before we came to the United States we were right across the water from England during the time of the Beatles, the Dave Clark Five, and all the British Invasion bands, but it wasn't until we moved to America that I heard them. Once we moved here, I got into rock and roll, which eventually led to me giving up playing piano when I was twelve.

But even before I started playing guitar, Alex and I formed a little rock band that we called the Broken Combs when I was in the fourth or fifth grade. He played saxophone and I played piano, and we wrote a couple of original songs called "Boogie Booger" and "Rumpus."

**You played drums for a short while.**

I played drums before Alex. I had a paper route to pay for the drums because my parents couldn't afford it. But while I was out throwin' papers, my brother played my drums and he got better at it. When he gave up piano, my mother and dad coerced him into taking flamenco guitar lessons, so we had a guitar around the house. He kept playing my drums, and when he got better, I started playing his guitar. That was the real beginning of Van Halen—that's where it all started.

**Your playing is pianistic in some ways. You can hear an influence from the way you use chords and the way you use both hands on the fretboard.**

I'm a very rhythmic player. I think it's just inherently built in, although I guess it subconsciously comes from piano, which is a percussion instrument. When I was growing up and listening to bands like the Dave Clark Five, the groove was what initially got me going. I really liked that funky, heavy groove on songs like "Bits and Pieces" and "Glad All Over." The only reason why I stopped playing drums was because my brother got better than me, so I said, "Fuck you, I'll play your guitar!" If you have enough dexterity in your fingers to play keyboards and drums, you can play anything.

And obviously, you have to have rhythm. If you have rhythm, then you can play anything you need. If you have rhythm and you love music, then play and play and play until you get to where you want to get. If you can pay the rent, great. If you can't, then you'd better be having fun. Playing guitar is the only thing I ever knew how to do.

**Was shifting to the guitar from piano easy?**

The piano is the universal instrument. When you start there, learn your theory and how to read, you can go on to any other instrument. Without sounding egotistical, I was always a natural player. My father was a professional musician his entire life, and he told me, "Kid, you've got it." Some people do and some people don't. There's a difference between those that have "the feel" and those that don't, and I'm not sure if it's something you can learn. You can really hear the difference in classical music. I've heard examples of two pianists play the same piece by Debussy that were like night and day. Both could play the notes, but one made every note sound beautiful, and the other was like noise to my ears—like they had lead fingers.

**Do you think your dad would've preferred you play violin or piano instead of guitar?**

It's hard to say exactly what he wanted us to be. He just wanted us to be successful in life. I think deep down he wanted us to be musicians, but it was my mom who really cracked the whip and wanted us to be proper musicians. She didn't want us to struggle playing nightclubs like our dad.

The whole time I was growing up, whenever I didn't practice or when I started playing guitar, my mom used to call me a "nothing nut, just like your father." When you grow up that way, it's not conducive for self-esteem.

**In addition to the Dave Clark Five, what are some other songs or bands that caught your ear when you were a kid?**

There were quite a few. The first solo I ever learned on the guitar was from the song "Pushin' Too Hard" by The Seeds. They were a Stonesy garage band from the mid-sixties. When Alex and I heard it on the radio for the first time, I thought, "What the hell is he doing?" American bands usually didn't play guitar solos in those days, but it was very tasty, with lots of sustain and distortion. I didn't know he was using a fuzz box, and when I found out, it didn't matter because I couldn't afford one anyway. So, I went home and just turned the volume up to ten and realized, "Hey, this natural distortion sounds even better."

The Kinks' guitar riffs would also just tear through your car speakers. They sounded so powerful at the time and they still hold up. I liked "All Day and All of the Night" even more than "You Really Got Me"—especially that wood-chop snare that rocked it along. I heard that [Kinks singer-songwriter] Ray Davies told *Guitar World* that I did the riff from "You Really Got Me" better than they did. I don't want to claim it was an updated version, but ours sounded more like a jet plane as opposed to a prop. But the prop version is the classic, Ray. The prop is the real shit.

"It's My Life" by The Animals was another one. (*sings*) "It's my life and I'll do what I want . . . don't push me!" If that ain't rebellion, I don't know what is. The Animals would have these great bass riff intros, followed by a bluesy verse, capped with big, anthemic choruses, like on this song and on "We Gotta Get Out of This Place." Emotionally, I just dug those lyrics.

**What about the Beatles?**
I liked *Abbey Road*. It takes you for a ride, and the song "I Want You (She's So Heavy)" takes you on a ride within that ride. Those monster riffs seem to go on forever and then just drop you off a cliff, and Lennon's singing is just so passionate.

**Did you see many concerts when you were growing up?**
The first concert I ever saw was Derek and the Dominos with Eric Clapton at the Pasadena Civic Auditorium [November 21, 1970]. A friend of mine won two tickets from a local radio station and, knowing what a Clapton fan I was, gave them to me and Al. The show wasn't sold out when I got there, so I paid a little extra money, upgraded my tickets, and ended up in the sixth row. It was great, even though I wasn't into Clapton as much as I'd been when he was in Cream. I was still carrying a torch for him, but it was wavering a bit. (*laughs*)

To be honest with you, I was expecting something more powerful. If I would've seen Cream, I probably would've been blown away, because that's the era of Clapton that I really loved. The show I saw was more of a Doobie Brothers kind of thing—there was, like, this tambourine and bongo player. The power wasn't there.

I don't want to knock Clapton. It's just that he had shifted gears and I didn't like it as much. But in spite of all that, Al and I tried to get backstage—we were just hoping to see Eric walk by. Unfortunately, he had left already, but we did get to meet the tambourine player! Swear to God! Al and I cracked up because the guy actually had a little flight case for his tambourine. I'm not kidding. (*laughs*)

**Were there any shows that lived up to your expectations?**
Oh yeah. Grand Funk used to kick ass live! I loved Grand Funk. I can still play all of their stuff. Black Sabbath, too. People may think this is weird, but Jethro Tull was pretty happening then—the Thick as a Brick tour was amazing!

**What was your biggest "takeaway" from those early years?**
My dad gave me the best advice. He said if I make a mistake, just keep going . . . or do it again and people will think you did it on purpose. (*laughs*)

# 2

# RIOT ON
# THE SUNSET STRIP

*Van Halen emerge from the backyards of suburban
Pasadena to become kings of the Hollywood club scene.*

---

" Stop! I hired you to play Top 40. What is this shit?! "

ON THURSDAY, APRIL 4, 1974, Eddie Van Halen walked
onstage for Van Halen's first official gig at Gazzarri's, an
all-ages nightclub on West Hollywood's Sunset Strip.
Temporarily blinded by the overhead stage lights as he peered into the
crowd, once Ed's eyes adjusted to the glare, he was dismayed to see
nothing but an empty dance floor before him.

Brushing off the disappointing turnout, Ed unleashed a vicious flurry
of notes from his Gibson Les Paul, with singer David Lee Roth whoop-
ing and hollering as the band ripped into Deep Purple's "Hallelujah," the
first song of four 45-minute sets they played that night. By evening's end,
only four people had shown up to hear the band perform cover versions
of songs by Bad Company, the James Gang, and ZZ Top—and all were
friends the band had put on the club's guest list.

Fortunately, turnout improved for the band's appearances over the weekend, and at the end of the Sunday night show Bill Gazzarri came backstage with a seventy-five-dollar cash payment for their first run. The money was barely enough to cover gas, parking, chili dog dinners, and liquid refreshments for the four nights, but the band dutifully showed up again the next week to play another four nights in a row with the same energy and enthusiasm.

Van Halen went on to become Gazzarri's house band for June, August, and September that year, and by January 14, 1977, when they performed their last gig at the club, they'd played more than 140 shows at this Sunset Strip hot spot.

LOOKING BACK, IT'S SHOCKING THAT the band managed to wiggle their way into one gig at the club, let alone 140. When Van Halen first auditioned for owner Gazzarri, he was far from impressed.

He complained that Eddie was too loud, and he hated that everyone except the lead singer was dressed casually in T-shirts and jeans. To his eyes, they looked like hippies in an era when flamboyant glitter-rock fashion was becoming de rigueur.

The critique of their appearance was especially surprising to the group. Gazzarri, who called himself the "Godfather of Rock and Roll," dressed like a sixties B-movie version of a Chicago mobster and seemed like the furthest thing from "cool." His gaunt forty-nine-going-on-seventy facial features made him look like an out-of-touch grandpa to four young guys who hadn't yet reached legal drinking age. Regardless of his eccentric personal style, the club owner had his ear to the ground and was a canny judge of youth culture and what would fill his venue.

Van Halen were disappointed when he told them to beat it, but they didn't give up—they couldn't. Playing backyard beer bashes and high school dances was all well and good, but Roth knew the group desperately needed to break into the Hollywood club scene. Nobody was going to discover them in some dive bar in Pomona—the Sunset Strip was the place to be.

"Gazzarri's was where all the heat was coming from," said Roth. "And Bill had all these dancing girls—the Gazzarri dancers, go-go girls. I determined that his club was the next step, our entrée to Hollywood."[2]

But it wasn't that easy. The band groveled for a second audition and struck out again. Roth panicked, unsure of what their next move was going to be, when, miraculously, the quartet's luck changed.

Two young bookers, Mark Algorri and Mario Miranda, hired to scout bands by—of all people—the cigar-chomping Gazzarri, happened to see Van Halen perform to a packed room at Pasadena City College. They could see the excitement the group generated, and they were certain that the Hollywood kids would love them, too. They talked the reluctant Gazzarri into giving Van Halen a third shot—but this time playing a few nights for people from their own element.

After witnessing an early evening set at his club, attended by a small but enthusiastic crowd, Gazzarri finally relented. Why he changed his mind is unknown, but it's likely that he detected a certain "teen idol" charm in David and Eddie from the way girls in the audience crowded right in front of the stage. For business reasons—and, it was said, a personal fixation—the club owner aspired to fill his venue with attractive girls. He knew that where the girls were, the boys would follow, with spending money in hand, so he also hired sexy go-go girls and hosted female dance contests that offered cash prizes.

In Van Halen's case, Gazzarri's instincts proved correct. As word of mouth spread from Hollywood to the beaches of Santa Monica and beyond, thousands of young women, including blonde-haired surfer chicks, UCLA college co-eds, and fans from their Pasadena hometown, flocked to the club. Most came to see either Dave, the lean and lascivious singer who would escort them to the back seat of his car, or Eddie, the phenomenally talented guitarist and somewhat shy nice guy they wanted to take home to meet their parents.

"The girls would always say to me, 'Godfather, could you introduce me to Eddie?'" recalled Gazzarri, who died in 1991. "Eddie was the quiet one, but he was the most popular. [He] would be on one side of the stage, and every week that we played 'em here, there would be at least fifty girls who would come and pay and sit on Eddie's side all night long."[3]

After packing the house for a few hundred Hollywood gigs at places like Gazzarri's and the Starwood over the next few years, the band finally managed to catch the attention of Warner Bros. and landed a record deal. But the question remains: Why did it take *so fucking long?*

THE ANSWER IS A BIT complicated. In the mid-seventies, the rock and roll scene on the Sunset Strip was a mere shadow of what it had been in its heyday. Nearly a decade had passed since the Strip's initial rock and roll peak in 1966, when bands like The Byrds, Buffalo Springfield, The Doors, and Love catapulted to fame after making the rounds on the legendary Los Angeles club scene. During the psychedelic sixties, almost every night of the week hundreds—if not thousands—of teenagers jam-packed the sidewalks between Doheny Drive and Larrabee Street, where clubs like the Whisky a Go Go, Pandora's Box, Ciro's, and the Central (now the Viper Room) were located.

It was a virtual Mardi Gras in the streets nearly every evening, but when local residents and merchants complained, the Los Angeles City Council enacted strict curfew and loitering laws. Young music fans, band members, and a few club owners felt that the curfew was a violation of the kids' civils rights, and a protest was organized for Saturday, November 12, 1966. That night, a crowd of about a thousand demonstrators clashed with police officers in an encounter now known as the "riot on the Sunset Strip."

In its aftermath, the city rescinded the youth permits of twelve clubs, limiting attendance to audiences over twenty-one; predictably, profits dropped sharply and several venues closed. By the early seventies, the Strip was a ghost town, and kids almost abandoned nightclubs altogether in favor of attending larger rock concerts at theaters and arenas.

Meanwhile, Hollywood nightclubs booked only up-and-coming national acts or local artists like Jackson Browne, the Eagles, Linda Ronstadt, and Buckingham Nicks, showcasing a mellow sound that appealed to more mature audiences.

If you were a Los Angeles record executive in the seventies, Hollywood clubs became the place you went to scout introverted singer-songwriters like J. D. Souther or to discover the next James Taylor. If you were looking for the next great hard rock band like Led Zeppelin, Bad Company, or Aerosmith, it probably wouldn't have even occurred to you to look in your own backyard.

EDDIE VAN HALEN WAS ONLY eleven years old when the Sunset Strip riot took place in the mid-sixties, and he probably wasn't even aware of its occurrence. Ed and Al were still living in their suburban home, studying classical piano under the strict supervision of their mother, Eugenia. Although the boys were progressing, neither particularly enjoyed the music they were forced to learn; they were far more attracted to the rock and roll they heard on the radio. But their rigorous formal study of the piano—which taught them rhythm, harmony, left- and right-hand independence, and, more generally, the diligence required of any musician—would serve them well down the line.

Alex drifted to the guitar, while Ed took to the drums. Eventually, they decided to trade—or at least Ed was forced to take the guitar when his older brother became more interested in pounding the skins.

"When I first picked up the guitar there was no message from God or anything," Eddie told *Guitar World* writer Steven Rosen. "Some things were easy and some things were hard. But I didn't even think about whether it was easy or hard; it was something I wanted to do, to have fun and feel good about doing it. Whether it took me a week to learn a half a song or one day to learn five songs, I never thought of it that way."

Those days and weeks became years, and he continued to improve. "I used to sit on the edge of my bed with a six-pack of Schlitz Malt talls," he said. "My brother would go out at seven p.m. to party and get laid, and when he'd come back at three a.m., I'd still be sitting in the same place, playing guitar."

Ed bought his first electric six-string—a Teisco Del Rey WG-4L—from the Sears department store with money he earned delivering newspapers. The inexpensive Japanese guitar was a good beginner's instrument, but Ed soon discovered that its four pickups and confusing array of switches were much more than he needed.

One day in 1968, Ed walked into Lafayette Electronics on Colorado Boulevard in downtown Pasadena and saw a red-and-black sunburst hollow body thinline Univox Custom twelve-string electric. The instrument looked similar to the cool guitars his neighborhood friends like Bill Maxwell were playing, but the only problem was that it was a twelve-string model and Ed wanted a six-string. He purchased it anyway and removed all of the upper-octave strings to convert it to a standard guitar.

"That was my very, very first successful attempt at changing something on a guitar that was not up to my liking," said Edward. "Since the beginning, everything I picked up off the rack at a music store—even the expensive stuff—did not do what I wanted it to do. Either it didn't have enough of something, or it had a bunch of Bozo bells and whistles that I didn't need. A lot of it had to do with the fact that I never took guitar lessons, so I didn't know right from wrong. I didn't know there were rules. I just knew what I liked and wanted to feel and hear."

Meanwhile, Eugenia Van Halen was less than thrilled that the boys were losing interest in the piano the family had gone through so much trouble transporting to California, but their musician father was much more understanding. After seeing Ed's and Al's enthusiasm for guitar and drums, respectively, he decided to encourage their interest by buying them the instruments they wanted to play. In August 1969, Jan took his kids to a store called Music for Everyone, in Sierra Madre, California, and bought a $200 Cooper drum kit made in Japan by Pearl for Alex and a brand-new $400 gold top Gibson Les Paul Standard for Ed, making a $143 down payment for both that included a $20 bill and $123 in trade-in credit for a Bundy flute and Ed's Univox guitar.

Any kid would've been thrilled to own such a beautiful guitar, but as would be the case throughout his entire life, Ed found things about it that weren't quite up to his exacting standards. He was soon disappointed to discover that the gold top's single-coil P90 soapbar pickups didn't deliver the same fat, harmonically rich tone as the dual-coil humbucking pickups found on the Les Paul guitars and Gibson SG played by his hero, British blues virtuoso Eric Clapton.

Clapton, who played on Ed's favorite albums by Cream and the Blues Breakers, was one of the only players Ed would ever idolize, and replicating his sound on songs like "Crossroads," "I'm So Glad," and "Sunshine of Your Love" became a sort of sonic Holy Grail for the teen.

"Eric Clapton while he was in Cream is the only guitarist that really influenced me," Edward said hundreds of times over the years. "He was the one that made me want to pick up a guitar. He just basically took a Gibson guitar and plugged it straight into a Marshall, and that was it. His solos were always melodic and memorable. After Cream broke up, I pretty much took what I learned from him and went my own way."

Rather than bitch and moan about what he perceived were his guitar's deficiencies, Ed altered his Les Paul by taking a chisel to the new instrument and installed a humbucking pickup in the bridge position himself. He also removed the cover on the neck-position P90 pickup to increase its output. He later took what others would regard as a desecration further when he decided he wasn't a fan of the instrument's gold finish, so he stripped it and repainted the guitar black. The modifications gave Edward more of what he wanted and were a hint of things to come.

MODIFYING A GUITAR WITH NEW or spare parts was a radical idea in the early seventies, but it was easy to see where Ed might've gotten his inspiration, consciously or not. Southern California was the birthplace of hot rod culture, where backyard car mechanics, working with junkyard parts, would compete with each other to see who could make the fastest or coolest car.

His Pasadena hometown was filled with these DIY mechanics, and custom cars were literally everywhere. Don Blair's legendary Speed Shop, one of the first dealers to sell custom parts in Southern California, was located less than two miles from where Ed grew up, and many teenagers in his neighborhood were transforming and improving their old cars by inserting different engines, painting the bodies, and adding racing stripes. Replacing a pickup or painting his guitar black probably seemed like no big deal by comparison.

And after he had fabricated a guitar he wanted, the next critical event that enabled Ed to become a serious tinkerer took place in 1970, when, to make the remaining payments on the Les Paul, he took a job moving pianos and organs for Pasadena's Berry & Grassmueck Music Co.

While working there, a full Marshall stack consisting of a 100-watt amplifier head and two speaker cabinets, each with four 12-inch speakers, appeared in the store's showroom. The Marshall was previously the house amp at Pasadena's Rose Palace, which had recently stopped presenting rock concerts. It was the exact same type of amplifier played by Jimi Hendrix, Led Zeppelin's Jimmy Page, and, of course, Eric Clapton.

At the time, Marshall amps were a scarce commodity in the United States, with a new stack selling for about $1,500 on the rare occasions they appeared on the market. Thanks to his employee's discount, Ed paid less than that for the used amp, although he had to work throughout his high school years to pay off the debt.

A Gibson Les Paul and Marshall stack were the preeminent electric guitar rig of the late sixties and seventies. Equipped with his now-formidable gear and boasting prodigious playing skills, Ed began forming bands, including one he and Alex named the Trojan Rubber

Company—later changed to the more commercially viable Space Brothers for gigs at the Saint James United Methodist Church—and another named Genesis.

Playing the guitar was a hobby for most of his musician pals, but for Ed it was everything. His ability to master Cream's difficult "Crossroads" note for note was more than an accomplishment, it was an immigrant's passport to friendship, acceptance, and respect. When he got up to play the latest Black Sabbath song at a backyard party, he was no longer that "quiet freak from Holland" who struggled in class—he was a genuine high school superstar.

Playing in a band was also a balm for his social anxiety. As long as he was onstage and his Marshall stack was turned up to 10, he could be with his friends without actually having to awkwardly interact with them. "I'm actually a shy, nervous person," he told *Rolling Stone* in 1998. "I used to be easily intimidated. That's why I used to drink."

At first, the bands were formed from a loose collection of friends, including Dennis Travis or Kevin Ford on bass, Bill Maxwell on guitar, and singer Gary Booth, with Ed and Alex (who had upgraded his drums to a Ludwig kit that included double bass drums) as the mainstays. When Mark Stone joined Genesis on bass in the spring of 1971, the band became a power trio featuring Ed as lead singer. A short while later, after learning of the existence of a British band called Genesis, they changed their name to Mammoth.

Genesis/Mammoth mostly played songs that featured extended instrumental jams, including covers of Cream's "Crossroads" and "White Room," Black Sabbath's "Iron Man," The Who's *Live at Leeds* version of "My Generation," and Ten Years After's frantic boogie "I'm Going Home." Although the band's instrumental prowess was impressive, Ed's lead vocals were merely serviceable. After seeing a Genesis performance, an aspiring vocalist and outgoing motormouth named David Lee Roth told Ed and Alex that their band needed a new singer—namely, himself. By that time, Ed wanted to shift away from singing to concentrate more on his guitar playing, so he and Alex asked Roth to learn a few of their songs and come back for an audition. For all of Roth's bravado, when he did return to play with them they weren't impressed with his singing and turned him down.

Undeterred, Roth went on to form his own band called Red Ball Jets, named after the popular sneaker whose ads promised to make kids "run faster and jump higher." When the Van Halen brothers and Stone later shared a gig with Red Ball Jets, they were surprised to see a flamboyantly dressed character with a familiar face strutting across the stage. What Roth lacked in vocal prowess he made up for in energy, charisma, and stage presence. The two bands soon competed for dominance in the local scene, pitting Mammoth's virtuosity against Red Ball Jets' showmanship.

David Lee Roth and the Van Halen brothers finally got together when a series of events led to the singer's joining Mammoth during the summer of 1973. Red Ball Jets had disbanded earlier that year, leaving Roth without a band. Around that same time, the Van Halen brothers were looking to rent a sound system after their usual sources had raised their prices.

Aware that Roth owned an Acoustic PA system that he wasn't using, the Van Halens turned to him for help. Roth agreed, but over time he went from charging them a modest rental fee to demanding they allow him to perform a few songs with the band at their shows in exchange. Eventually, the members of Mammoth decided to accept the determined Roth into the band, both to save the money they were spending renting his PA and to finally relieve Ed of his role as reluctant lead singer.

"Ed and I couldn't stand [Red Ball Jets] or their music," Alex told *Classic Rock* magazine. "But I realized Ed couldn't be the singer. At the time Roth was a very cocky guy; he had long blond hair and walked around with a certain confidence. I figured his singing would improve as time went by, because he couldn't sing for shit. Seriously. He compensated for it by being outspoken and different-looking."

Shortly before Roth joined Mammoth, the band added keyboardist Jim Pewsey to the lineup, which gave them more freedom to expand their sound and repertoire.

With Roth as their new lead singer, Mammoth's sound transformed away from heavy rock with extended instrumental jams to favor shorter pop songs with a few funky dance tunes thrown in. The change was mainly influenced by the band's desire to get themselves booked in clubs where pop was the main fare. Although Mammoth attracted growing crowds to the backyard parties they played, they also attracted attention from local police forces, and their gigs were often shut down within minutes after they began playing. If they wanted to appear in clubs, pop, at least temporarily, represented the way forward.

As Mammoth started booking shows beyond Pasadena and its vicinity, they caught the attention of another band named Mammoth, which was based in the San Fernando Valley. This band, older and better established than the teenagers from Pasadena, had a lawyer send them a cease-and-desist notice. Forced to come up with a new name, the Van Halen brothers suggested Rat Salad, inspired by an instrumental track on Black Sabbath's *Paranoid* album. That's when Roth made the brilliant move of suggesting that they should rename themselves Van Halen, which was obviously appropriate, sounded cool, and would certainly be unique to them. The suggestion also strengthened Roth's bond with the brothers.

By the time Van Halen booked its first gig at Gazzarri's, Pewsey had left the band. Although they could still perform dozens of songs as a three-piece band with a lead singer, they sought ways to add to their repertoire to make it easier to play cover material for all-night sets four to five times a week. Roth thought that three-part vocal harmonies could make the band sound bigger and could even serve as a surrogate horn section for the funk and R&B songs he wanted to play. The problem was that Mark Stone couldn't sing and refused to even try. Another issue was that Stone had trouble memorizing many of the three hundred songs in their expanded repertoire. The upshot was that the band needed to hire a new bass player.

Van Halen already had a replacement in mind when this decision was made: Mike Anthony, the bass-playing front man of Snake, a band based in nearby Arcadia. Anthony had an impressive vocal range, and he could easily hit higher notes that Roth and Ed could not. Although he'd previously crossed paths with the brothers, the first time he caught their attention was when Snake opened a concert headlined by Van Halen on May 3, 1974, at Pasadena High School Auditorium.

After the show, the Van Halen brothers struck up a conversation with Anthony, who suggested that they all get together to jam sometime. A few weeks later, Ed reached out to the bassist through a mutual friend and invited him to bring his bass and amp to Van Halen's rehearsal space. After a session with Alex and Ed, the brothers invited Anthony to join the band.

"He was a really energetic performer and had a great voice, although I didn't care for the rest of his band," recalled Alex.

Playing at Gazzarri's was not the most glamorous gig, but it eventually led to bigger and better things for Van Halen. In April 1976, the influential

# EDDIE'S ODDITIES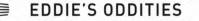

**GUITAR:** 1955 Gibson Les Paul Junior
**USED:** Early Hollywood club years

Ed's black and white "Frankenstein" super Strat became an instant celebrity in the guitar community when he posed with the instrument on the cover of Van Halen's debut album. However, several outtake images from that photo session show Ed holding an entirely different guitar—this battered 1955 Gibson Les Paul Junior, which Ed occasionally played during Van Halen's club days. Although Ed didn't play the Junior on the album, history could have been very different if one of the outtake photos with the guitar was featured on the cover instead.

"I wanted to remove the paint so I could refinish this guitar, so I put liquid paint remover on it," Ed recalled. "As I was doing that, the paint wasn't coming off, but it started to look really interesting, so I just left it like that. It looked tripped out. I did that right after I destroyed my ES-335 [see main story] with a belt sander, trying to get the paint off. I didn't realize that the body was contoured, and I sanded a hole right through the wood! I should have used the belt sander on the Junior instead, because it has a flat surface, but when I went to the paint shop they told me to try paint remover."

This guitar, along with Ed's original Frankenstein and Ibanez Destroyer, was one of a handful of instruments from Van Halen's club days that remained in the guitarist's personal collection.

Hollywood tastemaker Rodney Bingenheimer dropped by the club with a friend to have a few drinks and laugh at the struggling cover bands that usually played there. Instead, they were surprised to find a highly talented band and a club filled with attractive girls, including a few that frequented Bingenheimer's English Disco, which had been located about two miles east of Gazzarri's on Sunset Boulevard before closing in December 1975.

"[Van Halen] were just doing Top 40 stuff," Bingenheimer told Robert Hilburn of the *Los Angeles Times* in early January 1977. "I was impressed and asked them if they had any original material. They told me I should drop by and see their show at the Pasadena Civic. When I got there, they had something like two thousand kids in the place. They had put the show together themselves. Amazing."

Bingenheimer helped Van Halen book bigger and better gigs, including shows opening for international acts like UFO, at the Golden West Ballroom in Norwalk and at the Starwood on Santa Monica Boulevard, which presented national acts and local bands that performed original material. "I took Gene Simmons of Kiss to see them [at the Starwood], and he liked them so much he flew them to New York to record a demo," Bingenheimer said. He also was the first DJ to play Van Halen on the radio, broadcasting "Runnin' with the Devil" from the band's demo tape and interviewing the vociferous Roth on his new program on the Pasadena station KROQ in December 1976.

The band's involvement with Simmons was bittersweet. Although recording the demo was exciting—they worked at Jimi Hendrix's Electric Lady Studios in New York as well as at Village Recorders in West LA, where the Rolling Stones had recorded *Goats Head Soup* and Eric Clapton had tracked "After Midnight"—they weren't happy with the results. They were further disappointed when Kiss's manager, Bill Aucoin, didn't share Simmons's enthusiasm for them and opted instead to sign a band called Piper, fronted by Billy Squier.

In late 1976, Van Halen resumed playing shows in Hollywood at clubs like the Starwood and Whisky a Go Go, which had just started booking live music again after spending the previous year and a half hosting cabaret revues and stage shows like *Let My People Come*. Van Halen also landed a handful of concert opening-act gigs, including a New Year's Eve show at the Santa Monica Civic for Sparks and a show headlined by Santana on January 30, 1977, at the Long Beach Arena. But their band's most successful performances were those they booked and promoted themselves at the Pasadena Civic Auditorium, which they packed with thousands of homegrown fans.

Van Halen's persistence in playing original music at Hollywood nightclubs finally paid off later in 1977. It took the band longer than it should have to land a contract with a major record label, but once they did, their days of playing clubs ended, replaced by gigs at arenas and stadiums across the United States and beyond. But they were able to make that transition seamlessly, in part because of all the experience they had garnered playing those same small clubs.

**What inspired you to play music?**

My dad. He was a soulful guy. He was a professional musician, and he played saxophone and clarinet like a motherfucker. But he didn't make enough money playing music to make ends meet, so he also had to do things like washing dishes and working as a janitor. My mom had to work full-time, too. She was a maid. I'll never forget helping my dad wax floors at the Masonic Temple in Pasadena. I learned how to operate a floor waxer and helped my mom clean houses.

But what saved all of us was music. Music was just the environment that I grew up around. That was his life, and it became my life. I don't know if it was in the genes or the environment . . . or both. My mom didn't play professionally, but she had this huge organ with a rhythm box in it. On holidays my mom and dad would play oldies, with her on the organ and my dad on sax.

Music became my escape. Every week the cops would show up at our house because my mom would be chasing my dad with a pan and slamming him on the head. They loved each other, but they fought a lot. To escape from that, I would play the piano or hide in my room playing guitar.

My dad died when he was sixty-six because he was an alcoholic, but he led a full life. My mom was eighty, and she didn't do anything. I'm trying to find a balance. I don't want to be like my mom and live to be eighty, but do nothing. But I don't want to die at sixty-six, either, like my dad did.

**What was your first electric guitar?**

It was a Teisco. It's ironic because it had four pickups and I'm known for having guitars with just one pickup. The first songs I learned how to play on that guitar were "Pipeline," "Wipeout," and "Walk, Don't Run" by The Ventures. I actually have Super 8 footage of me playing at my sixth-grade talent show. There's no sound, though. After that I started playing songs by Cream and eventually things by Grand Funk and Black Sabbath. I got rid of my original Teisco a long time ago, but I found another one that's exactly the same. [See photo index.]

### How did you learn to play guitar?

I would listen to records or the radio and play by ear. I was very shy when I was young. I never talked much, so a lot of people at school thought I was a prick. I started drinking when I was twelve—my dad gave me a shot of vodka and a cigarette after a German shepherd bit me—and I kept drinking after that because I was shy and nervous. I also drank every time we played with my dad's band to calm my nerves.

When I got drunk, I would say all kinds of shit that I didn't mean. I struggled a lot in school, getting fucked around by girlfriends and not fitting in with the jocks, so I would just stay home and play guitar for hours at a time. I locked myself up in my room all throughout high school and said to myself, "Hey, this guitar is never going to fuck me in the ass like some chick." The more effort and attention I put into it, the more I got back.

### When did you start playing guitar in bands?

When I first learned to play guitar, it would be just Alex and me. We played together for so long. We never had a bass player in the very beginning. I played so fucking loud you couldn't hear the guy anyway. Alex and I would play with my dad's band—the country club circuit, weddings, bar mitzvahs, and shit. My dad would play at the Continental Club every Sunday night and we would sit in with him. We would play at the La Mirada Country Club, and he'd play at a place called the Alpine Haus in San Fernando in the Valley and we'd wear the lederhosen. Those polka songs are so weird. They're all I-IV-V, but they're like some odd country song. Alex would sit in and play drums with them, then I'd come up and play guitar with Alex. When the band took breaks, Alex and I would play by ourselves for the crowd, and my dad would pass the hat around for tips. It was a lot of fun.

All those bands that played the Hollywood clubs after us missed the most important part. They didn't play weddings, bar mitzvahs, polkas, and all that other shit like we did way before the club days. I'm not saying that you have to do that to play clubs, but it helps you understand how to make different audiences happy.

**Van Halen really didn't sound like any of the other bands in the clubs back in the seventies, whereas many of the bands that played in Hollywood clubs during the eighties sounded like Van Halen.**

Back then, record companies played a big part in defining trends. When punk and New Wave first happened, they signed a bunch of punk and New Wave bands and promoted them. It was the same thing when Nirvana and Pearl Jam first came out—then every record company had to sign a grunge band. After a while, people can only take so much of one thing, so it goes in cycles. But it always comes back to the simplicity of rock and roll. When we started out, there was no path to fame. You just played.

**I remember all of those ads for bands seeking members in the eighties: "Must have hair." It was like they cared more about how you looked than how well you played.**

It was like a bad dating service. There were some good bands playing in the clubs after us, but after a while the music became secondary, and it was all about image.

Nowadays people have these workstations at home, and they can piece anything together, but they can't play it for me live. They can dance around while they lip-synch it, but they can't actually perform it. Music was played live way before there was any technology to record it. Do you think Beethoven or Mozart would have wasted their time writing their music out if they had a twenty-four-track recording studio or Pro Tools? They would have just recorded it and let someone else transcribe it. Think of all the music they could have made.

**How did you go from playing covers to playing original material?**

When we used to play clubs, we learned just enough Top 40 songs to get hired. But you had to play five 45-minute sets. Even if you knew thirty songs, that was only enough to get you through two sets, because most Top 40 songs are only three minutes long. We figured we could play our own stuff, and no one would care as long as the beat was there.

One day we were playing at this club in Covina called Posh. I'll never forget this. We ran out of Top 40 tunes, so we started playing our own music. The owner of the club walks up to us while we were playing a song and goes, "Stop! I hired you to play Top 40. What is this shit?!" He told us to get the fuck out of there and he wouldn't let us take our equipment. We had to come back the next week to pick up our equipment. It was always that way. It was either the guitarist is too loud or plays too psychedelic. They always complained about me.

It's funny, but no matter how hard I tried to sound like the records—and I really tried—I always ended up sounding like me. We used to play "It's Your Thing" by the Isley Brothers, but everyone thought it was a Black Sabbath song because I was playing it through a Marshall. It was Black Sabbath funk! We would play "Get Down Tonight" by KC and the Sunshine Band—all that stuff. But the stuff that was closest to my heart was Black Sabbath. But it was a blessing. If you play and play and play, after a while you discover the essence of yourself.

**In the very early days of Van Halen, you originally wanted to call the band Rat Salad. You obviously were a huge Black Sabbath fan back then.**

We played just about every Black Sabbath song. I used to sing lead on every Black Sabbath song we did—things like "Into the Void," "Paranoid," and "Lord of This World." I grew up listening to Tony Iommi, but just because he wore a cross and played left-handed didn't mean that I had to do the same thing. Just because Clapton had an afro didn't mean that I did. I just liked the music. One thing that David Lee Roth always used to say that was kind of funny but true is that people just need to know where to look. It wasn't about image. I never emulated anyone and thought if I dressed like that, I'll make it. If I write a song like that, I'll make it. I just listened to people play so I could play.

To me, Tony Iommi of Black Sabbath is the master of riffs. That's what I loved. I'm not knocking Ozzy or his singing, but listen to "Into the Void." That riff is some badass shit. It was beyond surf music and jazz. It was beyond anything else I had ever heard. It was so fuckin' heavy. I put it right up there with (*sings the four-note intro to Beethoven's Fifth Symphony*). What are you going to sing over that? Listen to the main riff where he chugs on the E string. It hits you like a brick wall. Every band on the planet still does that. That is a staple of rock and roll.

**You've mentioned that Eric Clapton was also an early influence.**
He was. I figured out a few of his guitar solos note for note, but that was about as far as it went. With me, it was all about the live Cream stuff. To me, that is where Clapton's style came from. Clapton was the only guy doing that kind of soloing back then. His live jams with Cream also helped me find my own voice on the guitar because I was limited gear-wise. Back in '68, he was using natural distortion from his Marshall stacks on those live tracks on *Wheels of Fire* and *Goodbye*. I had no money and couldn't afford a fuzz box or wah pedal, or whatever else it was that Hendrix had in his rig. I just plugged straight into the amp and turned everything up to 11. To get a different or unique sound, I had to use just my fingers and my imagination.

I don't mean to downplay anything Clapton did, but for me it was also about Cream's rhythm section. Listen to "I'm So Glad" on *Goodbye* and adjust the balance to the right—Jack Bruce and Ginger Baker were playing jazz through distorted Marshall stacks. Jack is an insane player. It's just E to D on the entire song, but what Jack does sonically, how he plays around those two chords and makes it interesting is just out there. The bass playing is the most insane twisting and changing thing I've ever heard in my life, and it's just two chords. It's so out, but it's brilliant. Clapton sounds lost.

**How did you start your quest to find your own individual sound on the guitar?**
A lot of it had to do with the fact that I never took lessons, which also influenced the way I play. I bought one of my first guitars from Lafayette Electronics, which was like RadioShack. They had a twelve-string Univox guitar that I really liked, but I didn't want twelve strings. I wanted six. I asked the sales guy if I could take six strings off and try it and he said, "No." I said, "Why not? I want to buy the guitar. You should give me a discount for taking six of the strings off."

**What was your first good guitar?**
I saved my money and bought myself a 1969 gold top Les Paul with soap-bar P90 pickups. It was the first real guitar that I ever owned, but I didn't

like the pickups at the time. I wanted a humbucker. I got a humbucker from somewhere, crammed it in the guitar, and replaced the bridge pickup.

Back when we used to play the Starwood and Whisky, people were tripping at the sound I was getting from that guitar. Everyone who heard me wondered how I got that sound from a soapbar pickup. They didn't realize I put a humbucker in there because my right hand covered the pickup. They thought I was getting that sound with soapbar pickups. I wasn't trying to fool anyone, but that was the sound I wanted. I didn't like the way the gold finish looked, so I painted it black. I always fucked with everything. I never left anything the way it was when I bought it. Eighty-seven percent of the time I was successful. Thirteen percent of the time I ruined it, but I learned.

**What was your first good amp?**
I got a 100-watt Marshall stack, which was the same amp that I used on our first six albums. I was working for a music store called Berry & Grassmueck in Pasadena, moving pianos and organs, and a Marshall amp that had belonged to the Rose Palace came in one day. The Rose Palace is a concrete building where they build Rose Parade floats, and they used to have concerts there with bands like Iron Butterfly and Jimi Hendrix. When they stopped having concerts there [the last concert at the Rose Palace took place on January 17, 1970, featuring Eric Burdon and War and Alice Cooper], that Marshall ended up in the store. I had never seen a Marshall before, except in pictures. I told them that I didn't care how long I had to work there, but I wanted that amp. All I cared about was that it was a Marshall.

When I first plugged it in, I blew it up. When you'd plug the amp straight into the wall, it would go "poof!" When I got it fixed, it was too loud. I remember playing a gig with it once when it was still working and as I looked behind it, I could see the tubes melting! It was too hot.

I just used to sit in my room and stare at it. I just couldn't believe I had Marshall. I eventually met someone who worked at the Rose Palace who told me it was the house amp. Probably everyone and their brother played through it. It remained stock throughout its life.

The first time I opened up my 100-watt Marshall, I was taking advice from some guy who knew less about electronics than I did, but I listened to him. He kept saying, "It's the rectifier. It's the rectifier." I asked my dad if he knew what a rectifier was, and he showed me this big old square thing, which didn't belong in an amp at all. I was poking around in the amp, trying to figure out where the rectifier was. Of course, I touched the wrong thing, got shocked, and was knocked clear across the room. At least I found the rectifier! But I always wondered, "What will happen if I do this?"

That's how I stumbled onto the Variac [a variable transformer for adjusting power outlet voltage from 0 to 130 or more volts]. I bought a second Marshall head, but I didn't know that it was a British model instead of a US export model, like the one I had. The British models are wired to run on 240 volts, and US voltage is 120. When I first plugged in the Marshall, it didn't make any sound because the voltage was half of what it needed to work properly. I left it on for a few hours, thinking that it just needed to warm up, and when I played it again you could barely hear it. It sounded distorted like a Marshall turned all the way up, but it was really, really quiet. Later I discovered that the British Marshall was supposed to run on 240 volts.

That made me wonder if my first Marshall would still work if I lowered the voltage. I thought that might enable me to get the same tone as when I turned the amp all the way up but at a lower volume level. I actually started out with just a light dimmer. I hooked it up to the house and fried a fuse. I went, "There's got to be a better way to do this." Then I went to Dow Radio and bought a Variac. That worked. The Variac was the key to making that amp work, and it worked for years. I used the Variac to lower the voltage to about 89 volts, so I could turn the amp up without blowing it up. Sylvania 6CA7 tubes sound great in it, but the best set of tubes I ever had in that amp was a matched set of Telefunkens.

**Do you still use a Variac?**

No. The only reason I ever used that was in the club days to get my sound, but quieter. The only way I could make that Marshall work is with everything all the way up. In a club it would be too uncontrollable. It would be too loud, and it would feed back. I actually used it for recording in the early days, too, before I started sitting in the control room. I always play back here [behind the mixing console at 5150]. Alex is the only one out there. I play in here so I can get the vibe. I hate wearing headphones. In the old days of recording, I would stand out there and use headphones. I'd be too close to the cabinet, so it would feed back, so I would turn down the volume with the Variac. I stopped doing that a long time ago, back in '83 when I built the studio.

**In photos of some of the band's early performances, you have a blond Fender amp head onstage.**

That was a Fender Bandmaster. I used that amp for years in two ways. I already had the Marshall, but I had not stumbled onto the Variac thing yet, so I would use the Bandmaster through the Marshall cabinet when we gigged at places like Gazzarri's because the Marshall was too loud. In the little house in Pasadena that I grew up in, my mom always hated what she called "that high crying noise"—in other words, soloing. She'd always go, "Why do you have to make that high crying noise?"

I discovered that I could plug a speaker cabinet into the Bandmaster's external speaker output instead of the regular output and it was really quiet. I could turn everything all the way up, which is what I always did anyway, and there was this small amount of bleed that sounded exactly like when the regular output is turned all the way up, but it's really quiet. Everyone says that you can't do that because the transformer will blow, but the amp never blew up. It was really quiet, so my mom couldn't hear me, but it sounded amazing.

The beauty of that amp is how many songs I wrote with it. I wrote all of the early Van Halen songs for the first three albums that way, with that amp, sitting alone in my bedroom. My dog Monty would sit down next to me, and he dug it. When I wrote the intro to "Women in Love," he was sitting there with his ears perked up, like the RCA Victor dog. That Bandmaster was more important than the Marshall head, because I wrote everything with it.

**What were some of your other early guitar experiments?**

I bought a Gibson ES-335, which used to be my favorite guitar because it had a thin neck and low action. It was real easy to play, but the guys in the band hated how it looked. It had one of those Maestro Vibrola wiggle sticks with the bent metal tailpiece, like you find on an SG. I liked it, but it wouldn't stay in tune. I started messing with it to find out why it wouldn't stay in tune. I don't know if people to this day understand the reasons why a guitar won't stay in tune.

Since I was having problems with the vibrato making the guitar go out of tune, I figured that maybe I could make the E, A, and D strings solid and just have the high three strings affected by the wiggle stick, so I sawed the bent metal spring in half. I figured out how to hard-mount the low three strings, but I couldn't figure out how to bolt the wiggle stick part into the wood. I drilled a hole and put a screw in it, and it worked a little bit, but after a while the wood gave out.

I did all kinds of crazy shit to that 335. I took a belt sander to it when I wanted to strip the finish and repaint the guitar white, but I didn't realize it was an archtop so I ended up sanding a big hole through the wood. I've destroyed a lot of guitars, but to me it didn't mean anything. It was really about having a guitar do what I want.

**There are photos of you from the club days playing a Stratocaster with a humbucking pickup installed at the bridge.**

I played that guitar for a while before I built my Frankenstein guitar. I just slapped a humbucker in there, and that got me closer to the sound I wanted, but it still wasn't right. The tone was too thin, probably because of the wood that the body was made of.

After I tore that Strat apart, I had no idea where all the wires should go. I hooked up the pickup to the volume knob and it worked, so I just left it at that. That's all I needed. For years after that, all of my guitars that I built by myself had just one pickup. That was just simply due to my ignorance.

**How did you promote Van Halen in the early days?**

A lot of bands make a demo tape. We did that also. We went to New York with Gene Simmons from Kiss in 1976. He saw us in a club and asked us, "Are you guys on a label or anything? Do you have a manager?" and we said, "No." So he said, "Wow, you guys are a hot band, I'd like to work with you." And we were going, "What do you mean?" What it boiled down to was he wanted to take a shot at producing a rock band, so we said, "Sure," because he was paying for it all. We went to New York, made the world's most expensive demo tape, and never ended up using it. Even though we had a demo tape, we didn't know where in the hell to take it. We didn't know anyone.

Bands will take demos to a record company where some clown sitting on a couch and smoking a joint listens to your tape, but usually nothing ever happens that way. We basically just kept playing everywhere around the LA area. We used to put on our own shows in our hometown and draw three thousand people, selling tickets for four dollars. This was way before Warner Bros. We just developed a following that way, and the word got out.

**What did you learn from recording the demos with Gene Simmons?**
I learned that I didn't like overdubbing. Gene just naturally assumed that I knew that was how it's done, but I said, "Oh no, I can't do that." I wanted to stick to my normal way of playing, where I would noodle in between chord lines. Instead, I had to fill in those spots on the tape after I recorded the rhythm part, so it was rather uncomfortable.

**What do you miss the most about playing in clubs?**
I miss how things back then were unknown. I miss the mystique. There was no internet or YouTube, so we got away with a lot of things in certain aspects of life that bands would never get away with today. It was easier to build things up and get a reputation. Look at a band like Zeppelin. Their whole thing was mystique. Half the shit that was talked about back then never happened, but if there was YouTube, you'd know.

# MUSICAL INTERLUDE

*A conversation with Van Halen bassist*
**Michael Anthony**, *Part I*

---

The bearded and barrel-chested Michael Anthony, much beloved by the group's fan base for his friendly, everyman appeal, was Van Halen's bassist and backing vocalist for over three decades, from 1974 to 2006. His steady playing and distinctive harmonies were an integral part of the band's sound. Mike always took a certain amount of pride in avoiding any mudslinging when recounting the band's numerous public battles, and this is one reason he's regarded as the beating heart of classic Van Halen.

Mike met Ed when both were playing in Pasadena-area bands and attending music classes at Pasadena City College in the early seventies. Anthony was the respected lead singer and bassist in a boogie rock unit called Snake, and when Ed and Al were looking to replace Van Halen's bass player Mark Stone, it seemed only natural to give Mike a call [see main story].

After a memorable jam session, the Van Halen brothers asked Anthony to join their group. And though he was fronting his own band, Mike recognized Ed's extraordinary talent and immediately agreed to sign up as bassist and backing vocalist to front man David Lee Roth.

In the first half of this two-part interview (the second appears on page 240), Mike fondly remembers the band's carefree early days and his ringside seat to the evolution of Eddie Van Halen.

**What was your initial impression of Edward?**

I saw him play at a school fair with Alex and their bassist Mark Stone. Ed was lead singing and playing guitar at the time. I was really impressed because they did a lot of Cream and Ed was blowing that stuff note for note. There weren't many guys around at that time that could play that well.

Later, when I first joined the band, I was impressed by how humble he was. Unlike a lot of the local guitar players, who would act like, "Hey, I'm badass—check me out," Ed just did his thing. And obviously, why I joined the band was Ed and Al's musicianship. I was also impressed by their ideas. The band already had four or five original songs that were just great.

*Did Ed ever talk about his childhood?*

Yeah, a little bit. He would talk more about his father's hardships. He was bothered by the fact that his dad was a respected musician in Europe but had to work as a janitor to make ends meet in the United States.

*You were a solid bassist and well-trained musician when you joined Van Halen. What did you think you could contribute?*

I played bass and often sang lead in my previous bands. I didn't mind being the front man because I've never really had a problem with playing and singing at the same time, but I didn't love it either. When I joined Van Halen, Dave was singing lead and Al and Ed were singing background vocals, so I thought, "Oh shit, this is great. I can finally just focus on my bass playing. I don't have to sing." But the second time I jammed with the band, they said, "Hey, why don't you try a background?" As soon as they heard me sing, it was like, "Oh man." All of a sudden, I was enlisted to sing *all* the backgrounds.

*During that period, outside of Cheap Trick or AC/DC, there weren't a lot of hard rock bands doing background vocals. You guys really embraced it. Your approach was almost like the Beatles or Motown.*

That's true. Many of the bands during that time, like Led Zeppelin, Deep Purple, or Black Sabbath, were more focused on the lead singer. I'm not sure where it came from, but we always wanted that element in our music. Whenever Dave would come up with lyrics, we'd automatically start thinking of ways to fit in background vocals. I listened to the Beatles, and Ed and Al were always into British Invasion bands; that was probably a big influence.

But regarding style, I don't think Ed and I ever gave it much thought. We just had our own way of doing things and we knew we were unique sounding. Our background vocals were like Ed's guitar sound: you knew it was Van Halen when you heard them.

*How was Ed's singing?*

His pitch was good, and he sang fine. All the early stuff is me and Ed. His smoking took a bit of a toll later on. But when Sammy joined the band, I even tried to elevate the backgrounds to another level. On the later albums I started singing both parts myself.

*Getting back to your bass playing. On the first five albums, Ed and Dave could wander pretty far from the foundational chords of any given song. Did you see your role as holding down the harmonic integrity of the song?*

Yeah. As much as I liked bands like Cream, it always amazed me how far they would stray from the song, especially when Eric Clapton soloed. Sometimes it sounded like the band members were playing three different songs. It was cool, especially when they would fall right back into place, but I always wanted to keep a really good foundation. I was stifled a little bit as a player, because it's fun to go off and do your own thing, but more often than not, the band relied on me to keep things solid.

*Ed always seemed pretty disciplined when it came to soloing. Most of the time he'd take his twelve bars and be done, even though most fans would've been thrilled to hear him stretch out.*

Yeah, you're right. But it wasn't a conscious thing. We just gravitated to tighter structures.

*When did you first recognize that Ed was something beyond just a good guitarist?*

Early on. He was obviously a great lead player, but when he started doing the hammer-on stuff, it was like, "Wow." And we just tripped because none of the other guitar players in the local bands were doing anything like that. There were plenty of times we would rehearse in a garage in Pasadena, and the other local guitar players would start hanging to watch Ed. Finally, Dave intervened. He told Ed, "Man, don't let these guys rip you off." When we would play, he always told Ed, "When you tap, turn your back to the crowd so that they can't see what you're doing."

We knew what he was doing was pretty special. He was playing things that nobody had ever heard before. It wasn't just like a guy who was fast or good or . . . it was a whole different thing. And we're like, "Man, keep that canned up. We don't want that to get out. That's your thing."

*Did he develop those techniques over a long period of time?*

Yeah. It wasn't overnight. It evolved over time. But it really came together when he started putting it in his solo spot. Long before we were signed, he would play an unaccompanied solo that would eventually become "Eruption." But Ed was always developing and evolving. "Eruption" on the first album is great, but you can hear how his playing became more sophisticated on later albums.

*Do you remember the first time he brought one of his Frankenstrats into rehearsal?*

Not the exact date, but yeah, I remember him bringing it to rehearsal. It always amazed me how fearless he was in that respect. He was always fucking around with his guitars. I remember him buying this Gibson ES-335—it was a beautiful guitar—and the next time I saw it, it was completely gutted and ripped apart and the pieces would be on some other junkie-looking guitar. I'd be like, "Damn, what are you doing?" And he'd say, "Oh no, man, check out how this sounds."

But the Frankenstrat was the culmination of a lot of failed experiments. There were a couple of earlier versions, but the body would get so hacked up that he couldn't play it anymore. And, believe me, he was no electronics mastermind, but that's how he found his sound. He couldn't really figure out how to wire all the pickups together, so he finally slapped in one humbucker and wired it to one knob, and he got the tone he wanted. He was like, "Hey, check this out!" It was all very unorthodox.

He never followed the rules. If someone told him, "Well, this is how you wire a pickup," his tendency was to take it somewhere else. Like, "Wow, what if I put this wire on that." Sometimes it wouldn't work at all, and other times he'd be like, "Hey, that sounds pretty good." But I watched him destroy some really nice guitars. It was sorta funny.

*What kind of music did you guys listen to?*

It was weird. Ed never listened to the radio. He had a couple of bands that he liked, like Cream and Black Sabbath, but when we cruised around, he never put the radio on.

*Can you tell me a bit about the Hollywood club scene before you were signed?*

We were playing the Sunset Strip in Hollywood during the early and mid-seventies, between when the scene was shifting from Bowie-era glam to punk. It wasn't until after we got signed that the hair bands like Poison and Mötley Crüe started getting popular—all the bands that had singers with bleached blond hair that wanted to be David Lee Roth.

*You regularly played Gazzarri's, which was one of the legendary clubs of the era. What was that like?*

Dave was our real connection to Gazzarri's. The owner, Bill Gazzarri, would say "hi" to us or whatever, but Dave was the guy that would hang out and work the room. I wasn't really a Sunset Strip guy. When I joined the band, I wore jeans and T-shirts most of the time, but that didn't fly in Hollywood. I remember, the first gig I played with Van Halen was at the Proud Bird out by LAX airport. They had a night called the Freaker's Ball, which was a total mix of everything that was hip and trendy at the time. I remember my wife made me a pair of gold lamé pants and vest so I could fit in. Eddie was wearing silver lamé. It was pretty crazy, because we'd dress one way for Hollywood and then go back to our regular clothes when we'd play parties in Pasadena.

*You guys used to play at dance contests at Gazzarri's.*

Yeah. It'd be like, "Hey, contestant number one!" And we'd play about ten bars of "Tush" by ZZ Top, and these girls would dance.

*Eddie and Randy Rhoads were the two big guitarists on the scene back then. Was there a rivalry?*

Not really. I mean, there was a bit of rivalry between every band that was playing the area. That's only natural. We were all competing for gigs. But I think the only time Quiet Riot played with us was at Glendale College in one of their theaters [April 23, 1977]. I believe Randy was with them, but I never met him personally. I mean, there were a lot of guitar players that were trying to copy and catch Eddie.

*Do you remember ever seeing bands like Mötley Crüe or Ratt? A lot of them talk about seeing Van Halen when they were still on the Strip.*

Not really. We were about three or four years ahead of a lot of those guys. We played in Hollywood almost right up until our first tour in '78. But after that, we were pretty much off and running. It sounds hard to believe because it was happening in our own backyard, but I don't think we paid too much attention to the hair metal thing in LA because we were just so busy. The biggest thing that I can recollect is that suddenly a lot of the comparisons started popping up between Eddie and these other guitar players that were all starting to cop his stuff.

*All these bands said they were influenced by Van Halen, but you guys never teased your hair or wore makeup.*

I'm proud to say we never wore makeup! (*laughs*) I don't know where that look came from. Maybe from the glam scene. It's like anything else, one of those bands probably started doing it and then they all started, but it didn't come from us. I mean, the clothes? Maybe. I had about fifteen pair of platform shoes in my closet, but not the makeup.

I felt the scene that came after us was totally different. It was a different kind of music. We were on the tail end of bands like Humble Pie, Zeppelin, and stuff like that. We weren't a "so-called" eighties band. I think we were more classic rock.

*They all happily point to you guys as the forefathers. Is that acceptable to you that you kind of spawned this in a way?*

Oh yeah. I mean, that's fine. That's flattering. But that wasn't what we were all about. To me, a lot of eighties music has a certain flavor to it. A certain sound. I don't think we had that. We were more influenced by people we grew up listening to—Zeppelin, Cream, and all those bands.

*After your success, did you go ever go back to the Strip in the eighties? Were you amazed at how insane it had gotten?*

I wasn't really amazed. We could see it changing while we were playing. We weren't against being visual, but it was important to have talent, too. We always used to say, we wanted our music to hold up even if we were playing naked with one light bulb hanging over our head. We would say that in a lot of the interviews—"Hey, hang a light bulb over our head and we'll still kick your ass."

The Sunset Strip rock scene became more about the fashion. It was like Hollywood punk. In Europe, the punk kids lived that shit. When we went to England on our first tour, our record company told us not to go into certain areas of town at night because we'd get killed. The punks were real punks. They were living it. Over here in the States, it was more of a pose, you know, "I'm going to rip my pants up and do all that." And the eighties metal music was almost like that. Talent was fine, but boy, if you have the big hair and clothes, even better!

*In addition to Gazzarri's, you guys played the Starwood. What was that like in the seventies?*

It was the top club if you were an actual rock band. We'd open for people like Ray Manzarek [whose band at the time was called Nite City] of The Doors after Jim Morrison died, and we'd open for Y&T, who were actually pretty big. The Starwood didn't book top-name acts, but they had a lot of up-and-coming recording artists play there.

We actually lucked out when Warner Bros. saw us there. The club had just told us that they really couldn't afford to book any local acts anymore. We were about ready to pack up our bags and focus on Pasadena again. We were able to play to fifteen hundred, two thousand people there and make a lot of money. We thought if we had a big enough following that the record companies couldn't help but take notice of what we were doing.

*The upstairs area of the Starwood was legendary. What was that like?*

It was like a VIP area—you had to be invited. But it wasn't that special. It was just where the cool people or celebrity types could go if they didn't want to be hassled. They didn't let the general crowd go up there. The kind of decadent stuff that probably went on in Gazzarri's basement wasn't happening—it was just a place famous people could go to do blow. (*laughs*)

*Rodney Bingenheimer was one of the major movers and shakers of the Sunset Strip music scene. He liked you guys.*

Yeah, Rodney was actually pretty instrumental in helping us out, maybe more than anybody else. I think he helped us get our first gig at the Starwood, and he booked us at a place called the Golden West Ballroom in Norwalk, California, that held about fifteen hundred people [May 9, 1976]. That was the first show that we played all original music. We opened up for UFO, and Rodney was the emcee. He took a liking to the band, and he and Dave got along well. Rodney would play us on KROQ radio in Pasadena, which was a big deal.

**When Gene Simmons and Paul Stanley of Kiss came to see you at the Starwood, were you excited?**

Oh yeah, Kiss were big! This is when people still didn't know what they looked like under their makeup. There was still a lot of mystery. Right after we finished doing the demo with Simmons [see main story], we actually played a set at SIR [Studio Instrument Rentals] rehearsal studios in New York for their manager, Bill Aucoin, who was interested in comanaging us with Gene. Alex was like, "Okay, where do we sign? Where's the dotted line?" But Bill was signing a band called Piper at the time, and Gene was getting ready to do a big Japanese tour. They decided they didn't have time for us, and that's how the deal kind of died. We all flew back to LA with our tail between our legs, but it ended up working out well for us.

**About two months later, Ted Templeman and Mo Ostin from Warner Bros. showed up at the Starwood.**

Yeah, and the timing was perfect, because we were just about finished with Hollywood. The Starwood was about to stop booking unsigned local bands, and we got fired from Gazzarri's because Bill Gazzarri got really upset when he found out we were playing the Whisky, which was his competition just down the street on Sunset. All we had left was the Whisky, but you had to sell tickets and stuff. We could get our friends from Pasadena to come out to Hollywood, but what was the point? We could just play Pasadena.

# 3

# ON FIRE

*Edward builds his Frankenstein, makes an "Eruption,"*
*and goes runnin' with those devils in Black Sabbath all*
*over the globe.*

*" I wasn't trying to show off . . . it was just fun! "*

THE STORY GOES that no one seemed to notice when Ted Templeman walked into the Starwood club in Hollywood just before ten on Wednesday night, February 2, 1977, and immediately made his way upstairs to the balcony. With his shoulder-length golden-blond hair parted in the middle and casual attire, the thirty-four-year-old vice president and staff producer at Warner Bros. looked more like a Malibu hippie surfer than a record company executive.

Although he might've looked unconventional for a "suit," Templeman was a rising star in the music industry and instantly recognizable to anyone who was familiar with the record business. Surprised to see that the nightclub was nearly empty, he was relieved to sit in the shadows, unrecognized.

Having previously produced hit records by the Doobie Brothers, Little Feat, and Van Morrison, Templeman was at a stage in his career where he didn't need to prowl nightclubs to scout new talent. But he found himself at the Starwood that night in response to an enthusiastic invitation from Marshall Berle, a respected figure in the music industry who was best known for signing the Beach Boys to a management contract with the William Morris Agency in 1960. Berle was booking talent at the recently reopened Whisky a Go Go at the time, and he'd called Templeman a few days earlier to ask him to drop by the Starwood to see a promising new band that was playing on consecutive nights at the club.

After the band's techs finished setting up the gear and made one final check of the microphones, Van Halen took the stage and blasted into their first song like the Roman army laying siege to Carthage. Templeman was impressed that the band played for that sparse a crowd with the kind of energy one would expect if they were onstage before twenty thousand screaming fans at the LA Forum. The lead singer was charismatic and confident to the point of cockiness; the drummer played with power and precision; and the bass player delivered muscular bottom-end punch along with dazzling high-tenor vocal harmonies.

But it was the band's guitarist who particularly caught Templeman's eyes and ears. "Right out of the gate, I was just knocked out by Ed Van Halen," he recalled. "I had never been as impressed with a musician as I was with him that night. I'd seen Miles Davis, Dave Brubeck, Dizzy Gillespie, all of those transcendent artists, but Ed was one of the best musicians I'd ever seen live. His choice of notes, the way he approached his instrument, reminded me of saxophonist Charlie Parker. When Ed played, he looked completely natural and unaffected; he was so nonchalant in his greatness. Here he was playing the most incredible shit and acting as if it were no more challenging than snapping his fingers. Right away, I knew I wanted him on Warner Bros."[4]

Templeman quietly slipped out the Starwood's front door when Van Halen retreated backstage after finishing their first set. The next morning, the producer called Warner Bros. chairman and CEO Mo Ostin and urged him to come to the Starwood that night to see his new discovery, echoing the fervor with which Berle had pitched him just a few days earlier.

Ostin accepted the invitation, and when, seated next to Templeman, he saw Van Halen at the Starwood, he too was blown away and agreed that that they needed to sign the band without delay.

The next day, Friday, February 4, the four members of Van Halen drove to the Warner Bros. offices in Burbank to sign a letter of intent. Templeman insisted on producing the band himself. News of the letter appeared in the February 11–17 issue of the *LA Free Press*, which noted that Van Halen was "the first band of the new wave of young groups to work their way through the local clubs onto a major label."

About a month later, the band returned to Warner Bros. to sign an official recording contract. While attending a concert by Queen at the Los Angeles Forum that night, the Van Halen brothers couldn't contain their excitement as they shared the news with friends and fans they encountered in the audience. Little did they know that, less than three years later, they and the rest of their band would be headlining the same venue.

That is how Van Halen is said to have climbed from semi-obscurity to a position from which they could scale the heights of stardom. Ed would later say that it was like something "out of the movies."

He was right—it *was* like something out of the movies, where true stories are embellished to a point where they assume the trappings of a myth. The fact is that well before Templeman was wowed by them in the mostly empty Starwood, Van Halen was already on their way to a record deal. The rags-to-riches story of their "discovery" was likely the concoction of the Warner Bros. publicity department.

In May 1976, nine months before Templeman saw Van Halen for the first time, the band's reputation in Los Angeles skyrocketed after they performed their first shows at the Starwood. Van Halen quickly became the frontrunners among a group of other aspiring hard rock groups that featured talented guitarists and that were playing the Hollywood club circuit, including Quiet Riot with Randy Rhoads, The Boyz featuring George Lynch, and Eulogy, whose guitarist, Rusty Anderson, would later become Paul McCartney's sideman.

Gene Simmons of Kiss was the first notable figure to show interest in signing Van Halen, and when that news became public knowledge in early December, the buzz surrounding them exploded.

"We became known as the band that Gene Simmons secretly flew to New York to record a demo with," said bassist Michael Anthony. "After that we had no problem getting a lot of people in Hollywood to come and see us. It also really helped stoke up our following."

By the end of 1976, their shows were being reviewed by the *Los Angeles Times* and *LA Free Press*, which described Van Halen as "local favorites" in its music gossip column. Additionally, several record companies were beginning to circle the water. Kim Fowley, manager of The Runaways, made a failed attempt to sign Van Halen to Mercury. A&M Records founder Herb Alpert also scouted the band, and Danny Goldberg, former vice president of Led Zeppelin's Swan Song Records (and later Nirvana's manager), was interested in becoming the band's manager in hopes of landing them a contract with CBS.

During the last week of January 1977, just prior to Van Halen's "discovery" by Templeman at the Starwood, the band played several high-profile gigs. They packed the Whisky for a successful three-night headline run from Thursday, January 27, through Saturday, January 29, and completed the week by opening for Santana at the Long Beach Arena the next day.

So, with all this buzz around the band, why was the Starwood nearly empty on the nights Templeman and Ostin saw them? It's likely that Van Halen's devoted fans had either just seen them or were preparing to attend the band's upcoming February 18 blowout at the Pasadena Civic Auditorium.

TEMPLEMAN'S REPUTATION HAD MOSTLY BEEN established by his production of slick, middle-of-the-road records for the Doobie Brothers and Van Morrison, so it seemed odd to some that he took so much interest in a heavy guitar-dominated band. But he actually had experience producing hard rock, having worked, in 1973 and 1974, respectively, on the first two albums by Montrose, a band featuring a singer named Sammy Hagar. Songs from those records, like "Rock Candy," "Bad Motor Scooter," and "I Got the Fire," were still staples of FM radio in early 1977. They also happened to be favorites of Van Halen, who often performed covers of Montrose songs at their shows at Gazzarri's. So, their partnership with Templeman actually made perfect sense. Also, the producer's approach to recording Montrose—live, in the studio—proved to be a helpful blueprint for his work on Van Halen's debut.

In April 1977, Templeman, his engineer Donn Landee, and Van Halen recorded demos from which they would choose the material for the band's first album. After setting up his stage rig at Sunset Sound, which consisted of a '75 Ibanez Destroyer and a homemade Strat copy with a humbucking pickup, a '68 Marshall 100-watt Super Lead plexi amp, an MXR Phase 90, and a Maestro Echoplex, Ed asked Templeman and Landee if he could play the songs exactly as he performed them live. The guitarist admitted that his previous attempts at recording overdubs were frustrating, and the production duo agreed that it would be best for him to do whatever he found most comfortable.

To Templeman and Landee's surprise, the band's live performances in the studio were nearly perfect. Only a few songs needed more than one take, and by the end of the first day they'd already recorded twenty-five remarkably polished demos. The second day was spent recording lead and harmony vocal overdubs, and mixing was taken care of one day later. And that was it—in the course of just seventy-two hours, Van Halen's Warner Bros. demo was done.

Templeman didn't record Van Halen's debut album right away, as he had to take a few months to complete the Doobie Brothers' album *Livin' on the Fault Line*. Warner Bros. wanted the band to cut back on their local shows (Van Halen mostly fulfilled their monthly commitment to the Whisky and played a handful of gigs at the Pasadena Civic Auditorium and Magic Mountain before starting work on the album), so the brothers, Roth, and Anthony found themselves with an unusual amount of free time on their hands. Ed did not let it go to waste.

IN ANTICIPATION OF THEIR UPCOMING recording sessions, he spent much of the hiatus working on his playing and tinkering with his guitars. During this period, he refined what would become his signature technique—something he called "tapping," for which he used fingers from both hands to strike the fretboard, enabling him to play intervals and lightning-fast passages no guitarist could with just their fretting hand.

"Tapping is like having a sixth finger on your left hand," Ed explained. "Instead of picking, you're hitting a note on the fretboard. I was just sitting in my room at home, drinking a beer, and I remembered seeing other players using the technique for one quick note in a solo. I thought, 'Well, nobody is really capitalizing on that idea.' So, I started dickin' around and realized the potential. I had never seen anyone take it as far as I did."

Producer Templeman often likened Ed to the legendary jazz saxophonist Charlie Parker for the natural ease and flow of his phrasing, but perhaps it would be more accurate to compare him to another jazz giant, John Coltrane. Also a sax player, he played extremely dense improvisational lines consisting of high-speed arpeggios and scale patterns that *Down Beat* magazine jazz critic Ira Gitler described as "sheets of sound." With his tapping technique, Eddie Van Halen, like Coltrane, was able to peel off wild combinations of notes that flowed from his amp like red-hot lava. No one had ever heard anything quite like it. One thing for sure, it was an electrifying departure from typical blues-rock chord progressions and the solos played by most guitarists.

Ed had wisely kept the technique a secret, using it sparingly while performing onstage and not at all on the Warner Bros. demos. He understood the revolutionary implications of tapping, the possibilities it would open up for every guitarist, and he didn't want anyone to steal his discovery before he had a chance to exploit it. But with his major label debut looming, he knew it was time to unveil his secret weapon.

But that wasn't the only surprise he had up his sleeve. For years Ed had been experimenting with his guitars, ripping them apart and putting them back together as he searched for an instrument that would replicate the sounds heard in his head. But he still hadn't found what he was looking for.

Incredibly, in those few months of downtime before Van Halen recorded their first album, Ed's years of experimentation with instruments bore fruit, and he came up with a finished product that, like tapping, would change guitar history, this time in design.

Ed had never been particularly happy with the thin sound of his '61 Fender Stratocaster, yet the instrument's whammy bar had become an essential part of his sound. He had wrestled for months with the dilemma of how to make the guitar sound bigger, and suddenly he had a eureka moment: Edward routed out the body of his '61 Strat and installed a fat-sounding Gibson humbucking pickup in the bridge position. It was an innovative solution, "but it still wasn't right," he remembered. "The tone was still too thin, probably because of the wood that the body was made of."

With his first recording sessions just a few months away, Ed decided to refine his homemade guitar and build his own "super Strat," using hardware that he liked from previous instruments and parts he purchased from his buddy Wayne Charvel, who owned a guitar workshop in Azusa, not far from Pasadena.

"Eddie would come by the shop a lot," Wayne Charvel recalled. "Sometimes he would sit on the floor and play the guitar while I repaired some of his other guitars. He also did some of his own work. Eddie and Michael Anthony would hang out, and we would talk about show business, managers, etc. I gave them some World War II atom bomb blast glasses and some old paint respirators. They used to wear those onstage for some of their Hollywood shows!"

At the time, Charvel sold Boogie Bodies brand replacement guitar bodies and necks that were made by Lynn Ellsworth. Ed dropped by the factory in late 1976 or early 1977 and bought an ash Strat body for fifty dollars. It was, he recalled, a "piece-of-shit" second he found on the bottom of a stack of other bodies. For another eighty bucks, he picked up an unfinished maple neck.

Because the body was prerouted for three narrow, Fender-style pickups, Ed chiseled out a larger cavity near the bridge to install a standard humbucking pickup, which was bigger—a change that enhanced the guitar's bass response, output, and sustain.

He also put jumbo Gibson frets on the fretboard and a brass nut on the neck and installed on the body a vibrato tailpiece he'd removed from his Stratocaster guitar. Though empty chambers for two Fender-size pickups remained, Ed decided to leave them that way, as he was unable to remember how to wire the additional pickups and tone controls. So, he simply screwed a crudely cut piece of black vinyl over the chambers.

The final and most distinctive touch, at least visually, was a black-and-white-striped finish. Ed applied this by spraying the body with several coats of black acrylic lacquer paint and then, after winding a network of masking tape around the instrument, he sprayed it again with several coats of white lacquer. He removed the tape once the final coat was dry, leaving a crisscross pattern of black stripes that instantly became and remained his signature.

The result of these modifications was a guitar that combined Ed's favorite aspects of his Gibson guitars and his Strat and looked and sounded like nothing else. Thus did Edward Van Halen give birth to his Frankenstein—or, as he sometimes called it, his Frankenstrat—a legendary guitar played by a legendary guitarist.

Made for next to nothing, the mongrel guitar not only would go on to become one of the most famous in rock history but also would inspire countless imitations. During the eighties, Eddie's "super Strat" design became the most popular guitar model to emerge since the Gibson Les Paul and Fender Stratocaster and Telecaster designs of the fifties, and it remains one of the most successful guitar models today. (See Chapter 11.) But more important to Ed at the time, as he prepared to record the band's debut, the Frankenstein was indeed a monster of a guitar.

But where did Ed get the idea for the guitar's now-iconic paint job? Several theories are out there, one of which is that Ed was subliminally influenced by the De Stijl/Mondrian art and design movement, founded in the Netherlands and still popular when he was growing up in Nijmegen. De Stijl painters, sculptors, and architects were minimalists who employed vertical and horizontal patterns and only black, white, and primary colors in their work. Anyone familiar with Ed's guitars and De Stijl art can immediately see the similarities.

Another far less highbrow explanation for Eddie's striking stripes is that he was influenced by the custom paint jobs he saw on the hot rods that were seemingly everywhere in Pasadena (see previous chapter). Or perhaps he was inspired by a white Les Paul copy played by Chip Kinman of the punk rock band The Dils, which Kinman had adorned with black electrical tape. Ed had seen The Dils perform at the Whisky during the summer of '77, so he would've been familiar with the guitar.

Regardless of how he came up with the concept, the guitar's striped artwork and its subsequent iterations became universally associated with Ed, who copyrighted the design in 2001.

Van Halen returned to Sunset Sound on August 29, 1977, to begin work on their debut album. Templeman and the band chose five songs from the demos for the initial sessions, but the band also wanted to record four new songs they'd written during the break—"Ain't Talkin' 'Bout Love," "Atomic Punk," "Loss of Control," and "Jamie's Cryin'." With much darker lyrics and a heavier sound than in their previous work, the first three were clearly the band's nod to LA's burgeoning punk scene, while "Jamie's Cryin'," featuring Van Halen's catchiest melody to date, was a successful attempt at penning a radio-friendly hit.

ED WASN'T THE ONLY BAND member who took advantage of the hiatus before the album's recording to up his game. During the break, Roth worked with a vocal coach to improve his often-wobbly pitch and enhance his projection and power to ensure that he wouldn't blow out his voice box when delivering his distinctive lusty shouts and hollers.

The recording sessions progressed rapidly, with the band completing two to four songs during each daily six-hour session. As was the case with the demos, the songs were recorded live, with Ed playing his solos, accents, and fills, as well as his rhythm parts, exactly as he did onstage.

The basic instrumental tracks were completed in about a week, after which Ed added a handful of guitar overdubs to "Ain't Talkin' 'Bout Love," "Feel Your Love Tonight," "Ice Cream Man," "Jamie's Cryin'," and "Runnin' with the Devil." Lead and harmony vocals were recorded over the next week, and the band stepped away in mid-September while Landee and Templeman mixed the tracks. Work on the debut was finished on October 4, 1977. The final cost was a modest $54,000—considerably less than the six- and sometimes seven-figure sums it typically took to record an album at that time.

Van Halen finished 1977 playing farewell shows for their devoted local fans at the Pasadena Civic Auditorium and, on New Year's Eve, at the Whisky a Go Go. The band returned to the Whisky stage one last time to film promotional videos for "Jamie's Cryin'," "Runnin' with the Devil," and "You Really Got Me." Warner Bros. released their debut album, *Van Halen*, on February 10, 1978 and selected "You Really Got Me" as the album's first single.

*Van Halen* sounded unlike anything rock music fans had heard before. The yin and yang of aggressive, heavy sounds contrasted by catchy melodies and slick vocal harmonies was truly unique, like a Birmingham brawl and a Beach Boys beer bash happening at the same time. Those disparate yet somehow complementary attributes broadened the band's appeal, attracting everyone from angst-ridden teen males to pop-loving young females.

Although Roth was the front man, the spotlight focused on Ed, whose guitar remained prominent throughout the entire mix. Almost every song featured a distinctive six-string flourish—pick scrapes in "Runnin' with the Devil," stuttering staccato bursts in "You Really Got Me," phase-shifted dissonance in "Atomic Punk"—plus squealing artificial harmonics, chiming natural harmonics, and deep whammy bar dives throughout.

Ed's wild assortment of bends, growls, and zany sound effects had almost nothing in common with the traditional blues or rock textbook that most guitarists drew from. They were like something from another universe—a whacked-out Looney Tunes cartoon soundtrack to Roth's outrageously hypersexual Bugs Bunny persona. It was almost deliciously ironic that the band was signed to Warner Bros., the same company that produced the animated adventures of Bugs, Daffy Duck, and their pals.

"When I recorded Van Halen's debut, my strategy was just to take the guitar and blow it up all over the face of the damn map," said Templeman. "I thought it was the most amazing thing I'd ever heard."

But the album's coup de grâce undoubtedly was Edward's mind-blowing solo instrumental "Eruption." Just 1 minute and 42 seconds long, it forever changed the way electric players looked at their instrument. As the song's title suggests, the track was an explosion of musical ideas—sounds and techniques that would give players new avenues for expression for decades to come.

With his Frankenstein guitar, tuned down a half step to E-flat, plugged into a 1968 Marshall Super Lead tube amp turned up to 10 and supplemented by an MXR Phase 90 and Univox echo unit, all subject to the ambience of the Sunset Sound studio reverb room, Edward offered a brief but devastating summary of everything he had been working on for years.

Then there was the tone of his homemade guitar itself, which Van Halen described as his "brown sound." He had always admired the rich, liquid textures of Eric Clapton's playing on his Gibson SG during his time with Cream, but Ed's guitar equaled it in beauty while adding extra bite. His sound was big and round, even majestic when needed, but it could also ring out with sharp clarity during rapid passages. Engineer Landee's deft use of reverb contributed to the concert hall vibe of his sound.

Over the course of *Van Halen*'s thirty-five-minute run time, Ed redefined the rock guitar vernacular. He may not have pioneered every single trick and technique he employed on the album, but he made them uniquely his. Most guitarists who heard the album for the first time responded with slack-jawed wonder, realizing that the bar for guitar playing had been raised significantly.

Even the most jaded giants of the guitar community were impressed . . . and maybe a little intimidated by his virtuosity. Led Zeppelin's Jimmy Page raved, "For my money, Van Halen is the first significant new kid on the block. Very dazzling." Even the famously cynical Frank Zappa thanked Eddie for "reinventing the guitar."

LESS THAN A MONTH AFTER the album's release, Van Halen went on tour as the opening act for Journey and Ronnie Montrose. Their debut in Chicago, on March 3, was the band's first gig anywhere more than two hours' drive from Pasadena. Over the next nine months, Van Halen played shows across the entire United States, as well as in England, Scotland, Belgium, the Netherlands, Germany, France, and Japan. During the summer, they performed at large outdoor festivals in stadiums, sharing the stage with bands like Aerosmith, the Doobie Brothers, and the Rolling Stones. They also booked a handful of headline shows, including a triumphant homecoming appearance at the Long Beach Arena on July 8.

Most of the shows Van Halen played in 1978 were as the opening act for one of Eddie and Alex's biggest influences, Black Sabbath. The excited and energetic newcomers upstaged their heroes from their first show together in Sheffield, England, on May 16. Less than two weeks into the tour, on May 24, Van Halen celebrated their record's attaining the Recording Industry Association of America's (RIAA) Gold status. By October, when the band was with Black Sabbath in Germany, the album went Platinum.

Meanwhile, Black Sabbath's most recent album, *Never Say Die!*, failed to reach Gold, even in their UK homeland. But if this caused the heavy metal veterans some anxiety, it ceased once ticket sales for the tour's shows in the United States surged, thanks to the opening act's rising star.

Van Halen played its final show with Black Sabbath on December 3, 1978, at the San Diego Sports Arena, leaving the tour a few days early to begin work on their second album. The band was now living a life beyond their wildest dreams, and they were on top of the world. But the work they needed to do to stay there was only just beginning.

**How did you get discovered by Warner Bros.?**

Ted Templeman and Mo Ostin came to the Starwood in Hollywood, which was always kind of a bad place for us because we weren't a Hollywood band. Pasadena is really not like Hollywood at all. We were playing and somebody said, "There's somebody real important out there, so play good." It was just a weeknight, and there was hardly anyone in the crowd. Mo and Ted came backstage and said they loved it. They said, "If you don't negotiate with anyone else, we've got what you want right here." We were happy. Warner Bros. was always the company I wanted to be with. On top of that, we got Ted Templeman to produce the record.

**How did you write songs for the first album?**

A lot of the basic ideas were things that I came up with when I used to practice on the edge of my bed. I would take those ideas to band practice. At the time, we were rehearsing in David's father's basement, so Al and I would go over there by ourselves and jam on the ideas for hours until we came up with something we were happy with.

Sometimes you really have to work for inspiration. But ultimately, it's not really work, because my brother and I genuinely love to jam. I'd say that's the way most things happen in our band. It usually begins with me and Al, which is funny in a way, because most people don't usually think of the guitar and drums as a unit. It's usually bass and drums. I think Al's drumming is more musical because he listens to me rather than just being concerned with maintaining a steady groove.

**What were your feelings about recording the first album?**

Before we recorded the album, we went into the studio to record demos of about twenty-five songs with Ted and Donn. When we got in the studio, I asked them if it would be okay to play the way I do live instead of doing overdubs, and they said, "Sure. That would make it easier for all of us." We recorded the instrument parts for all twenty-five songs in one day and then came back the next day to record vocals. The idea was for us to choose the best songs for the album, but in between recording the demo and the sessions for the album, we had written some new songs that we liked better, like "Ain't Talkin' 'Bout Love," "Atomic Punk," and "Jamie's Cryin'." We also wrote "Loss of Control" and recorded it during the first album sessions, but it didn't make it to the finished record, so we saved it for later.

I remember when Al and I went to Warner Bros. to pick up the cassettes of the first twenty-five-song demo tape we did for them. We popped it into the player in my van and expected to hear Led Zeppelin coming out, but we were kind of appalled by what we heard. It just didn't sound the way we wanted to sound. The first album sounds a little better, but it still wasn't the way we imagined it should sound. The drums sound small and you can barely hear the bass. I guess you can say that it's very unique sounding. I wouldn't even know how to duplicate it, to tell you the truth.

The overall package of how the whole band sounded was not what Alex and I expected it would be. We figured that the drums would sound different. There is so much EMT plate reverb on the mix, which is something I never had really heard before. It still holds up today to a certain extent. It's not in your face or all that heavy, but the songs are great. If you heard us live, we sounded different. We were much heavier than what you heard on the record, and that's what Alex and I expected to hear on the record.

We didn't have a whole lot to say about much of anything. The songs basically got recorded the way we played them with very few overdubs. I guess it was Ted's idea to make it come off as pure, simple, and honest as it was live. I wasn't sure about that at first, but by the time Donn got through with it, I went, "Wow!" I really liked it. I didn't know what making a record was, and I guess it was good that we did approach it that way, because when we played live you were only going to get more.

**Whose idea was it to record at Sunset Sound?**
Donn and Ted had basically done all the Doobie Brothers stuff there. It was one of their favorite places. I didn't know anything about studios, so wherever they wanted to go was okay. I liked that room [Studio 2]. It was just a big room like our basement rehearsal space, actually. The guys who ran the studio and maintained the place, they'd walk in after we were done, and there were beer cans all over the floor and Pink's hot dog smears all over the place. But in order for us to be comfortable, we needed to do whatever we wanted.

**Was Ted important in bringing out the best in you?**

Oh, sure. What he managed to do was put our live sound on a record. He knows his shit. It was cool. I'm not saying I couldn't do better, but for a first album it took us only about a week just to do the music. Everything was basically done in a first or second take.

I hated overdubbing back then because it wasn't the same as playing with the guys. I needed to feed off them to play well. "Runnin' with the Devil" was one of the few exceptions because it had a melodic solo, so I overdubbed a rhythm guitar track underneath it. Songs that had a spontaneous solo, like "I'm the One," "Atomic Punk," and most of the songs on the album, Ted felt they were good enough on their own without fattening it up. Recording that way meant when we played those songs live, it sounded the same. I didn't like it when bands overproduced in the studio and then when they played live it didn't sound the same. With us, it sounded exactly the same and maybe even better because you got to see us doing it at the same time. We were very energetic. We'd get you up and shake your ass.

**Do any solos on the first album stand out for you?**

I really liked the solo in "I'm the One." It was spontaneous—whereas "Runnin' with the Devil," "On Fire," and some of the other ones were set. "I'm the One" gave me a chance to space off a little bit and noodle around.

**"Ain't Talkin' 'Bout Love" is another song where you recorded overdubs.**

That's right. If you listen closely, you can hear I doubled the guitar solo melody with an electric sitar. Either Donn or Ted suggested that I overdub a sitar underneath that melodic part. I told them that I didn't know how to play a sitar, and they explained that there was an electric guitar that sounded like a sitar. Donn rented the Coral Sitar that I used on "Ain't Talkin' 'Bout Love" from Studio Instrument Rentals.

**Why was "You Really Got Me" released as the band's first single?**

Looking back at things, that was my fault. A few months before the album came out, I went to the Rainbow or some other club, and I had a tape with a rough mix of the album. I was telling everyone about it. Barry Brandt, who was the drummer for Angel, was there, and he said we should go to his house to listen to it. So, we all went up there and listened to it. Everyone was blown away and paid really close attention to it. I thought that was cool, and I was really proud of how everyone reacted to it.

A couple of days later, Ted called me and asked if I had played the tape for anyone. I told him that I played it for a bunch of people a few nights ago and that everyone dug it. He asked me who was there, and I mentioned Barry. He got really pissed off at me and told me that he had just heard that Angel went into the studio to record "You Really Got Me" and that they were going to put it out as a single before our album was scheduled to come out.

Ted got on the phone with Warner Bros. and they decided to send "You Really Got Me" to radio stations as soon as possible. I was really bummed that they did that, because I wanted one of our own songs, like "Jamie's Cryin'," to be our first single.

### How was the decision made to place "Eruption" as the second song on the album?

The funny thing is that it wasn't meant to be on there at all. I was rehearsing for a show at the Whisky and Ted heard me playing a version of "Eruption" as a warm-up. He thought it sounded great and said we should put it on the record, so he had Donn record it. I did it about two or three times before we got a version that I liked. It wasn't perfect, though. When I got up to the top, I made a mistake, and I can't reproduce it. I'm still trying to figure out how I did it on the record.

With the tapping thing, I'm sure somebody did it before me. What made me think of doing it was something Jimmy Page played on "Heartbreaker." He was doing pull-offs to an open string and I thought, Fuck, if you can do that there, you can kind of capo it and move it anywhere you want. Instead of doing it like that (*holds right hand over left hand*), I used this finger (*holds up left index finger*) to barre. Basically, all this finger does is barre everything, and if I put that over here, I can move it around and play it anywhere. I realized that you could do that anywhere if you used your forefinger as a nut. I wasn't trying to show off. It was just fun.

### You really developed that technique to an advanced state.

It's not a trick with me. It's part of my playing now. When I was doing interviews for the *Balance* album, a writer said, "I didn't really hear you do any tapping." I went, "Well, because I do it so naturally now it's not a trick anymore." It's not like, "Here I go!" It has more of a flow—like one continuous thing. I've heard other people doing it, and I'm not knocking anyone for using the technique, but they should try to do something different with it.

**Do you remember how you came up with the intro to "Atomic Punk"?**
That basic idea for that sound originally came from "Light Up the Sky," which I had written before "Atomic Punk," even though "Light Up the Sky" appeared on our second record. After the guitar solo, there is a drum break, and you can hear me rubbing my palm on the low E string. One day I decided to try that with the Phase 90. It was an interesting sound, and it turned into a cool song. I've never really ever heard that sound from anyone else, neither before nor after I did that. After the solo, I actually also used the MXR Flanger for a quick bit.

**You didn't use many pedals in the early days—a phaser, a flanger, tape delay, and a wah-wah—but they became an essential part of your sound.**
I'd use a pedal if it enhanced the sound of what I played. I would use them in certain spots if I needed them. It wasn't a set thing. I'd just wing it, and nine times out of ten it would work. I had to have an idea or a song first, then I'll putz around and add or take away things. It's like making a steak. You have to have the steak first, then you can make it better by adding a little seasoning, but not too much because you want to taste the steak, not the seasoning.

All my pedals were stock, as well. I've gone back to using a homemade pedalboard again with my Phase 90 and the Flanger, plus a wah-wah, but I'm using the new MXR stuff. It sounds really, really good. When we first went on tour and were opening for bands, the other guitarists used to laugh their asses off when they saw my pedalboard. They stopped laughing when they heard me play, and then they asked if they could try my rig. They always sounded like themselves—nothing like me at all.

One time on our first tour after we finished sound check and went backstage, I heard this awful noise coming from the stage. When I went to check it out, there was Ted Nugent playing my guitar through my pedals

# EDDIE'S ODDITIES

**GUITAR:** John F. Sterry custom dragon guitar
**USED:** Early Van Halen tours

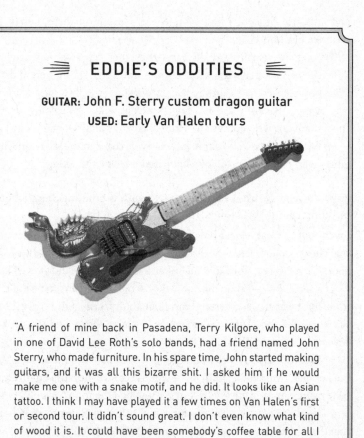

"A friend of mine back in Pasadena, Terry Kilgore, who played in one of David Lee Roth's solo bands, had a friend named John Sterry, who made furniture. In his spare time, John started making guitars, and it was all this bizarre shit. I asked him if he would make me one with a snake motif, and he did. It looks like an Asian tattoo. I think I may have played it a few times on Van Halen's first or second tour. It didn't sound great. I don't even know what kind of wood it is. It could have been somebody's coffee table for all I know. That's the kind of thing that he did."

Ed posed with this guitar for his first *Guitar World* magazine cover story, which appeared on newsstands in January 1981.

and amp. He thought I had some secret weapon in there, but he just sounded like himself.

People are usually way off base when they try to copy what I did. When I see fans playing a song of ours, I ask myself, "Where did they learn how to play that?" They're usually playing it totally wrong. I simplify everything. I basically use two fingers except when I'm soloing. When I show them how I do it, they go, "Huh?" Like my guitars, it's all pretty basic to me. It all boils down to simplicity. Now I'm back in the studio playing a guitar with one pickup and one knob and it sounds smoking.

**How did you go from playing a Strat with a humbucking pickup to building your own Frankenstein guitar?**
I went out to Charvel and bought a Strat-shaped Boogie Body that was a real cheap second. It was at the bottom of the pile of junk that they were about to throw out. They told me it was a "second," and I didn't even know what a second was. I thought it was the second one in line to be built, but it meant it was flawed in some way. I bought it from [guitar maker] Lynn Ellsworth for about fifty dollars because it was cheap, and the neck for seventy or eighty dollars.

Like I did with my Strat, I just gouged out the body and put one humbucker in it. I wired it up with just a volume control because I didn't know how to wire in the tone knobs. I never touched the tone controls anyway, and I could never get both the neck and bridge pickups to sound right together through the amp, so I just put in the rear one.

What I wanted wasn't necessarily a Strat-style body, but a Strat came with a vibrato bar that was the best one available at the time before the Floyd Rose. The Bigsby is more of a wiggle stick, whereas I just like going down in pitch. A floating tailpiece doesn't work for the way I play. It sounds like a warped record because I rest my hand on the bridge. I always like to have the tailpiece connected to the body for tone. If it's floating, it's not connected to anything and you might as well not have the wooden body at all. It's just in the air. Somehow, I came across an old Strat tailpiece and I put together the Boogie Body guitar, which is now known as the Frankenstein.

I discovered so many things building that guitar, especially why a guitar goes out of tune. On the first Van Halen record and tour, people were floored by how I could do all this crazy shit with a standard Fender vibrato bar. Here's the secret: if the string is not straight from the saddle to the nut to the tuning peg, you're going to have friction. On most guitars the headstock is at an angle. When you loosen the strings, they will loosen between the nut and the tuner, but they won't go back to where they were before because of the friction at the nut.

I got a brass nut, and I made the slots really big and put 3-in-One oil in the slots. I wound the strings up the tuning peg instead of down so the line from the saddle to the tuning peg was straight as an arrow. That provided the least amount of friction. From the back of the guitar where you put the string through the block on the Strat tailpiece, every time I turned the tuning peg, I would grab the ball end and turn it also so the string itself wasn't twisting.

It worked really well, but there were a few problems. If I hit an open string too hard, it would pop out of the nut, so when I played a low E or an A, I would hold the string in place with my forefinger at the nut. Sometimes halfway through the gig the oil would dissipate, and the strings would get stuck, so I'd have to pop them back.

**When you recorded the first album you were still playing the Ibanez Destroyer as well.**

I used that a lot on the first album. It's the guitar on every song that doesn't have any vibrato bar parts on it, like "You Really Got Me," "On Fire," and the rhythm track of "Jamie's Cryin'." I can't remember what pickups were in it when I recorded the album—I was always changing them—but that was before I cut that big chunk out of it. It was a really great-sounding guitar before I did that. A few months after I first bought the Destroyer in 1975, I painted it white. Then after we finished recording the first album, I decided to make it look different, so I cut it into a different shape that I thought looked really cool and painted it silver and red. That just fucked it up. All the bass was gone, and it sounded really thin. It went from sounding like a huge Les Paul into a weak, tinny Strat.

**Was your Marshall amp really 100 percent stock?**

I told people that [amp repairman] Jose Arredondo modified my amp to throw him a bone and help him out. Jose made most of his money by doing modifications to people's amps, but he never did anything to my amps other than re-tube them, set the bias, and replace things that blew, like the transformers. For years people thought that I had my amps hot-rodded, but they were stock. My Marshall had no line output or master volume. All I did was turn every knob all the way up, plug in, and play. That was the only way I could get the sound I wanted from that amp. In a funny way, I feel a bit guilty about telling people about Jose's mods because I lied, but a lot of people dug them. I don't own any of those modified amps. All of my Marshalls are just stock 100-watt heads.

**You lost your main Marshall amp on the first tour.**
Yeah. We had just toured Japan and the next gig in the States was supposed to be the Dallas Music Festival, the Texxas Jam. We were sitting there waiting for our equipment to arrive and it ended up in Chicago somewhere. We ended up playing in front of eighty thousand people on rented equipment. It was a drag. I had my guitars, but I was using Music Man amps. It sounded terrible. They were good amps back then, but they weren't the Marshall I was used to. When it finally showed up a few months later, I was so relieved. I sent it home and only used it to record albums in the studio. I never took it out on the road again.

**What were the first tours like?**
Back in 1978, we were on tour with Journey and Montrose for two months in three-thousand-seat auditoriums before we went out with Black Sabbath. The sound guy at those shows sucked, so I decided to play so loud that I didn't need a PA. He couldn't do anything because it was so goddamn loud. We also did the Day on the Green festival in Oakland with everyone from AC/DC to Foreigner. That was a hell of an experience.

**Were you playing well then, by your own standards?**
Yeah, I think so. I wasn't ashamed of my playing. I didn't feel I had a lot to learn. I had a lot to learn about dealing with people, but I felt we held our ground pretty well. If anything, we took a little too much ground, unintentionally. Not like, "Hey, fuck you, we're the best!" We just did our gig and whatever happened, happened. Everyone else was a victim of their own bullshit. It didn't come from us.

**What was it like to tour in 1978 with Black Sabbath, who were one of your biggest influences?**

They scared the shit out of us! I'll tell you a funny story that I'll never forget. After one of our first shows together, I walked up to Tony Iommi and began to ask him, "Second song on side two of *Master of Reality* . . ." Tony looked at me and went, "What the fuck, mate?" He didn't have a clue about what I was talking about.

By that time, Black Sabbath had so many records out, he had no idea what the track listings of any of his albums were. We only had one album out, so I knew where every track on our first record was. A few years later somebody asked me the same question, and I started saying, "Oh, you've gotta be kiddin' me." Then the first thing that popped in my head was that incident with Tony. I thought it was odd that he couldn't remember what was on his records, and then it happened to me!

Touring with Black Sabbath was great. I had a lot of good times on the road with Tony. Out of all the people I've ever met—all the celebrities and rock and roll stars—I fuckin' love Tony. After all of these years, he's still like a brother.

# MUSICAL INTERLUDE

*A conversation with **Eddie Van Halen** and Black Sabbath guitarist **Tony Iommi***

---

For a new band going on tour for the first time, performing as an opening act can be a challenging rite of passage. Some of the pitfalls include having cramped space onstage, not being allowed to do sound checks, and dealing with indifferent sound and lighting crews that are more likely to wreck your performance than enhance it. One of the biggest disappointments can be dealing with the inflated egos of the acts headlining the show and being subjected to their disdain and disrespect.

Van Halen encountered more than a few instances of the latter during their first world tour in 1978. After seeing the prop atomic bomb that housed Ed's Univox echo unit—a crucial part of his performance of "Eruption"—Mick Jagger sternly told the guitarist to remove it from the stage before the band opened for the Rolling Stones. When the band was playing festivals with Aerosmith, Ed was thrilled to run into guitarist Joe Perry backstage but quickly became crestfallen when Perry silently gave him the cold shoulder as he tried to shake Perry's hand. (The two eventually became good friends years later.)

Van Halen was given a similar icy reception during its first shows as the opening act for Black Sabbath's Never Say Die! tour. Not wanting to be upstaged, singer Ozzy Osbourne had told the booking agency before the tour to find a bar band from Los Angeles as the opening act. What they got instead was the hottest thing to come from the City of Angels since Jayne Mansfield, and Ozzy was not pleased.

Because Black Sabbath was a huge influence on Ed and Al, the members of Van Halen treated their heroes with respect. As the tour went on, Black Sabbath warmed up to the newcomers and became supportive and friendly. Drummer Bill Ward allowed Alex Van Halen to sit at the back of the stage to watch the Sabbath drummer play, and the two often talked shop. Ed and Tony Iommi forged a particularly tight bond, and the guitarists would often hang out after every show to drink and commiserate until the early hours of the morning.

Ed and Tony stayed in close touch over the years after that, so it wasn't difficult to get the two guitarists together for an interview. The following discussion took place in August 2010 at a photography studio in Los Angeles. Iommi showed up dressed in black from head to toe in characteristic metal god attire. Ed brought along the same hot-pink jumpsuit that he wore in 1980 during the album art photo shoot for *Women and Children First*. The outfit still fit him like a glove.

### Tony, what was your first impression of Van Halen?

**TONY IOMMI:** From the very first minute I heard them, I knew straight away that they were something special. The way that Ed plays is very different. He came up with a style that's been imitated a million times. And they had great songs. Often after the shows we would get together in my room and chat about guitars. We'd ramble on for about ten hours before we'd go to bed.

**EDWARD VAN HALEN:** Or not. (*laughs*) "What time is show time? The bus has left without me!" That was awesome.

**IOMMI:** That's right! (*laughs*) I really enjoyed that tour. Brian May is the only other guitar player I've ever associated with, and we've never been on tour together.

**VAN HALEN:** Tony is the sweetest, most humble, down-to-earth, normal guy. He has no attitude . . . and look at what this guy has done! I could name a handful of people who I still respect but I no longer look up to. After I met them, I was like, Fuck you! You're no better than I am as a person. So many people are a bunch of pompous fuckin' pricks. What makes them think their shit doesn't stink?

IOMMI: We lost contact for a bit, but ever since the early days it was like we were always together.

VAN HALEN: And you live in England. It's not like you're right around the corner.

IOMMI: When Van Halen came to England, we would get together again. But then there was a gap where we lost contact. But we hooked up again, and it's been really brilliant.

*Tony, your playing on Black Sabbath's* Heaven and Hell *album, which was the first record you released after touring with Van Halen and after Ozzy left Black Sabbath, progressed significantly. Was that partially inspired by touring with Ed?*

IOMMI: The whole thing was different because we had a different singer, and we developed a different sound. It was a different approach, really.

VAN HALEN: It's just the chemistry.

IOMMI: Yeah. Ronnie [James Dio] was someone who we could sit down and work with. He brought new life to the band. When Black Sabbath did *Never Say Die!*, which we probably shouldn't have called the album since we broke up after it came out, it was really tough. Ozzy left after we wrote the first song, and then about three days before we were due to record the album, he wanted to come back.

VAN HALEN: I'll say it for him. Dealing with singers is like pulling teeth. I should have been a fuckin' dentist! (*laughs*)

IOMMI: Working with a different singer influenced me to approach my playing in a different way. It injected the band with a bit of life. Ozzy didn't participate that much towards the end and wasn't coming up with any ideas, and when Ronnie came along, he came in with some input.

VAN HALEN: It's similar to when Hagar joined the band. It's just the element that a different person brings to the band. It's just like my son being the band's bassist now. He approaches everything differently, and the rhythm section is now like this huge wall behind me. I'd want to play with him regardless of whether he was my son or not. It's not to knock anyone. It's just when you change elements of a band the chemistry also changes. One little change can change the whole dynamic. It's not that it's getting any better or worse. A lot of people ask me which Van Halen singer was better. You can't compare them. It's like asking which guitarist is better. Nobody is better than anybody. Every player is their own person.

**IOMMI:** I get asked that question about singers all the time and I can't really answer it.

**VAN HALEN:** Music is not the Olympics. It's not a sport. It's a form of expression. There is no such thing as bad music. There may be music that you personally don't like, but if you don't like it, don't listen to it and shut the fuck up! Don't listen to it and complain about it. There's lots of music that I don't care for, but you can't say it's bad. That's subjective. That would happen if we put out something new now also. After we released our first album and were done touring, we recorded our second album. When it came out, the critics and some fans went, "Hey! It's different than the first one." Well, yeah! It's a different record. If it sounded like the first one, then fans and critics would complain that it sounded the same. What the fuck?

**IOMMI:** You can't ever win no matter what you do.

**VAN HALEN:** You just do what you do. If anyone has a better way, show me how to please everyone all the time! For some reason, people love to complain about everything. The internet has made it easy for people to do that. Shut the fuck up and get a life or show me how good you can do it.

People think they know what *I* should do. A lot of fans are complaining that Van Halen should put out a new record now. Everybody is going, Eddie should do this. Eddie should do that. I've got all kinds of music that I could put out if I wanted to. But they don't take into consideration the other members of the band. Maybe the singer doesn't want to do that. And if we do put something out, the first thing people are going to say is that it isn't as good as the classics. Okay. Put it in your closet for twenty years and then it will be classic.

People seem to forget that we put three new songs—"It's About Time," "Learning to See," and "Up for Breakfast"—on *Best of Both Worlds* in 2004. The reviews didn't even mention those songs. When we played the new songs live, people would just stand there. Why go to all the trouble, spend all of that time in the studio, and spend tons of your own money—there aren't even any record labels anymore to put our shit out—to record a new album when people are only going to complain about it or ignore it or some cocksucker is going to download it from the internet for free? We might not record something new. There's an element of satisfaction and joy to creating something new, but not when it comes solely at your own expense and when people are just going to shoot it down no matter what you do.

**IOMMI:** Whenever we do a show, people are always saying that we didn't play enough songs. Nobody understands that you only have a limited time. There are curfews and union rules that you have to obey.

**VAN HALEN:** Or you've got a guy with a decibel meter telling you how loud you can play.

**IOMMI:** And then people complain that the band wasn't loud enough. What can you do? You can try to fight these things, but you can't refuse to go on. I wish that people had a better understanding of what is going on.

**VAN HALEN:** People only see the end result of something. It's like today's photo shoot. They'll only see the cover shot and go, "Wow! It must be neat to be a rock star." They have no idea what goes into this or how many hours it takes. They don't see the wardrobe person hemming and pinning things up. When you walk onstage, they don't take into consideration the years of practice, the attitudes and egos of other people that you have to deal with, the songwriting, the recording, the record producer, the crew, designing the stage. All they see is the show.

**IOMMI:** And then they complain that you didn't play a certain song.

**VAN HALEN:** When people see Van Halen or Black Sabbath, it conjures up a certain image in their minds. If there's just one albino pubic hair outside of that image, they won't accept it. I play classical piano. I play a little bit of cello. I write all kinds of different music that certain singers or certain musicians don't want anything to do with. So what do I do?

*It wouldn't make sense for Ed to record the first Van Halen album again or for Tony to make* **Paranoid** *again because you've already done that. You've both moved on considerably from then, so going back would be counterproductive.*

**IOMMI:** Early on with Sabbath I had done a couple of instrumentals on *Master of Reality*. For *Sabotage*, I wrote this song called "Supertzar" and I wanted to have a choir on it. I got a choir in the studio, and even my own band members were wondering what I was doing. People from the record company came to visit and when they saw the choir and this harp player, they thought they were in the wrong studio. At the time, they were telling me I couldn't put this heavy guitar with choir and harp on an album, although it did finally make it there. I was just experimenting and trying something new, but even my own band was against the idea. I feel that as long as you write it, it's you.

*It's interesting how you both made your initial impact and found success by coming up with something that was very original. Then after thousands of imitators copied you and you wanted to go onto something else, the fans didn't want you to change. It seems like the more successful you become, the harder it is to do what initially made you successful.*

**IOMMI:** That's why I just do what I like.

**VAN HALEN:** I'm just glad to be able to play. I recently had hand surgery and arthritis treatment. I just found out that Tony was having the same problems I was, so I turned him on to my doctor. It's funny how there are so many parallels between Tony and me.

**IOMMI:** I was already booked for surgery in London with this specialist. Then Eddie told me about this guy in Germany who he went to for the same problem, so now I'm going to see him instead.

**VAN HALEN:** My hand hurt so much I couldn't even play. On the last half of the last tour, I was in pain. Tony is in pain now, and people are giving him shit about not wanting to tour. This is what we do for a living. It's not only our livelihood and our income—it's the only thing I know how to do! You don't know how I felt not being able to stretch my hand to play because of that pain. And then I had to go under the knife. I was scared shitless that it wasn't going to work.

**IOMMI:** I know that as soon as I go in, all of these things are going to come out on the internet and in the press.

**VAN HALEN:** It's nice to have some avenue to explain this to people.

*Why wouldn't you want to get a problem fixed? You want to be able to play. Everyone should understand that. Les Paul suffered with arthritis for years. It's too bad he didn't find out about your doctor.*

**VAN HALEN:** I knew Les very well. I'm glad that my son and I got to hang out with Les when we were on tour in New Jersey. He lived a long life and he always did what he wanted to do. He didn't do it for fame or vanity.

**IOMMI:** He played right up until the very end.

**VAN HALEN:** He was a musician. His death was a loss as a friend, but the guy had a rich, full life and he did what he wanted. He was still cracking jokes about pussy to Wolfie and me.

*I was just looking at your guitars and I noticed that Tony uses the same type of fluted knobs as Eddie has on his guitar, only larger.*

**IOMMI:** It's so ironic.

**VAN HALEN:** And the back of his guitar's neck is stripped, just like mine. I never liked having any kind of paint or lacquer on the neck. Tony took all of his off—the same thing!

*You both also liked to modify your guitars. Tony, you changed pickups on your guitars very early on when it wasn't common practice to do that. The only people I can think of who did that before you guys were Les Paul and Eddie Cochran.*

IOMMI: It's weird how we've both done a lot of the same things. I bought a guitar company because I couldn't get anybody to make the guitar that I wanted. Back in those days, Gibson didn't want to know me. So I started a company and I had a guy build me guitars with twenty-four frets and everything else that I wanted. Gibson told me that it couldn't be done.

VAN HALEN: Personal need is where it all comes from.

IOMMI: You've got to do it for yourself.

VAN HALEN: And then people want one. You try to give people what they want, but if the company that makes it is substandard, the people blame you. It ain't my fault the thing broke off! Mine broke too! Don't blame me because my name is on it. I just invented it for myself. Do you think people blame Henry Ford for a bad Mustang?

IOMMI: Companies always try to keep costs down. It's expensive to make things right.

*What were some of the most significant events for you over the last thirty years?*

IOMMI: The band broke up and got back together again.

*Both of your bands did!*

VAN HALEN: Some things have changed, but with me it's always been a family thing. It still is. My son joined the band. Contrary to people's beliefs, I didn't get rid of anyone to get him in the band. We needed a bass player and when I asked if he wanted to play bass, he said sure. It's always been my brother and I and whoever else. It used to be my dad, a lead singer, and a saxophone.

IOMMI: People would ask me over the years, "Why did you get rid of so and so?" They don't understand that sometimes people don't want to stay or they don't want to work hard anymore. You have to replace them. You may not be happy about it, but it's like a factory. Just because somebody leaves, you don't close the factory down.

**VAN HALEN:** You don't stop making music just because one of the guys doesn't want to play with you anymore.

**IOMMI:** There are so many different aspects to it. Sometimes they don't want to carry on and want to do their own thing, so you replace them.

*And sometimes you don't know when hell is going to freeze over and you'll work with someone again.*

**VAN HALEN:** Whoever thought we'd be back again with Roth? He went off and did his own thing. He just got tired of what we were doing. We did our thing and now we're back together.

**IOMMI:** Black Sabbath got back together with Ozzy. Even when Heaven and Hell got together with Ronnie James Dio a few years ago, we didn't think we were going to record a new album, but things worked out so well that we did it.

*You've both worked with personalities who became larger than life.*

**IOMMI:** Yeah, but we became the arseholes.

**VAN HALEN:** I was thinking about that old joke while I was on the way over here: What do you call a guy who hangs out with musicians? A drummer. But I beg to differ. In my experience, it's been singers.

*They never have to pack up any gear after gigs, so they're always out there after the show chatting up the hottest chicks.*

**VAN HALEN:** They're not musicians. They like to vocalize. They remember every goddamn thing under the sun except the lyrics. It does take a special breed to be a singer.

*The best singers usually have the biggest personalities and that comes with a lot of baggage.*

**VAN HALEN:** The problem is when they start believing that they're larger than life. The bottom line for me is I'm just happy to be here with my friend Tony. I've had a hip replacement, I've beaten cancer, I had my hand operation, and I stopped drinking. Something inside of me just went, I'm done. People always ask me if I'm in a program. AA didn't do anything for me. It's a strange thing. If you don't want to quit, you won't. Rehab didn't work. Nothing worked. I can't tell you what happened. It just did. I don't need to drink. I'm not jonesing for one. I don't even think about it anymore. It's like God gave me one big bottle and I drank it all, so now it's gone. I'm done. I'm just happy to be alive and to still be able to play.

### How would you like to be remembered?

VAN HALEN: What, do you want an epitaph here? I just want to be remembered for being a nice guy. I'd say for both of us that not a hell of a lot keeps us down.

IOMMI: We've done an awful lot.

VAN HALEN: We've made a lot of mistakes.

IOMMI: And you learn from it.

VAN HALEN: We've come up with a lot of cool stuff and we're far from done. We're certainly not the assholes people think we are!

# 4

# WARNING SIGNS

*Van Halen records four hit albums, each bigger than its predecessor, but there is trouble in paradise.*

---

" What do you got, Eddie? "

---

E DWARD VAN HALEN should have been in a celebratory mood on New Year's Eve 1978. He was attending a party at the home of his band's producer, Ted Templeman, and work on Van Halen's second album was almost finished. Less than a month had passed since the band ended its first world tour, and with the album's basic tracking completed a few weeks before, the young guitarist had his first opportunity to finally relax and catch his breath since March.

But Ed didn't feel like mingling with the small gathering of music industry figures—record company executives and employees, studio musicians, and members of various bands from the LA area—who were enjoying more than a few drinks before the countdown began. Parties made him nervous and he could feel his social anxiety beginning to kick in. It was the same unsettling feeling he'd felt in the pit of his stomach a million times when he was a young immigrant trying fit in at school.

Spotting an acoustic guitar in a side room, Ed picked it up and started to noodle on a few familiar patterns and the licks he played on his electrics. Almost instantly, he felt a sense of calm, as he had on so many nights alone in his room long before Van Halen became world famous. He lost himself in his playing and forgot all about the world around him.

Minutes or possibly even an hour had passed before Ed opened his eyes and realized that Templeman was watching him. Seeing Ed come out of his trance-like state, the producer exclaimed, "That sounds amazing! I didn't know you played acoustic guitar so well. We should put that on the record." It was almost an exact repetition of the scenario during the first album sessions when Templeman overheard Ed rehearsing the solo guitar piece that eventually became "Eruption."

The guitarist was more than happy to indulge Templeman's request, and a few days later he walked into a music store and bought a nylon-string Ovation acoustic. While paying for the instrument, he felt a wave of anxiety: "Can I even afford this?" he thought to himself.

Less than a month earlier, only a few days after getting home from the tour, the band reached out to Warner Bros. to learn how much money they'd earned from the tour and album sales. The answer they received shocked them. Instead of making a substantial profit, they actually owed the record company more than $1.2 million. That was a staggering debt for anyone, but particularly for the Van Halen brothers, who were so broke they were still living at home with their parents. It wasn't unusual for a new band to owe some money back to the label for tour support, especially if they weren't headliners. The band had been more than a little rowdy, causing damage to hotel rooms and shelling out for expensive room service and bar tabs. But still, the debt came as a jolt.

Ed felt that Van Halen's second album was better than their debut, but he also knew that the music industry could be unpredictable, and that success wasn't necessarily guaranteed. The band would now be a headline act on its second tour, and although that meant they would be taking in a larger share of the ticket sales, it also meant that they'd be responsible for a lot more upfront costs. Would the album and tour get them out of trouble, or would the expenses continue to pile up even higher?

There were a few signs that things were going to get better. Most significantly, during the downtime between tours, Van Halen fired their manager, Marshall Berle, who'd been largely absent during their first year as a signed band. He rarely gave them advice and left them to fend for themselves on their initial tour, practically guaranteeing their towering debt to the label.

When the manager did finally appear at one of the band's shows in Japan, he hosted a lavish dinner for the group and its entourage in Tokyo. Assuming that Berle was picking up the tab, the boys blew a gasket when they later discovered that he'd put his entire trip—including the celebratory dinner—on Van Halen's expense spreadsheet to the tune of more than $10,000.

Berle's replacement was the band's road manager, Noel Monk, a no-nonsense hardliner who oversaw the Sex Pistols' US tour just prior to working with Van Halen. Monk steadfastly accounted for every expenditure on Van Halen's 1978 tour, and once he became the band's manager, he looked out for their interests honestly and to the smallest detail.

Despite the pressures roiling Van Halen at the time, no signs of trouble were discernible on *Van Halen II*. With the exception of Ed's acoustic solo showpiece, "Spanish Fly," the band completed the album's tracks in less than a week. Several of the songs that were two years old or older had been road-tested prior to the recording sessions, and because the band had just finished touring, the arrangements and performances were solid and tight.

Featuring upbeat songs like "Bottoms Up!," "Beautiful Girls," and the band's strongest contender for a hit to date, the newly written "Dance the Night Away," there was a joyous party vibe to *Van Halen II* that captured the energy of their stage shows. Like its predecessor, the album did feature a fair share of darker material, including "Outta Love Again," "D.O.A.," and a sinister remake of Linda Ronstadt's cover of "You're No Good." The overall sound of *Van Halen II* was less aggressive than its predecessor, and its stronger pop melodies helped the band appeal to a wider audience—including a growing influx of female fans who joined the ranks of metal heads and guitar geeks.

Ed stepped up to the plate with admirable conviction, delivering an entirely new set of guitar licks and tricks to solidify his burgeoning guitar hero status. These included volume swells, palm-muted harmonic sweeps, tapped harmonics that sounded like they were produced by a windup music box, and an assortment of his signature moves performed on acoustic guitar.

# EDDIE'S ODDITIES

**GUITAR:** 1962 Gibson SG TV Junior
**USED:** Slide guitar part on "Dirty Movies"
(*Fair Warning*)

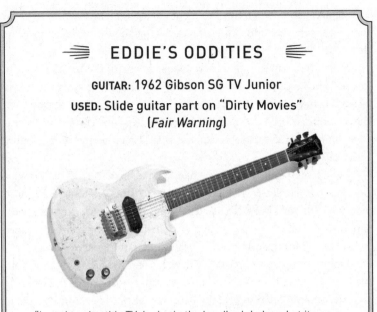

"I used to play this TV Junior in the band's club days, but it was a bitch to keep in tune. The neck is heavier than the body. I didn't play it for very long because it's uncomfortable to play a guitar when you have to support the neck and play at the same time. The neck joint on TV Juniors often break, but this one never cracked or broke, which is surprising considering all of the abuse I put it through.

"I took this guitar to Sunset Sound when we were recording 'Dirty Movies' for *Fair Warning*. I used it to play the slide part. I kept recording takes over and over, and finally I asked Donn Landee to get me a hacksaw. He asked me what I was going to do, and I told him not to worry about it. I hacked off the horn on the treble side because I couldn't hit the high notes with the slide. Everybody looked at me like I fell out of my tree, but it was by necessity.

"People trip when I do things like that right in front of them. I've destroyed a lot of vintage guitars over the years. Some people might think, 'How could you desecrate the *Mona Lisa*?' But I don't really care what something looks like or if it's 100 percent stock. I tear things apart to try and make them work and do what I need them to do. I'm more concerned with a guitar's functionality, sound, and playability."

In some ways, "Spanish Fly," performed on a nylon-string instrument, was one of the best demonstrations of what made Ed's *electric* playing so explosive. The listener can hear how well each note is articulated without the aid of an amplifier. Ed rarely approached his instrument "casually," and his tone was as much a product of that physicality as his Marshall. Whatever he played through or whatever guitar he was using, it always sounded like Ed.

On *Van Halen II*, you hear the awesome force and precision of his right hand and the unique tone it produced, whether it was the wonderfully syncopated rhythms on "Beautiful Girls" or the wildly spikey solo on "You're No Good." Special guitars and amps aside, Ed's real secret weapons were his hands.

*Van Halen II* hit record store shelves on March 23, 1979, and two days later the band played the first show of its second world tour in Fresno, California. Charvel built Ed a new guitar to his specifications, featuring black and yellow stripes, with which the guitarist posed for the album cover photo session. Just before the tour began, Ed modified his signature black and white Frankenstein guitar by installing dummy single-coil pickups and applying an extra top layer of fire-engine-red bicycle paint in an attempt to confuse the guitar companies that had started to copy his designs.

"What trips me out is that when I painted the Frankenstein red that made it more famous," he said. "A lot of people still don't know that it's the same guitar as the black and white guitar on the cover of the first Van Halen album. That guitar went through a lot of different phases and changes. On the first record it had a stock vintage Fender Strat vibrato, then the Floyd came around, and then I added the dummy pickup at the neck. I kept changing it because I was tired of people copying my guitar."

*Van Halen II* enjoyed greater initial success than the band's debut had, earning Platinum certification and peaking at number six on the *Billboard* album chart within two months of its release. The album's first single, "Dance the Night Away," peaked at number fifteen on the *Billboard* Hot 100 chart about two months later. Thanks to its calypso-style melody and rhythm—Ed's guitar even sounded like steel drums—"Dance" became the unofficial song of the summer of '79.

Van Halen's 1979 World Vacation tour was a financial success, even with the added cost of carrying thirty-six tons of sound and lighting equipment on the road. They regularly sold out arena-size venues across North America, and when they returned to Europe and Japan they attracted considerably larger crowds than on their previous visit. With Monk watching every penny like a hawk and the band conscientiously cutting down on laying waste to hotel rooms, Van Halen's expenditures diminished drastically, leaving them considerably in the black.

"The first thing I'm going to do is get my dad to retire," Ed told Steve Rosen, who regularly interviewed the guitarist in the seventies (portions of which were used in the following conversation). "The weekly checks out of our corporation pay us a lot more than he's making, so Al and I said, 'Quit your job.' He's been working seven days a week ever since we came to this country, and we're going to retire him and buy him a boat so he can go fishing."

During a brief midtour break, Ed and Al returned home and bought that boat for their dad.

The World Vacation tour concluded October 7, 1979, with a homecoming show at the Los Angeles Forum. This was the same venue where Ed and Alex so often watched their heroes like Led Zeppelin, Deep Purple, and Black Sabbath perform. Now they were headlining on the same stage, as their parents watched proudly from the audience; particularly, their father, Jan, was brought to tears during his sons' drum and guitar solos. After the show the Van Halen brothers partied with a few hundred of their friends until the early hours of the morning.

Still buzzing from a potent combination of adrenaline, alcohol, and cocaine, Ed and Al abruptly plummeted down to earth when they returned to their parents' home and discovered that it had been burglarized. The valuables stolen from the household included all of their Gold and Platinum record awards.

At that moment, Ed and Al finally decided to make good on their plans to buy their parents a new home and finance their retirements. They were able to do this thanks to Monk's negotiating more favorable terms for the band after Warner Bros. overlooked the deadline to exercise a contract-extension option for their third and fourth albums.

In addition to looking after their parents, the brothers enjoyed a few personal indulgences. Each bought himself a car—for both, the first of many that would grow into large collections—with Ed driving home a Porsche 911E Targa. Their days of driving junky clunkers with doors held shut by guitar strings were in the rearview mirror. Ed also went to Norman's Rare Guitars in Tarzana and bought a pair of vintage late-fifties Les Paul Standard guitars, though more as an investment than anything else. As David Lee Roth sang in "Beautiful Girls," Ed was truly "on top of world." All he needed was the girl. And that would come soon enough.

AFTER A WELL-DESERVED TWO-MONTH BREAK from touring, Van Halen returned to Sunset Sound in early December 1979 to start recording *Women and Children First*. This time around, the band decided to make a statement by recording only original material. Ed had written several new songs during the interlude, including what became a perennial favorite, "Everybody Wants Some!!," but they weren't enough to fill the album. To make up for the shortage, the band dug deep into the past and polished some of their earliest material.

Most of these songs—"Fools," "In a Simple Rhyme," and "Take Your Whiskey Home"—dated back to 1974, with the last two included on a tape the band gave Michael Anthony for him to learn when he first joined Van Halen. Ed reconfigured parts of "Get the Show on the Road" from the Warner Bros. demos for "Romeo Delight," and the band also recorded a new version of "Loss of Control," which was left over from the first album sessions.

The new song "And the Cradle Will Rock . . ." began its life as a guitar riff Ed wrote on the tour bus, but after the guitarist bought a second-hand Wurlitzer electric piano from a pawnshop, it was transformed into a keyboard-dominated song. Purportedly, the first thing Ed wrote on the Wurlitzer were the chords to "Jump."

"After we got back from tour, Al and I jammed on the basic riff from 'And the Cradle Will Rock . . .' two hours a day for two straight weeks," Ed said. "We didn't really know what to do with it, but we were having fun because it just sounded so wicked. Then, out of nowhere, the chorus came to us and it was finished."

The addition of keyboards expanded Van Halen's sound, but it was a subtle shift thanks to Ed's playing the Wurlitzer through his distorted Marshall amp and using an MXR Flanger to create jet-like sounds. Ed also used a rented Rickenbacker twelve-string electric to perform "In a Simple Rhyme," and he played slide on "Could This Be Magic?"

But, by far, the most significant guitar innovation on *Women and Children First* was not a sound or a technique but rather a piece of hardware that Ed had been dreaming of since he started playing guitar: the locking vibrato system. Using a vibrato bar was a major part of his playing technique, allowing him to bend notes dramatically. But excessive use often caused his strings to fall hopelessly out of tune. He had developed a number of strategies to minimize the problem, but he was unable to come up with a solution that worked all the time.

As Ed's star was rising, a guitarist named Floyd Rose was dealing with the same set of issues. Rose was playing in a rock band and wanted to use his whammy bar the way his hero Jimi Hendrix did but was frustrated when his guitar wouldn't stay in tune. Using skills acquired from years of jewelry making, he devised an ingenious system of clamps that would lock the strings at the nut (where the neck meets the headstock) and again at the bridge. Together, they'd keep the guitar in tune even under the most extreme twang bar duress.

Rose shared this "double-locking" system with his friend Lynn Ellsworth of Boogie Bodies, who immediately thought of Ed. Ellsworth's company had provided the body for Ed's Frankenstein guitar, so he called Ed to set up a meeting.

"So, I went with him to show Eddie the locking system I created," said Rose. "He liked it and gave me a guitar to put one on."

Ed picked up the story from there: "My role in the design and development of the Floyd was adding the fine tuners to the bridge. . . . Strings stretch, temperature changes, and depending on how hard you play, your guitar would go out of tune, even with the Floyd Rose system. So, you'd have to unclamp the nut, which involves loosening three screws with an Allen wrench, tune the guitar, and reclamp the nut down again. There wasn't enough time to do all that in between every song live. . . . To put it simply, it was a pain in the ass." So, Eddie suggested adding fine tuners to the bridge. That would allow a player to lock down the strings, so they'd essentially stay in tune, but still make subtle adjustments when needed. And it worked!

Ed could now use the whammy bar on his Frankenstein as much as he wanted without any fear of his strings going sharp or flat, which allowed him to explore a whole new universe of otherworldly sounds and subtle nuances. On *Women and Children First*, he wasted no time investigating the possibilities of his new toy, using it to produce a host of squeals and jungle sounds on the second song, "Everybody Wants Some!!" And as time progressed, the Floyd Rose locking system became more of an essential device for Ed . . . and many other rock players in the eighties and beyond.

*Women and Children First* was released almost exactly a year after its predecessor. By this point in the band's history, Van Halen had become locked in a repeating annual cycle where they would quickly record an album and then go on tour for most of the remaining year. The 1980 World Invasion tour began on March 19 in Victoria, British Columbia, a week before the March 26 release date of *Women and Children First*. Keyboards, played by Michael Anthony, made their first onstage appearance at a Van Halen show. This time around, the band decided to bypass Japan and focus mostly on reaching the farthest corners of the United States and Canada, with a one-month side excursion to Europe.

The World Invasion tour was pretty much like the previous tours, albeit on a grander scale. One performance turned out to be particularly special: When Van Halen rolled into Shreveport, Louisiana, on August 29, a VIP was in the audience: Valerie Bertinelli, one of the stars of the hit television sitcom *One Day at a Time*, who was attending with her brothers. The twenty-year-old actress, who'd already become interested in the guitarist from his photos on the band's album covers, made her way backstage after the concert to meet Eddie.

Although Ed never had much time to watch network television, he recognized the cute young actress and was instantly smitten. In Valerie's presence, he behaved gentlemanly and shy, like the old pre-fame Eddie Van Halen, without the cocky demeanor he often displayed in the presence of a seemingly endless string of groupies. The two chatted late into the night, and when Ed boarded the bus to travel to the tour's next destination, he asked for Bertinelli's phone number.

The couple instantly fell for each other. Valerie appeared at the band's shows with increasing frequency, at first flying in to wherever the band was playing for a few nights on weekends, followed by stayovers that lasted for a week or more. The two were inseparable by the time the tour wrapped up on November 15, in Lakeland, Florida, and Ed finally left his parents' house and moved in with Valerie. By the end of the year, the couple were engaged.

Van Halen had become one of the biggest rock bands in the world. They'd released a trio of multi-Platinum albums, and their sold-out tours and merchandise sales had made the band members millionaires. At this point, it appeared that Van Halen had nowhere to go but up, but trouble was brewing.

As Ed became happier and increasingly more successful, earning numerous accolades for his guitar playing and appearing in gossip magazines thanks to his blossoming relationship with a popular television star, David Lee Roth allegedly grew jealous and sometimes confrontational. Roth was used to being the center of attention and had carefully groomed himself for that role, but suddenly the spotlight was shining on Ed— a role the introspective and socially awkward guitarist only reluctantly accepted. Onstage, Ed and Dave seemed like best friends, but behind the scenes the singer often taunted and insulted Ed, stopping only when it looked as if the two would come to blows.

"I never would have pegged Ed as someone who would be remotely attracted to the idea of a celebrity girlfriend (or wife)," wrote Noel Monk in his book *Runnin' with the Devil*.[5] "But maybe it was precisely the fact that David had bragged for so long about marrying a movie star that encouraged Eddie to choose this path instead. They were competitive, after all; and at times they legitimately disliked each other. So maybe Edward's relationship to Valerie was on some level triggered by a desire to issue a public 'fuck you' to David."

That tension spilled over to the recording of Van Halen's fourth album, *Fair Warning*. Unlike the previous efforts, where the band all got together and quickly recorded the songs live with just a few takes, *Fair Warning* was put together in piecemeal fashion, with Ed, in particular, working apart from his bandmates after hours with engineer Donn Landee. Often when the others returned to the studio the morning after a session, they discovered that the songs they'd recorded just a day earlier sounded quite different, with some of their parts erased.

"The approach on *Fair Warning* was definitely different," Ed said. "My playing on the first three albums was pretty much live and straight ahead. On *Fair Warning*, I did a lot more guitar overdubs, and only three of the ten songs were done in the old style, with a solo recorded at the same time as the rhythm track. I approached my playing differently by writing rhythm parts that I intended to solo over."

Ed took almost complete control of the recording process, writing songs in the studio and staying there almost continuously throughout the entire project. He kept himself awake and inspired by ingesting copious amounts of alcohol and cocaine but barely any food, and by the time the album was completed, his weight had withered down to only 125 pounds. Ed spent so much time in the studio that Valerie probably wondered if their upcoming plan to get married was a good idea.

"Alcohol and cocaine were private things to me," Ed later explained in a *Billboard* interview. "I didn't drink to party. I used them for work. The blow keeps you awake and the alcohol lowers your inhibitions. I'm sure there were musical things I would not have attempted were I not in that mental state. You just play by yourself with a tape running, and after about an hour, your mind goes to a place where you're not thinking about anything."

Between the drugs and Ed's increasingly contentious relationship with Roth, the darkness shadowing the album carried over into the sessions. Ed's playing was furious and aggressive, particularly on the tracks that opened the two sides of the LP, "Mean Street" and "Unchained," respectively. His explosive tapped solo on "Sinner's Swing!" sounded like the work of a man possessed, while his slower-tempo performances on "Push Comes to Shove," "Dirty Movies," and "So This Is Love?" brought to mind a dive bar saxophonist's sleazy playing behind a burlesque stripper.

Roth matched the mood with lyrics that replaced his usual good-times attitude with something more ominous. "Dirty Movies" told the story of a prom queen's degeneration into a porn starlet, while "Mean Street" made good on the menace suggested by its title. As a result, the album was more a soundtrack for a late Saturday night fight than the party-startin' rock and roll weekend that characterized the band's previous efforts—a distinction enhanced by the album cover's grim earth-toned depiction of violent images, reconfigured from a work called *The Maze*, produced by Canadian artist William Kurelek while he was in a mental hospital.

*Fair Warning* also showcased a significant maturation of Ed's guitar playing and compositional skills. He explored a wider variety of sonic textures as he finally became comfortable with the creative potential of overdubbing, and his solos were adventurous and exploratory, with a sophisticated jazz-fusion character instead of the blues-based phrases still common in rock and metal at the time. Ed also ventured even further into adding keyboards to Van Halen's soundscape, including an Electro-Harmonix Mini-Synthesizer on "Saturday Afternoon in the Park" and "One Foot Out the Door."

*Fair Warning* is considered Van Halen's masterpiece by many of the band's fans who are also musicians, but for the band's more pop-oriented following, the album was too dark, complex, and challenging. All of the first seven songs on the album are strong and memorable, but, like a gymnast delivering a perfect performance on the uneven bars only to blow it by stumbling on the dismount, the final two songs ("Sunday Afternoon in the Park" and "One Foot Out the Door") sound like incomplete sketches that were tacked on at the last second to fill up the run time.

Ed unleashed his imagination on *Fair Warning* like never before, embracing the creative potential of the studio recording process for the first time in his career instead of just rushing through the task, but he still needed to figure out how to refine and polish his output to make it more pleasing to the masses. It would take him another few years before he achieved that elusive balance, but the seeds for his progress and growth as an artist were sowed and nurtured here.

Ed and Valerie exchanged wedding vows on April 11, 1981, and after a quick honeymoon Ed hit the road about a month later when the WDFA (We Don't Fuck Around) tour started on May 12. For the tour, Van Halen planned their biggest shows to date, equipped with 175,000 tons of equipment and a 90,000-watt sound system. The band performed over a six-month period in the United States and Canada only, and all but three of the shows sold out, resulting in gross ticket sales of more than $10 million.

Although *Fair Warning* managed to reach a higher position on the Billboard 200 Albums chart, peaking at number five compared to number six for each of their two previous efforts, it sold at a slower pace, earning Platinum certification seven months after its release—about the same time the tour wrapped up. Producer Templeman and singer Roth became nervous about the band's future, but Ed wasn't particularly concerned, noting how Van Halen's back catalog was still selling and their concert audiences were growing.

AFTER FOUR NONSTOP CYCLES OF recording an album and touring every year, the members of Van Halen were ready for an extended break.

However, at the beginning of 1982, Roth expressed concern that the band could lose momentum if they stayed out of the public eye for too long.

In January, he convinced his bandmates to release a single as a stop-gap between albums to remind fans that they were still around. To make the process as easy as possible, the singer suggested recording a cover of Martha and the Vandellas' "Dancing in the Street." After struggling to come up with a compelling guitar part, Ed recommended recording a cover of Roy Orbison's "(Oh) Pretty Woman" instead, and Roth enthusiastically assented.

Van Halen recorded "(Oh) Pretty Woman" in a single day at Sunset Sound, and Warner Bros. quickly issued the single on February 6. When the song unexpectedly rocketed up the pop charts, it caught everyone by surprise—especially the label. The very idea of having a hit single without an album to promote outraged the executives at Warner Bros., who immediately put pressure on the band to crank something out quickly. They obediently returned to the studio in March to see what they could whip up, but because Sunset Sound was booked, Templeman and the band convened for the first time at Amigo Studios.

"We jumped right back into the studio and started recording again without any rest or time to recuperate from the tour," Ed told *Guitar Player* magazine.[6] "We used a different studio, which was called Amigo but is now Warner Brothers Recording Studios. It was nice to have a change, because we did every other album at Sunset Sound. But we worked so fast on *Diver Down* that it was actually cheaper to make than our first album."

Like the band's first three albums, *Diver Down* was recorded in rapid-fire fashion, over a period of twelve days. Ed had not planned on doing it so quickly, and understandably had little new material to offer the band. To make up for the lack of new compositions, a decision was made—mostly by Roth and Templeman—to record some cover songs. "Dancing in the Street" was reworked with a sequenced and delay-processed Mini Moog riff Ed planned on using for an original song, and Roth dug into The Kinks' back catalog once again and chose "Where Have All the Good Times Gone."

Van Halen resurrected a couple of songs from their original Warner Bros. demo: an a cappella version of Roy Rogers's "Happy Trails" and the original composition "Last Night," which was reworked into "Hang 'Em High." Dave also suggested the Dixieland jazz standard "Big Bad Bill

(Is Sweet William Now)," sweetening his pitch by asking the Van Halen brothers if they could get their dad to play clarinet on the track.

Of the album's three instrumental tracks, two were brief intros to "Pretty Woman" ("Intruder") and "Little Guitars," while "Cathedral" was something Ed had previously developed for his live guitar solo. The three new songs—"Secrets," "Little Guitars," and "The Full Bug"—were arguably the album's strongest material, leaving some fans to wonder what Van Halen could have delivered if the album had been recorded the way Ed originally planned.

Providing a breezy assortment of pop ventures along with a few interjections of Roth's sense of humor and schmaltz, *Diver Down* marked a 180-degree turn in attitude from the dark and desperate *Fair Warning*. Ed still managed to supply several dazzling moments of fretboard fireworks, but he seemed free to truly express himself only during his solo showcases. Because *Diver Down* was recorded so quickly, it has more rough edges and considerably less finesse and flair than *Fair Warning*, but the bright tones and light attitude cover those flaws like a thickly applied coat of fire-engine-red paint.

*Diver Down* was an instant commercial success, becoming Van Halen's first release to go Platinum before the supporting tour even started. Ed, however, saw it as a hollow victory. Although *Diver Down* had sold boatloads of records, he believed it was by far the band's worst album, and he was embarrassed by all the cover songs and filler material.

Then and there he vowed that he would never again be browbeaten by a singer, a label, a producer—anyone—into putting out an inferior product. He'd been bullied in one way or another throughout his life, and it was time to seize the artistic control that the band's success had rightfully given him. There wouldn't have been any Van Halen or Platinum records without his hours of practice and sleepless nights trying to come up with the next mind-altering lick or chord progression. And how many people had become rich by freeloading off his talent? Too many to count, and he was sick of it. From then on, he was going to do things his way.

Edward's solution was to take his ball and go home. Literally. The guitarist decided to build his own recording studio on the property he and Valerie purchased in the hills above Studio City. There, he could work at his own pace and record whenever he pleased. Roth's "play it safe" approach on *Diver Down* may have been more commercially successful than the artistic, adventurous angle Ed pursued on *Fair Warning*, but the guitarist was motivated to show that, given time and his own space, he could deliver music that was both fresh and commercially viable.

**When did you start working on *Van Halen II*?**
We started on the Monday after our last gig of our first tour. We'd just played for ten straight months, so we were extremely tight and wanted to take advantage of that. At that point you're just tight without even knowing it.

**Did you think the first album would be as successful as it was?**
Hell no! I had no idea, but we felt pretty good about *Van Halen II*. We had gained a lot of confidence. We took the same approach as we did on our first album and just set up in a big room with my old Marshalls and played.

The Marshalls I used on the first two albums just sounded so good, but I stopped touring with them after they got lost in transit on one occasion. I bought some new ones and put the original in a closet and only pulled it out for recording.

**It doesn't sound like there's very much overdubbing on *Van Halen II*.**
Oh no, not at all. Only three of the songs had guitar overdubs. The rest were live.

**Did you consciously try to write another "Runnin' with the Devil"?**
No. I thought the songs were very different on the second album. I knew that some of the harder things like "Light Up the Sky" would never get any airplay, but those were the songs that I really liked.

**How would you compare *Van Halen* to *Van Halen II*?**
Ted and Donn Landee weren't sure of what they wanted to do with us on the first album. By the second album, they knew exactly what to do and so did we. We also grew. We were playing and writing better. Ted said several times, "God, I can't believe how tight you guys are compared to the first record." *Van Halen II* is just much fuller.

**In retrospect, what songs stand out to you?**

I liked "Outta Love Again" because it was a funkier sound for us, and it gave some room for the drums to shine. It reminded me of [Tower of Power's] "What Is Hip?" "Somebody Get Me a Doctor" was written around the same time as "Runnin' with the Devil" and was an early club favorite.

**The beginning instrumental section of "Women in Love" was quite different for you. It was unapologetically pretty.**

I was experimenting with my use of "tapped harmonics" [a bell-like sound that is created when the guitarist taps exactly twelve frets above any fretted note played]. I doubled everything and Donn put it in stereo, which made the sound sparkle a little more. Another reason it sounded different was because I used a new guitar that I put together myself. It had a junk Strat-style body and a Danelectro neck I had laying around, and I threw a Telecaster pickup in the bridge and I think there was a [Seymour Duncan] Fat Strat in there somewhere. I put it together in a day and I only used it for that intro because my Frankenstein guitar just sounded too ballsy for something that quiet and clean.

**You also did another cover song on this album, "You're No Good."**

When we were playing the clubs, we used to do a version that sounded more like Linda Ronstadt's version, but when we had the idea to do it in the studio, I couldn't really remember how it went, so I just started noodling and that's what came out.

**Did you have a favorite?**

Probably "Light Up the Sky." I wrote it right before our first record was recorded. When we were getting ready to record the second album, Ted asked to hear all our new ideas, and he really liked it. I was totally surprised because it was pretty progressive—the changes were a little more bent than some of the more commercial ideas we had. It made me happy that he liked it. It gave me hope!

I also liked "Beautiful Girls." It was a happy song to balance out some of the heavier stuff. I hate when albums are happy-happy or heavy-heavy all the way through. We had a little bit of both on *Van Halen II*—some songs that sound really poppy and the others were about drinking a bottle of booze and fucking, like "D.O.A."

# EDDIE'S ODDITIES

**GUITAR:** Homemade black and white guitar ("Rude")
**USED:** Fair Warning tour

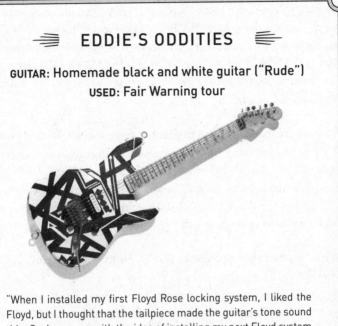

"When I installed my first Floyd Rose locking system, I liked the Floyd, but I thought that the tailpiece made the guitar's tone sound thin. So, I came up with the idea of installing my next Floyd system in a much thicker body, figuring the tone would improve. I had Lynn Ellsworth of Boogie Bodies make me a mahogany body that was two inches thick, like a Les Paul. I was just experimenting to see what it would sound like. It sounded a lot better and I played for a while on the *Fair Warning* tour. That's the one you see here.

"I built a similar guitar around the same time. I put circles and stripes on the finish and used it in the live performance video for 'Unchained.' I later added extra layers of red, yellow, and green paint to it, but I ended up giving it away because it wasn't really one of my favorites. I liked this one a lot better, even though it's big and chunky. It's a beast."

**Were you satisfied with your playing?**

Definitely. There were a lot of cool guitar tricks on it, but they were more subtle than on the first record. When *II* came out, most people weren't even sure whether some of the sounds were being made with a guitar, like the tapped harmonics on "Women in Love" and "Dance the Night Away." That gave me a lot of satisfaction—tricks that surprised people when they found out it was a guitar.

**Was the recording process similar on *Women and Children First*?**

It seemed like it took longer because we were renegotiating our contract with Warner, but we did most of the instrumental tracks in four days except for the acoustic song ["Could This Be Magic?"], which we did at the very end. All the vocal tracks and harmonies were knocked out in four days the following week, as well.

**What inspired your decision to play electric piano on "And the Cradle Will Rock . . ."?**

We were in the middle of a tour, and I was trying to decide what we were going to do different on the next record. One day I found this Wurlitzer electric piano and took it back on the bus with us. I would bang out chords on it and come up with all kinds of new ideas. I recall that the basic chords for "Jump" were actually one of the very first things I wrote on that piano. I had already written the riff for "And the Cradle Will Rock . . ." before then, but I thought it sounded better on the piano.

I blazed it through my pedalboard and my Marshalls. The noise that you hear in the beginning is an MXR Flanger and I'm banging on the lower register of the piano. I busted one of the keys on my piano while I was doing that.

**"Could This Be Magic?" is a fun take on country blues. When did you first start playing slide guitar?**

"Could This Be Magic?" was the first time I ever played slide! We were working on the song in the studio and we were all a little bit drunk and the guys went, "It doesn't sound right, Ed. Why don't you try playing slide?" I said, "Uh-oh, I've never played slide, guys." They told me to just fake it. A lot of people use different tunings when they play slide, but I wasn't really familiar with how to do it, so I just played in standard tuning.

**What is that little piece of music that fades into nothingness at the very end of side two?**
It was something Al and I were messing around with. We called it "Growth" or something like that. We thought that just for the hell of it we'd stick it at the end of the record and possibly start the next record with it. But it never amounted to anything, so we left it at that.

**You've mentioned that you like to leave mistakes on some of your tracks. Any good ones on _Women and Children First_?**
I love mistakes because you can never redo them in exactly the same way. They're just freak things. On "Fools" I accidentally made this weird noise, and to my ears it sounds like I'm slipping off the fretboard. At first, I wasn't sure whether I liked it or not, but now I love it.

**Was the homemade Frankenstrat still your main guitar on the album?**
Yeah, although I also used a Gibson ES-335 for the solo in "And the Cradle Will Rock . . ." For some reason when I play a 335, I can really blaze. It just has a different feel. I also borrowed an Ibanez Destroyer from Chris Holmes. I wanted to get a sound like I got on the songs on our first album where I used my Destroyer, before I ruined it by cutting a big chunk out of the body.

**Do you ever worry about living up to expectations as a guitarist?**
It seems like I should, but I don't. The way I got where I am is just by doing what I do without worrying about anything. I don't really think about getting better. I'm probably more concerned with change. You can only play so fast; you can only twang so much. It's more a matter of evolving than getting better.

I think my playing has changed quite a bit from the first album. I don't want to call it maturing or anything, but if you're exposed to different ideas, you tend to play different. I'll always sound like myself, but I'm always discovering different combinations of notes, riffs, and little noises that make my playing different.

**How do you feel when you hear other people playing like you?**
I don't mean to sound egotistical, but they don't play like me—they just _try_ to. Actually, I think it's better that they try to, because it comes off as

a little different, whereas if they play exactly like me, it's gonna sound like me. Just like when I started, I tried playing exactly like some people, but I just couldn't. That's how my style developed. Out of the mere fact that I couldn't play like someone else, I had to come up with something myself.

**Are there any guitarists you admire?**

I loved Allan Holdsworth. His playing on Bill Bruford's album *One of a Kind* still amazes me every time I hear it. That fucker was good. His band UK opened for us once in Reno [July 25, 1978] and I couldn't believe how good they were. Those guys were fucking playing their asses off even though people weren't very receptive to them. Holdsworth was a really strange player. You can never hear the attack of his pick. I'd love to hear him play with Tim Bogert on bass. If I ever played bass, that's how I'd want to play.

**_Fair Warning_ was the first album where you used the studio in a more sophisticated way.**

It was the first time I did a lot of overdubbing, and I was pretty happy with the results. I'm not unhappy with any solos I did on that record. I liked them all.

*Fair Warning* was the total opposite of *Diver Down* and the three albums that came before it. I wrote most of the songs in the studio. All I had were basic ideas. When we came off tour, everyone asked "Whadd'ya got, Eddie?" I showed them my basic ideas and we went from there. I came up with everything on it within two weeks. When we were done, I weighed only 125 pounds. I lost a lot of weight and a lot of sleep because I knew it had to be done.

**Which solos on the album do you like the most?**

"Sinner's Swing!" was spontaneous. That was a first take. It sounds like falling down a flight of stairs. The only problem I had while recording the album was playing the solo on "Push Comes to Shove." Usually, all my guitar parts are done in three takes or less. It took me ten takes to nail that one, but it was worth the effort. It's one of my favorites.

I don't like to overdub for the sake of laying an extra guitar on a track. I see no purpose in overdubbing just to double something. My attitude is if you can't do it with one guitar, why even bother? But that doesn't mean I won't overdub if the song needs it. Like on "Push Comes to Shove,"

I've got a distorted guitar and a clean guitar playing off each other like a countermelody to what I'm playing on the basic guitar track.

**What technique did you use at the beginning of "Mean Street"?**
I tapped on the twelfth fret of the low E and the twelfth fret of the high E and muffled both with my left hand down by the nut. I applied to guitar what bass players do when they slap. But it's not like I studied it or anything.

**How did you and Dave work together?**
I came up with 99.9 percent of the music, and Dave wrote 99.9 percent of the lyrics and vocal melodies.

**How did you feel about his vocals on *Fair Warning*?**
The truth is, I don't think he sang as well as I played. Like always, we went back into the studio pretty quickly after a tour. Dave took his two weeks off while I worked my ass off getting some ideas together. When he came back, it was the typical "What do you got, Eddie?" and I had pretty much most of the basic ideas for everything. But I love it; it's my life. I really shouldn't complain. At least Dave pulled his weight. Mike didn't. He didn't really ever do anything: he had zero input whatsoever. Period. But he remodeled his whole house and bought himself a Turbo Carrera off the money he made off of us. Whatever. I never even listened to his bass when we recorded.

**That sounds a little harsh.**
I'll tell you the honest-to-God fucking truth that since day one, I never liked Mike's sound and most of the time I could never hear him. All I had in my monitors when we played live was Al's drums, a little bit of Dave's vocals, a little bit of mine, and a little bit of Mike's vocals. But all I hear is myself and my brother. In the studio it's the same.

***Diver Down* was almost the exact opposite of *Fair Warning*. Why did the band take such a drastically different approach on that album?**
*Fair Warning*'s lack of commercial success prompted *Diver Down*. But to me, *Fair Warning* was more true to what I am and what I believe Van Halen is. We're a hard rock band, and we were an album band. We were lucky to enter the charts anywhere. Ted and Warner Bros. wanted singles, but there were no singles on *Fair Warning*. It wasn't a commercial flop,

but it wasn't exactly a commercial success either. For many guitarists and Van Halen fans, *Fair Warning* is a hot second between either *Van Halen* or *1984*. The album was full of things that I wanted, from "Unchained" to silly things like "Sunday Afternoon in the Park." I like odd things. I was not a pop guy, even though I have a good sense of how to write a pop song.

**You did five cover songs on *Diver Down*.**

Yeah, and it was five too many. It all started when we were in the middle of a break and Dave suggested that we should record a single to keep the fans interested. Dave always wanted to redo "Dancing in the Streets" and I remember him giving me a tape of it. I said, "I can't get a handle on anything out of this." I didn't really want to do it, so I suggested "Pretty Woman" because that seemed more of a Van Halen song to cover. It was us. The single became a surprise hit, and then Warner Bros. wanted us to record an album. I had only a few songs ready to go, so Dave came in with a bunch of songs he wanted to cover.

**What was the impetus for "Little Guitars"?**

The little flamenco-style introduction was inspired by the classical guitarist Carlos Montoya. I saw him on television, and he was doing these crazy things with his fingers. I knew it would take me years to learn how to fingerpick like him, so I came up with my own way to replicate what I liked about the sound of it.

Some other guitarists were in the studio while we were recording "Little Guitars," and that particular lick really blew them away. I remember Steve Lukather coming by and saying, "That's not you. How can you be doing that?" What threw him is that he was hearing a high trilling note and a low thing going on at the same time. When I showed him how I did it, he laughed himself silly because it was so simple. All I did was tremolo pick the high strings and hammer on the lower strings at the same time. People were always amazed when I played it live because they assumed that it was two guitars playing the part.

**The production of *Diver Down* is not as sophisticated as it was on *Fair Warning*.**

On *Diver Down* we went back to our old style of making records. We essentially played everything live and only two songs had overdubs. I was

# EDDIE'S ODDITIES

**GUITAR:** Dave Petschulat Mini Les Paul
**USED:** "Little Guitars" (*Diver Down*)

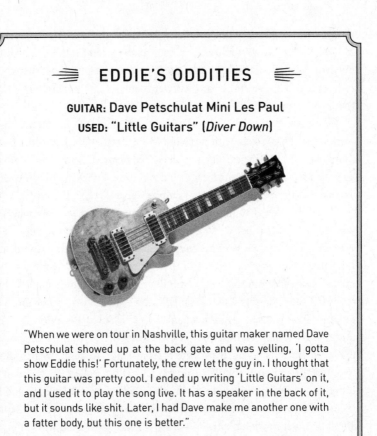

"When we were on tour in Nashville, this guitar maker named Dave Petschulat showed up at the back gate and was yelling, 'I gotta show Eddie this!' Fortunately, the crew let the guy in. I thought that this guitar was pretty cool. I ended up writing 'Little Guitars' on it, and I used it to play the song live. It has a speaker in the back of it, but it sounds like shit. Later, I had Dave make me another one with a fatter body, but this one is better."

always butting heads with Ted Templeman about what makes a good record. My philosophy has always been that I would rather bomb with my own music than make it with other people's music. Ted felt that if you redo a proven hit, you're already halfway there. I didn't want to be halfway there with someone else's shit.

The track that really made me crazy was "Dancing in the Street." I was working on a great song with this Mini Moog riff that I envisioned it being more like a Peter Gabriel song, but when Ted heard it, he decided it would be great for "Dancing in the Street." Ted and Dave were happy, but I wasn't. The riff was my original idea, and I didn't even get writing credits for it.

In some ways, I think *Diver Down* happened that way because Ted wanted his control back. When we were making *Fair Warning*, I was spending a lot more time with Donn Landee working on my sound, and I became much more involved in the recording process. Donn allowed me to engineer some stuff and comp the solo on "So This Is Love?" I had recorded four solos and Donn said, "I don't know how to put these all together. You want to give it a whack?" I said, "Sure. What do I do?" He told me to listen to all four and pick the best parts, and then he showed me what buttons to push to switch from track to track to put them together. I listened a couple of times, and Donn asked if I had something. I said, "What do you think of this?" and I played it for him, and he recorded it without me knowing. That's what ended up on the record, and it was just my demonstration of what I thought would work.

Then Ted walked in with this look on his face like, "Here we go . . . now he's engineering!" He obviously wasn't happy. He thought that Donn and I were getting a little too close and steering the ship in a direction that he didn't like. Ted said, "Hey, Ed! You could be a great engineer someday." And Donn replied, "He already is! Listen to this." He played him the solo that I had just comped.

*Fair Warning* was a big turning point. People were saying that I didn't know what I was doing and that it was a disaster. There was an inner struggle mostly between Ted and me. He was the A&R guy at Warner Bros. who signed us, and whenever he said to do something, people would do it. But with *Diver Down*, it was like I was being asked to turn back. After we made that album, I wanted to make sure that would never happen again, so Donn and I built our own studio.

# 5

# 1984

*By building his own recording studio and participating
in some outside projects, Ed spread his wings in new
directions that would inspire the creation of Van
Halen's masterpiece album, 1984.*

*" I wasn't going to allow them to control me anymore. "*

AFTER COMPLETING WORK on *Diver Down*, Ed Van Halen
felt unusually restless. Although he and the band had
worked almost nonstop for five years, the guitarist was in no
mood for rest and relaxation. The album may have been an unexpected
obligation forced upon Van Halen by Warner Bros., but instead of feeling
relieved that he'd gotten it out of the way, Ed had the uneasy sensation
that he could have done more.

Van Halen had more than four months of time off before their 1982
Hide Your Sheep tour was scheduled to begin in mid-July. With his bandmates away on vacation and his wife occupied with shooting *One Day
at a Time* and made-for-television movies, Ed spent most of his time off
alone, playing guitar or writing songs on his piano and synthesizers. The

many accolades he'd received for his playing never went to his head, and in fact they made him more determined to grow as a musician instead of resting on his laurels.

Ed's impact on the guitar world had by this time become incalculable. Besides being arguably the most innovative and most imitated guitarist on the planet, he'd also joined the ranks of the most influential guitar *designers* of his time. His DIY Frankenstein was hailed as a genuine breakthrough, even receiving a big thumbs-up from the genius of geniuses himself, Les Paul, a man notoriously difficult to impress.

A growing number of guitar manufacturers were shamelessly copying Ed's minimalist single humbucking pickup/volume control–only/vibrato bar "super Strat" design, with some even having the unmitigated gall to rip off his signature striped graphics. He was justifiably becoming angrier by the day as he watched others copy his ideas and rake in the dough. So, when the founding partner of Kramer Guitars, Dennis Berardi, approached Ed in February 1982 with a generous endorsement deal, the guitarist was ready to sign on the dotted line (see Chapter 11).

Meanwhile, Edward's revolutionary two-handed tapping technique, squealing harmonics, and deep whammy bar dives were also being brazenly cannibalized by other players and seemingly overnight incorporated into the arsenal of heavy metal, New Wave, pop, and even jazz players. Ozzy Osbourne's guitarist, Randy Rhoads—who rose to prominence with Quiet Riot on the Hollywood club scene along with Van Halen—was one of many who built upon Ed's foundation. The twenty-five-year-old Rhoads's tragic death in a plane crash on March 19, 1982, temporarily led to his superseding Ed as rock's preeminent guitarist.

But if he felt threatened in any way by Rhoads—or any of the other up-and-coming guitar virtuosos—he didn't show it. In fact, Ed went out of his way to befriend a number of guitar-playing peers he respected.

During the spring of 1982, one in particular caught his attention: the British jazz-fusion/progressive rock guitarist Allan Holdsworth, whom Ed had met on tour in 1978. Holdsworth's outlandish choice of notes and sophisticated left-handed legato work that produced horn-like tones and timbres captivated him like nothing since Eric Clapton's playing in his Cream years. He was thrilled when he discovered that Holdsworth was moving to Southern California, and Ed was determined to jam with him—and perhaps produce a record for him on Warner Bros.

"I took [him] to some meetings and somehow he ended up spending the night at my house," Ed recalled.[7] "When we woke up, Allan said, 'Shit, I have to be at GIT [the Guitar Institute of Technology] at noon to do a seminar.' I raced him down there just in time. Before I knew it, I was onstage with him and his band, and we were both answering questions and playing together. It was quite fun, actually, and very interesting, especially for the students. Because Allan and I play very different, we answered the same questions very differently."

This incident led to Ed's contributing a chapter to the Musicians' Institute/GIT instruction book *Ten*, published later that year. The guitarist's involvement with the Hollywood music school resulted in a surge in enrollment of wannabe rock guitar heroes, who would later form bands that became part of the "hair metal" scene that dominated Los Angeles clubs for the rest of the eighties. The notable Van Halen–inspired players who studied at GIT included Paul Gilbert (Racer X, Mr. Big) and Dave Kushner (Wasted Youth, Velvet Revolver).

GIT graduates weren't the only musicians trying to follow in Van Halen's footsteps to stardom via the now-exploding Hollywood club scene. The band Steeler imported hyperkinetic Euro-shredder Yngwie Malmsteen from Stockholm, Sweden, and Ed's club days accomplice George Lynch finally found fame with the band Dokken. Ratt and Stryper both worked their way up the scene by starting as house bands at Gazzarri's, and although Mötley Crüe and Poison might not have had guitarists with Eddie's chops, they had a similar pop-metal sensibility that eventually made them household names.

A short while after the GIT seminar, Holdsworth invited Van Halen to join him onstage once again for a show at Hollywood's Roxy Theatre on April 29. Ed jammed with the band during their last song, and backstage after the show he met a young guitarist named Steve Vai, who was playing in Frank Zappa's band. Vai gave Van Halen his phone number and offered to introduce him to Zappa (see Chapter 6 Musical Interlude).

After a series of phone calls the following week, Van Halen, Vai, and Zappa convened for a jam session at Zappa's home studio. "Oddly enough, Edward lived like a mile away from Frank," Vai recalled.[8] "While we were there, he ran home and came back with the new Van Halen record—I think it was [1982's] *Diver Down*—and we listened to it. At Frank's studio there are just tons of instruments, so Edward started playing and then

Frank started playing and then I started playing. It wasn't a song—it was just jamming. It was a lot of fun, and it went on for a while."

This encounter led to Zappa's asking Ed if he would produce a single by his son, Dweezil, who was a huge Van Halen fan. Ed agreed, and a short while later he returned to Zappa's home studio with engineer Donn Landee. Both were impressed with the sound quality they were able to coax from Zappa's studio, and after the sessions were finished, the two talked about building a similar studio at Ed's house. Having such a facility literally in his backyard would provide Ed with an ideal place to capture and work on ideas, leading to his reestablishment as the driving force behind Van Halen's subsequent albums. Thus, the concept for 5150 was born.

Around this time, Van Halen also frequently hung out with studio guitarist and Toto member Steve Lukather, one of the handful of players Ed respected (see this chapter's Musical Interlude). In addition to his membership in a chart-topping band, Lukather had recorded hundreds of sessions with rock, pop, jazz, and funk artists, including ripping solos on hits from Olivia Newton-John's "Physical" to "Talk to Ya Later" by The Tubes.

In 1982, Lukather was working in the studio with R&B giant Michael Jackson and legendary producer Quincy Jones on an album tentatively called *Thriller*. Jones suggested that Jackson compose a rock song, in the hope that it would cross over to MTV and the white teenage market. Jackson wrote "Beat It" and came up with the idea of having Eddie Van Halen play a guitar solo on the song.

When Jones first called Edward to inform him of Jackson's request, the guitarist thought it was a prank call and slammed down the receiver. This scenario repeated itself several times before Ed stayed on the line long enough to realize that it actually was the real Quincy Jones. Jackson and Jones dropped by the Coldwater Canyon house a few days later to play a rough version of "Beat It" for him, and, liking what he heard, Ed agreed to record a solo.

Since his bandmates were all away on vacation, Ed was unable to ask how they felt about his playing on the record. Truth be told, he didn't think too much about it. He was bored, had time on his hands, and it sounded like fun to work with Jones and Jackson. Besides, who'd ever notice his contribution to an R&B dance record?

The entire session took a mere two hours, and during that time Ed would write a new section for the song and record a thirty-second solo. The whole thing happened so quickly, Ed was too embarrassed to ask for compensation, but in an attempt to hide his infidelity from his bandmates, he did request that he not be credited on the album sleeve.

It didn't quite work out that way: "Beat It" went on to become a chart-topping, worldwide explosion of a song, winning Record of the Year at the 1984 Grammy Awards. Even though Ed's name was buried among the inner sleeve credits, the doorbell harmonics, distinctive vibrato bar dips, and frantic tapping could be the work of only one man.

David Lee Roth later was the first to take notice. "I was in a 7-Eleven parking lot," he recalled.[9] "There were a couple of butch Mexican gals with the doors open of their pickup truck, and the new Michael Jackson song 'Beat It' came on. I heard the guitar solo and thought, now that sounds familiar. Somebody's ripping off Ed Van Halen's licks. It was Ed, turns out, and he had gone and done the project without discussing it with anybody, feeling as though I would stand in the way. Actually, I wouldn't have at all. Quincy Jones is stellar company. If you're going to do something, climb the big one."

Ed's brother Al and bassist Michael Anthony were equally forgiving— it was hard to criticize something that was exploding into a global phenomenon. And the crossover to the Black listening market was beneficial for the Van Halen brand.

The band's Hide Your Sheep tour commenced on July 14, 1982, in Augusta, Georgia, and they remained focused on performing through mid-February of 1983, as the dates extended into their first-ever concerts in South America. After the band wrapped up the tour in Buenos Aires, Roth remained behind to go on an adventure up the Amazon River, giving Ed a few weeks of freedom to make some finishing touches on his 5150 studio and get a head start on Van Halen's next album.

Working mostly by himself, with Donn Landee behind the mixing board and Alex laying down drum tracks on a few occasions, Ed felt free to express himself as he never had before. The first tracks he recorded were synthesizer parts that became the genesis of "Jump." Ed's new fascination with keyboards would later become the source of much intraband tension during the album's recording, but because Ed owned the studio, the naysayers couldn't do much about it.

While Roth was still stranded up the Amazon, picking fire ants from his G-string (no wonder he selected Western Exterminator's intimidating hammer-toting "Mr. Little" character as the 1984 tour's mascot), Ed made yet another extracurricular guest appearance. In April 1983, he joined Queen guitarist Brian May and an ersatz band of Hollywood session pros at LA's Record Plant Studios to record three songs, including a twelve-minute blues jam called "Blues Breaker," a tribute to Eric Clapton, an early inspiration of both guitarists.

"After we played, [Brian May] called me up about four months later and asked what I thought about putting the stuff out," said Eddie. "I said, 'Send me a tape, let me hear it first,' because I didn't remember how it went. He did and I said, 'Sure, what the hell? It reeks of fun.'"

Meanwhile, manager Noel Monk announced that Van Halen would be playing at the second US Festival, scheduled for Memorial Day weekend in nearby Devore, California. The band's headlining set was billed as "The Musical Event of the 80s" and netted them a record $1.5 million. Playing for just two hours, Van Halen would gross more than they owed Warner Bros. in expenses from their first year with the label. Work on the album came to a halt as Van Halen shifted gears to put together its biggest stage production to date and rehearsed for the show.

On Sunday, May 29, Van Halen took the stage at Devore to close "Heavy Metal Day," the middle slot of the festival, bookended by "New Wave Day," headlined by the Clash, and "Rock Day," headlined by David Bowie. The festival stage covered more square footage than the footprint of entire clubs the band had played only six years earlier, and their five hundred plus backstage guest list was bigger than most of those clubs' attendance capacities. The crowd that showed up, estimated at more than three hundred thousand people, was the largest the band had ever seen.

Unfortunately, most of the work that went into preparing for the show, including rehearsals, went down the tubes when the band members—particularly David Lee Roth—overindulged during the preconcert festivities. Roth performed like the second coming of Johnny Rotten, slurring his words when he remembered them, scatting guttural noises when he didn't, and berating hecklers by threatening to fuck their girlfriends. Even heavy postproduction editing couldn't hide the ugliness captured by television cameras and later broadcast as select segments on Showtime.

Although Van Halen's US Festival performance was far from their best, fans didn't seem to care. The camera loved Roth even in his most inebriated state, and the exposure—particularly the overexposure of the singer's bare ass cheeks in backless chaps—made Van Halen bigger stars than ever. MTV might have banned the "Pretty Woman" video, but they still loved Van Halen. The music channel went on to play a critical role in the success of Van Halen's next album.

As work on the album that was to become *1984* progressed, the band was splintering into separate factions. The partnership between Ed and Donn Landee had become particularly tight, with the two working together after hours almost every night. Alex was a part of this grouping almost by default—he was Ed's brother. On the other side were Roth and producer Ted Templeman, who both found their input increasingly overruled by the guitarist. Roth, meanwhile, bonded with the band's lighting and creative director, Pete Angelus—a pairing that blossomed later when the two became the producers of Van Halen's music videos.

Amid all this creative tension, Van Halen somehow managed to deliver its masterpiece, *1984.* The album missed its planned New Year's Eve release date by a little more than a week, coming out on January 9, 1984, but by then the advance single "Jump" was working its way up the charts. By the end of February, it reached number one on the Billboard Hot 100, the only Van Halen song to do so. The album itself peaked at number two, with only Michael Jackson's *Thriller* ahead of it. The irony that Ed's contribution to "Beat It" probably kept their own album from reaching number one was not lost on the band.

The Roth and Angelus–directed videos for "Jump," "Panama," and "Hot For Teacher" quickly made heavy rotation on MTV, and those songs, along with "I'll Wait" and "Drop Dead Legs," were similarly successful on FM radio. The album's "deep" cuts, "Top Jimmy," "Girl Gone Bad," and the long-overdue "House of Pain," which dated back to the Gene Simmons demos, showcased Ed's guitar playing in its peak creative form. Keyboard synthesizers were front and center on the instrumental opener "1984," "Jump," and "I'll Wait"—in fact, listeners had to wait more than two minutes before Ed played the album's first guitar notes.

*1984* was a monumental breakthrough for Van Halen the band and Van Halen the guitarist. The album contained the most consistent set of material since their debut and broke new sales records for the group. That year Ed topped *Guitar Player* magazine's Best Rock Guitarist poll for the fifth consecutive time, earning him a place in the publication's "Gallery of the Greats." Thanks to Ed's endorsement, Kramer guitars were selling as quickly as retailers could stock them, and Kramer added dozens of big names to its endorsement roster.

*1984* also ushered in the age of the super guitar hero. Hundreds of bands were rising up the charts in Van Halen's wake, including Bon Jovi, featuring an Eddie doppelganger vocalist, and Night Ranger, with the dual-guitar tag team composed of whammy bar sound effects specialist Brad Gillis and eight-fingered tapping phenom Jeff Watson. Michael Sembello's Top 10 pop hit "Maniac," from the *Flashdance* soundtrack, prominently featured a two-handed tapping guitar solo. Funk and R&B bands even started incorporating rock guitar solos in their songs, hoping to capitalize on the crossover success of "Beat It."

The tour in support of *1984* was simply massive. The columns of speaker cabinets stacked onstage resembled city skylines, and the band was illuminated by a blinding rig consisting of two thousand lights. Every show sold out, but although the tour was a success on a financial level, it ultimately became a losing proposition as the band members' interpersonal relationships unraveled.

"On the 1984 tour, between all of our solo segments and Dave's stage raps we were never out onstage together for more than ten minutes at a time," Ed said. "It was the Johnny Carson Show. It wasn't a band anymore. It couldn't have gone on like that, so it was a good thing that Dave quit. The deterioration of it started when I built the studio. I was trying to take more control over the band and what I thought it should be. And there were other people who viewed the band in a more Las Vegas way. It was different motivation."

When Roth told Ed that he'd recorded four songs he wanted to release on his own, the guitarist questioned his singer's devotion to the band. Although Ed had participated in more than a handful of outside projects of his own, it was always as a guest. Releasing a solo work, as Roth was doing—particularly without prior blessing from his bandmates—was an act of betrayal.

When interviewed by the press in late 1984 and early 1985, Ed displayed a positive, supportive attitude to Dave's *Crazy from the Heat* EP. But when Roth later announced that he planned on making a movie

# EDDIE'S ODDITIES

## GUITAR: Custom Kramer double neck
## USED: 1982 Hide Your Sheep tour

After Ed signed an endorsement contract with Kramer Guitars in early 1982, he was often photographed with a purple Kramer Pacer and an identical white model that Kramer gave him. Shortly after that, Kramer luthier Paul Unkert made Ed this custom 6/12 double neck featuring an aluminum neck for the twelve-string and a wood neck for the six-string. Ed played it during Van Halen's Hide Your Sheep tour that summer in support of *Diver Down*.

"This is probably the first custom guitar I ever got from Kramer," said Ed. "I used it live to play 'Secrets.' [On *Diver Down* Ed used a Gibson EDS-1275 double neck.] But other than this guitar, no one at Kramer built any of my personal Kramer guitars. I built two of them myself—the '5150' and the '1984' guitars. I made both of those guitars when I visited the Kramer factory. Every other striped Kramer that's out there that's supposedly mine was a tour backup or giveaway guitar built by Kramer employees.

"Peter Morton of the Hard Rock Café once proudly showed me a guitar that was displayed at their Las Vegas location. He said it was my original Frankenstein, or so he thought. He told me that he had just bought it, and when I told him that it wasn't mine the blood drained from his face. He said he bought it through some big auction house. I told him that I'd call them right then and get his money back. So I did. The auction house asked me where the original was, and I told them I still had it at home. I felt really bad for Peter.

"The Kramer Baretta [originally styled to be a Van Halen signature guitar] had nothing to do with me. I didn't even know they were selling those things. In the early eighties, everyone was copying me. I'd walk around the NAMM [National Association of Music Merchants] show and see all of these guitars with one pickup and one knob. The people at Schecter even called them Van Halen models. Every company on the planet was making one."

with the same title, the guitarist could no longer hold back. Ed knew that something had to change, and that change had to happen quickly.

**What inspired you to build the 5150 studio at your home?**
I used to have a back room in my house where I set up a little studio with a Tascam four-track recorder to demo songs. I really wanted to record demos that sounded more professional than what I was doing. The bottom line is that I wanted more control.

When we started work on *1984*, I wanted to ram it up Ted's poop chute and show him that we could make a great record without any cover tunes and do it our way. Donn and I proceeded to figure out how to build a recording studio. I did not set out to build a full-blown studio. I just wanted a better place to put my music together so I could show it to the guys. I never imagined that it would turn into what it did until we started building it.

Back then, zoning laws disallowed building a home studio on your property. I suggested that we submit plans for a racquetball court. When the city inspector came up here, he was looking at things and going, "Let's see here. Two-foot-thick cinder blocks, concrete-filled, rebar-enforced . . . why so over the top for a racquetball court?" I told him, "Well, when we play, we play hard. We want to keep it quiet up here and not have the neighbors get pissed off." We got it approved.

Donn was involved with the design. I certainly didn't know how to build a studio. It was all Donn's magic. We built a main room and a separate control room. When we needed to find a console, Donn said that there was one at United Western we could buy that he was familiar with. We went to take a look at it, and it was this old and dilapidated piece of shit that looked like it was ready to go into the trash. Donn said, "Let's buy it," and I was going, "What the hell are you thinking?" He said that he could make it work, so we paid $6,000 for it and lugged it up here. He rewired the whole console himself using a punch-down tool. Donn used to work for the phone company, so he was an expert at wiring things.

Then we needed a tape machine, so we bought a 3M sixteen-track. Slowly, it turned into a lot more than I originally envisioned. Everybody else was even more surprised than I was, especially Ted. Everybody thought I was just building a little demo room. Then Donn said, "No, man! We're going to make records up here!" They weren't happy.

**It sounds like Donn wanted as much creative freedom as you did.**

Oh, definitely. We had grown really close and had a common vision. Everybody was afraid that Donn and I were taking control. Well . . . yes! That's exactly what we did, and the results proved that we weren't idiots. When you're making a record, you never know if the public is going to accept it, but we lucked out and succeeded at exactly what my goal was.

**It seems that Van Halen was splitting into two different production teams—you and Donn were one, and Dave and Ted Templeman were the other.**

Look at *Fair Warning, Diver Down*, and *1984*. I was very involved in *Fair Warning*, but it didn't do very well commercially. *Diver Down* was mostly Ted ramming it up my poop chute, going, "Here's how you make a record." *1984* was me ramming it back at Ted and saying, "No, *here's* how you make a record." That's truly what happened. I just didn't want to do things the way Ted wanted us to do them. I'm not knocking *Diver Down*. It's a good record, but it wasn't the record I wanted to do at the time.

*Diver Down* was the main reason why I built my own studio. That album was half cover tunes, because Ted Templeman and David Lee Roth thought that if you do a proven hit, you're halfway there. I didn't agree with that, so I built my own studio so I could write my own goddamn music. I demanded we record *1984* there. People were saying shit behind my back, like it was "little Eddie the drunk" taking control of the band. I'm sorry anyone felt that way, but it was my band and my life, too, and I wasn't going to allow them to control me anymore.

**You really were overflowing with creativity during that period between *Diver Down* and *1984*. You recorded with and produced other artists outside the band and you even did recorded music for *The Wild Life* and *The Seduction of Gina* soundtracks.**

Until you mentioned it, I had almost forgotten that I had done those soundtracks. Now I remember that Donn wasn't very happy because he had to mix it on his own because I had to leave to go on the tour we were doing with AC/DC in Europe. I remember we were rehearsing at Zoetrope Studios when Frank Zappa called me and asked if I would produce a single for his son Dweezil. I also did the Brian May Starfleet project then and the session with Michael Jackson. My wife asked me to write some music for a TV movie she was doing. I had a lot of music laying around because all I did was write. We did the US Festival in the middle of recording *1984*. I also had to build the studio during that period too! I don't know how I pulled all of that off.

**Then after completing *1984* the band went on its biggest tour ever.**
We toured in the US and did about 120 shows. Our live show for the *1984* tour just could not get any bigger. It was so over the top that we never made any money from it. We had eighteen trucks hauling the stage and equipment. That was unheard of. The standard lighting rig had five hundred to seven hundred lights, and we had over two thousand. We could never have topped that. We had the banners with the Western Exterminator guy on them. We filled the entire place with equipment and lights—great memories.

**The US Festival proved that you were the biggest band in the world at the time.**
What's funny is that we made the Guinness Book of World Records for making $1.5 million for one show. I remember hearing a DJ on the radio saying that we made so much per second. What he didn't realize is that we put every penny of that into the production. We didn't make a fucking dime when it was all over.

**You also spent a month or so just preparing for that one show.**
There was so much going on. We did that in the middle of making a record and I was doing all of this outside stuff. Then again, the Michael Jackson session only took two hours, so it wasn't like all of these things were taking that much time. I was recording pretty much everything. "Strung Out," which appeared on *Balance*, was recorded when Valerie and I were renting a house on the beach at Malibu that belonged to Marvin Hamlisch. I wrecked this beautiful white grand piano that he owned when I recorded that. Marvin was not very happy when he saw what I did. Donn and I were just into recording crazy shit.

**What did you record first once the studio was ready to go?**
The first song that I recorded at the studio was "Jump." Once Ted heard that, he was full hog in. He said, "That's great! Let's go to work." Alex

was supportive. He wasn't happy with his drum sound on the first and second records. There was only one room at 5150 at the time, so we were very restricted. It really was a racquetball court, where one-third of the space was the control room and the rest was the main room. Because the space was so limited, Alex had to use an electronic Simmons kit except for the snare, which was acoustic. We all played at the same time. I had my old faithful Marshall head and bare wooden four-by-twelve speaker cabinet facing off into a corner, and Al was in the other corner. We set up some baffles to have isolation between my guitar and the drums. I would sit right in front of my brother and play without headphones. All I needed to hear was his drums. There were a lot of limitations.

**You wouldn't know it, though, when you listen to the end product. The engineering on that record is impressive, especially when you know the situation.**

I have to give all the credit to Donn. His approach to everything was genius. He is one of those guys that is on the borderline of genius and insanity. I used the same Marshall amp to record the first six Van Halen albums, but my guitar sound on each album is different. The drum sounds, too. That was all Donn.

Alex and Donn got a lot closer on *1984* as well. "Drop Dead Legs" and "I'll Wait" were more towards Al's liking as opposed to the first record.

**Not only does *1984* sound different from Van Halen's previous records, but each song on the album also sounds different from other songs on the album.**

For the first six records and tours, we all traveled together on the same bus, which Dave called the disco sub. All I did was write. You can hear the bus generator on all of the demo tapes I recorded. Outside of "Jump," all of the other material was already written when we started to record the album. The guys asked me to write something with an AC/DC beat, and that ended up being "Panama." It really doesn't sound that much like AC/DC, but that was my interpretation of it.

I wrote "Jump" on a Sequential Circuits Prophet 10 in my bedroom while the studio was being built. I think I first wrote the main chord progression when I got the Wurlitzer electric piano I played on "And the Cradle Will Rock . . ." but I needed to turn that into a complete song. Every time I got the sound that I wanted on the right-hand split, the synth would start smoking and pop a fuse. I got another one and the same thing happened. A guy I knew said I should try an Oberheim OBxA, so I bought one of those and got the sound I wanted. I used to spend so much time getting sounds and writing. I have a tape of me playing in the living room at five a.m. and you can hear Valerie come in and yell that she's heard enough of that song. That was another reason why I built the studio.

I always carried a micro cassette recorder with me. I recorded my idea for "Girl Gone Bad" by humming and whistling into it in the closet of a hotel room while Valerie was sleeping. I could make sense of my own humming. I pretty much had the whole song in that state, and then when I got home I put it all together.

For "Top Jimmy," I had a melody in my head and I tuned the guitar to that melody. Steve Ripley had sent me one of his stereo guitars that had three pickups and ninety million knobs and switches on it that was too much for me to comprehend. I asked him for a simpler version, and he sent me one with a humbucker in the bridge and two single coils at the middle and neck positions. It was just a prototype. For some strange reason I picked up that guitar, tuned it to "Top Jimmy," and that's what I ended up using because it sounded interesting. That rhythm lick I play after the harmonics sounds cool ping-ponging back and forth. You can't really hear it unless you're wearing headphones. It just fit the track.

**"Drop Dead Legs" is one of the most unique songs on the album.**
That was inspired by "Back in Black." I was grooving on that beat, although I think that "Drop Dead Legs" is slower. Whatever I listen to somehow is filtered through me and comes out differently. "Drop Dead Legs" is almost a jazz version of "Back in Black." The descending progression is similar, but I put a lot more notes in there.

**Again, it's like what you did with "Panama." The open chords on the verse and chorus are somewhat similar to AC/DC, but the intro and especially the middle section after the solo are very Van Halen.**

From day one that was just the way that I write. I always start with some intro or theme and establish a riff, then after the solo there's some kind of breakdown section. It's there in almost every song, or else it returns to the intro.

**The solos on the album almost always go into a different place. Sometimes you even change keys, like on "Jump," "Top Jimmy," and "Panama."**

I view solos as a song within a song. Having the studio here gave Donn and me the luxury and freedom to do all kinds of things. They thought we were nuts to pull up my Lamborghini to the studio and mic it. We drove it around the city, and I revved the engine up to 8,000 rpm just to get the right sound.

We've done all kinds of silly things up here. One time a septic tank needed to be removed. Donn lowered a mic into it, and we threw an Electrolux vacuum in there. We called it "stereo septic." I have a tape of it around here somewhere. It's fucking hilarious. Donn really is a man-child genius. If you didn't know him all that well, you'd think he wore the same pants, shirt, socks, and shoes every day of his life. Then you go to his house and see that he has a closet full of all the same type of clothes. It's just like Einstein. He didn't want to waste brain cells deciding what to wear.

It was a bummer when we stopped working together. He just totally left the music business. I went to his house once and asked him to reconsider. He said, "Nah. I probably wouldn't even remember how to do it." I said, "That's bullshit. Everything we did we didn't know what the fuck we were doing anyway! We were just experimenting and having fun all the time."

I basically lived in the studio. If Valerie needed to find me, she just had to look in the studio because I was always there. Even when we weren't recording music for the band, Donn and I would be in there every day, putzing around, making noise, coming up with riffs, playing piano, or doing whatever.

**"Hot For Teacher" is basically a blues boogie, but it swings like a jazz tune.**

I'm a shuffle guy. I love fast shuffles. I think it stems from my dad's big-band days. Every record has a song like that—"I'm the One," "Sinner's Swing." It was an extension of that—more of me! I distinctly remember sitting in front of Al on a wooden stool and playing that part where it climbs. Well, I can't count, so Al needs to follow me. I'd sit right in front of him, and then he'd look at me like, "Now!"

**His drums on that intro sound phenomenal. It's like a dragster warming up before a race.**

When he started putzing around with that, we were going, "Holy shit!" It really does sound like a hot rod or dragster. You can only pull that off with the Simmons drums. It's so unique. On regular drums it doesn't sound the same. There's something to be said about the years that we used Simmons. The only bad part was how those drums affected Al's wrists. When you hit those things, there's no bounce or give. It's like pounding concrete, and thanks to the amounts of Schlitz malt liquor we drank, we hit everything twice as hard. Al would hit them with sticks that were like baseball bats.

**From old interviews it seems that "I'll Wait" got the most resistance.**
One of my favorite parts of that song is the first drum fill right before the vocals, and that was an accident. Al hit the hi-hat instead of the crash cymbal. The only way we could record in that room was to have Al play just the drums and then later overdub the cymbals. He just forgot to hit the cymbal. It reminds me of Ginger Baker on "White Room," where Ginger does a similar thing on the first verse.

Ted hated that song. When I played it for him, he kept humming "Hold Your Head Up" by Argent just to piss me off. It doesn't sound anything like that. We didn't have a chorus for the song. Ted played that track for Michael McDonald in his office to see what he would come up with. Little did we know that Ted was using a little microcassette recorder he held under his desk to record what Michael was improvising to it. Ted came up here the next day. I saw Ted with Dave in the control room and he was playing something to him on this cassette recorder. I asked, "What is that?" and they both went "Oh, nothing. Don't worry about it."

Of course, after the album came out, we got sued. Michael McDonald said that he came up with the chorus. There were only two other people in the world that knew that—Ted and Dave. I sure as fuck didn't. I don't know if Dave knew that it was Michael McDonald, but I knew that Ted played it for him. If Ted would have been on the up and up about it, we would have given Michael credit.

**"House of Pain" originally dates back to the demos you recorded with Gene Simmons and the Warner Bros. demos, but the version on *1984* is different. How did it finally make the cut six albums later?**

The only thing that's the same is the main riff. The intro and verses are different, I guess because nobody really liked it the way that it originally was. After "Jump" Ted was still involved, but all he cared about was the single. Ted was a funny guy. When I first played "Jump" for the guys, nobody wanted to have anything to do with it. Dave said that I was a guitar hero and I shouldn't be playing keyboards. My response was if I want to play a tuba or a Bavarian cheese whistle I will do it. As soon as Ted was on board with "Jump" and said that it was a stone-cold hit, everyone started to like it more. Ted only cared about "Jump." He really didn't care much about the rest of the record. He just wanted that one hit.

**"Jump" was by far the album's biggest hit, but *1984* included three other songs that became singles as well. In fact, almost any song on the album could have been a single. It was probably the strongest collection of songs that were ever on a Van Halen album.**

It's ironic. I'll never forget this one time where we were waiting to catch an airplane. *Rolling Stone* had just come out with a new issue. They never liked the band, but they loved this record. I couldn't believe it. They said that "Hot For Teacher" sounded like ZZ Top on speed.

The funniest story about the whole record was near the end when Donn and I were mixing it. Ted seemed to think that we were done, and we had a deadline to meet. The plan was to release the album on New Year's Eve of 1984, but Donn and I weren't happy with everything on it. Donn and I would be in there mixing and the phone would ring. It would be Ted at the front gate to my house, wanting to come in. To this day I don't think Ted knows what actually went on.

My whole driveway is like a big circle. So Donn would grab the master tapes, put them in his car, go out the back gate, and wait as Ted was coming through the front gate because Ted wanted the tapes. He'd ask where Donn and the tapes were, and I'd say that I had no idea. This went on for about two weeks. Little did he know that Donn was sitting outside the back gate. We had walkie-talkies and I would tell him when Ted was leaving. He'd drive down the hill and come back in through the front gate, and Ted never saw him as he was going out behind him. It was a circus!

Nobody was happy with Donn and me. They thought we were crazy and out of our minds. Ted thought that Donn had lost his mind and was going to threaten to burn the tapes. That was all BS. We just wanted an extra week to make sure that we were happy with everything. Ted just didn't see eye to eye with the way I looked at things. That was my whole premise for building the studio. I wanted to make a complete record from end to end, not just one hit. As soon as "Jump" was done, he looked at the rest of the album as filler. It wasn't that to me. It's a good record because it was different.

**Do you have any philosophy about sequencing the songs on your albums?**

Years ago, I had a conversation with Gene Simmons from Kiss about *Love Gun*—the one with "Christine Sixteen." I said, "Gene, how come every song has the same beat?" Most of the songs were even in the same key. I wondered why everything sounded the same. You could barely distinguish between the songs. He said, "Once you got the kids groovin', you don't want to lose them." I thought that was interesting, because I've always looked at it the other way around. I like more variety. Not that his way is wrong, or my way is right. I like to listen to records that go through changes and take you for a ride. I like things that come out of left field and keep your interest. I guess the philosophy of keeping everything the same is like what they do at raves. I like it better when each song holds up individually and makes a well-rounded collection.

I prefer to make records that you listen to from beginning to end. I'm really not into recording just singles. "Jump" was the only number one single we ever had.

**What's ironic is that the only thing that kept *1984* out of the number one spot of the Billboard 200 Albums chart was Michael Jackson's *Thriller*, which you also played on.**

We had the number one single, and he had the number one album. Of course everyone blamed me. They said, "If you hadn't played on 'Beat It' that album wouldn't be number one." We'll never really know who helped who more. Me playing on his record helped expose Van Halen to a different audience.

Some of the best-selling rock albums of all time never made it to number one on the US charts, like AC/DC's *Back in Black, Led Zeppelin IV,* and Boston's debut album. Peak chart positions aren't always an indicator of success.

As sales were projected, we were supposed to go number one. The week before that, Michael Jackson was filming that Pepsi commercial and burned his hair [on January 27, 1984]. When that happened, everyone was going, "Oh, poor Michael burned his hair. We'd better go buy his record."

You can never predict what can happen. A similar thing happened with *A Different Kind of Truth.* It was supposed to debut at number one, but at the end of the first sales week the Grammys happened and Adele won a bunch of awards, which suddenly spiked her album's sales.

I knew that was going to happen. We sold close to two hundred thousand records, which would have made the album number one almost any other week of the year. Being number one doesn't really mean jack fuck-all. We sold twice as many records as other records that year that landed in the number one position. *1984* and *Van Halen* are among a very small group of albums that have won RIAA diamond certification for selling more than ten million copies. Neither one of those records went to number one.

Was the Frankenstein still your main guitar in the studio?
I had actually retired the Frankenstein by then. I'm pretty sure I used the Kramer 5150 guitar the most on that album—"Panama," "Girl Gone Bad," "House of Pain," the solos on "Jump" and "I'll Wait." When I retired my Frankenstein, that became my main guitar. I played it in a lot of videos—"Panama" and "When It's Love"—and in the studio. I used the 5150 guitar up until I started using my Music Man EVH guitar. It's a workhorse. It served me for a very long time. It still sounds great.

Around that time, you patented a "guitar shelf" that supported the guitar horizontally so you could tap notes on the fretboard like a keyboard.
I got the idea for the patented guitar support from a room service tray table, you know, that cart they wheel into your room and they pull out a

tray so the food doesn't spill all over your lap? I took that concept, made it out of a piece of wood, and mounted it on the back of my guitar. I only used it on the 1984 tour. I thought that guys who play slide could play a guitar like a lap steel. I never marketed it or put it out there.

**You used a '58 Flying V on several songs as well, particularly "Hot For Teacher" and "Drop Dead Legs."**

You are very right. The ride out lick that I play on the end of "Drop Dead Legs" came afterwards. We had already finished recording the song, and then I came up with that part, which I thought would sound great at the end of the song. I'm not sure how Donn put it together, but we recorded it separately and added it to the end of the song even though it sounds like it was recorded at the same time. That ride out solo was very much inspired by Allan Holdsworth. I was playing whatever I wanted like jazz—a bunch of wrong notes here and there—but it seemed to work.

**Do you still have the Flying V and your late-fifties Les Paul Standards?**

No. I sold them a few years ago. I never played those guitars after the mid-eighties, so they were just sitting around. The value of them went up so much that I was almost afraid to touch them! Then some guy offered to buy them from me for a very generous price. Let's just say it was an offer that I couldn't refuse, especially since I had a lot of other guitars like my Wolfgangs that could do the same things and more.

**Your solos on the entire record are some of your most innovative playing ever. You really were going outside of your comfort zone and playing new, unusual lines, especially on your solo to "Girl Gone Bad."**

Allan really inspired me. There weren't any other guitarists out there who were blowing my mind at the time other than him. I don't think anyone can copy what he does. He can do with one hand what I need two to do. How he does it is beyond me. But sometimes his playing is so out there that people don't get it.

I got Allan a record deal with Warner Bros. and I was supposed to coproduce the record with him, but he wouldn't wait two or three weeks for me to get back from tour in South America, so he did it himself. I really wish he would have waited. I believe I could have helped him a lot. I heard his demos, and he had this one riff that I heard completely different than how it ended up on his record. That lick could have been a monstrous Zeppelin-style riff, but instead it turned into a lounge song.

Ted signed him, but I don't think he really cared about him, otherwise he would have been there for him. I feel bad for Allan because the album could have really been something good for him. I did everything I could to help him. It wasn't his only shot, but it was a hell of a shot. If he only would have waited a few weeks, things could have turned out very different.

**What is creating that chorus-like sound on the intro to "Drop Dead Legs"?**

I really don't remember. That was all Donn, although Donn never added any flanging or phasing to my guitar. I think I may have used a little MXR Phase 90 on that. I played through the Eventide Harmonizer all the time back then, but it was used mostly to split my guitar signal so it came out of both sides. Back then I didn't play in the control room—I was always out in the main room—so I never really knew what Donn was doing while I was recording tracks. I wouldn't hear it until we were done playing, and I usually liked what I heard.

**Your guitar tone became drier on each successive album. On *1984* I really only hear reverb on "Panama."**

That came from my dislike of that EMT plate reverb that our first album is bathed in. It had its time and place, but it strikes a bad nerve with my brother and me.

**You didn't get caught up in all of the production gimmicks that were prevalent during that period in the eighties. As a result, the album doesn't sound as dated as most other albums that came out during that period.**

I've never been in touch with what is going on in the world because I rarely ever listen to anything else. I think that the record did well because it was ahead of its time and simply different. It was even different for Van Halen. For one, it had two keyboard songs on it. It was a very special time in my life. That shows in the music. I have to credit Donn and myself for having the balls to build my own studio and demand how things were going to be done. Donn and I did a great job.

# MUSICAL INTERLUDE

*A conversation with Toto guitarist* **Steve Lukather**

―――――――――――

Edward Van Halen rarely participated in musical projects outside of his namesake band, but when he did, it often involved his fellow guitarist and good friend Steve Lukather. The two both played on Michael Jackson's mega-hit "Beat It" (although their parts were recorded separately); Ed appeared on two of Lukather's solo albums; and he joined Lukather and George Harrison onstage on December 14, 1992, for the Jeff Pocaro tribute concert, which was broadcast on KLOS-FM and later released as a live album.

Lukather is best known for his roles as a member of the chart-topping band Toto and as a first-call studio guitarist who played on dozens of hit singles recorded between the late seventies and the nineties. Ed greatly respected Lukather's guitar-playing talents, but their friendship was a deep bond that transcended their mutual interests in guitar. "We were friends for forty-plus years," says Lukather. "We went through life together—all the good times, bad times, ridiculous times, sad times, the whole shit. We were much more than just guitar pals. I adored the man as a human being."

Lukather and Van Halen may have had very different personalities as guitar players, with Steve being more musically schooled and disciplined in his approach compared to Ed's wild abandon, but the two were kindred souls when it came to other aspects of life. After Ed passed away, Lukather shared some insight about their friendship and Ed's work beyond Van Halen, including how Ed almost literally destroyed "Beat It."

### What did you think of Ed's playing when you first heard him?

The first time I heard him was when I was recording the solo for "Girl Goodbye" on Toto's debut album. David Paich [Toto keyboardist] came into the studio with the first Van Halen album and put it on the turntable. He said, "Luke, I want you to hear this before you record your solo." He dropped the needle on "Eruption," and I shit my pants! Everybody else in the studio did too. We were all going, "What the fuck! What is that? How do you do that?" It was a game changer. I felt my penis shrink, because I was thinking about what I was going to do on my solo.

I had heard the name "Van Halen" before, but I thought it was just the name of some guy, like Van Morrison. [Session guitarist] Mike Landau and I auditioned to play at Gazzarri's back in 1974 when we were sixteen years old and had a band together, and we got the gig until they found out we were only sixteen. Van Halen was the headlining band at Gazzarri's back then. We'd hang out at Guitar Center on Sunset Boulevard and we'd hear stories about this badass guitar player from Pasadena named Van Halen.

### How did you first meet Ed?

Toto ended up on the same bill as Van Halen at the CaliFFornia World Music Festival at the Los Angeles Coliseum in 1979. I wanted to meet Eddie, so I went backstage before they played. Eddie had heard of me, too, since he had heard "Hold the Line," so he let me sit on the side of the stage. He'd look over and smile at me, and I was just shaking my head in disbelief. I gave him back the best vibe I could. We talked after the show and exchanged phone numbers. He invited me to come over, and I never left. We bonded hard that night over a lot of things that cemented our relationship. It just got stronger over the years.

### It seems like Ed really liked to hang out with other guitar players that he respected.

He was super nice to everybody—kids, fans, or just random people he would meet. He was a beautiful soul. He always made time for everybody. He might say something like, "Could you wait until I'm done with my meal and I'll make time for you," and he would. He was a gentleman. He was a crazy motherfucker too, and so was I. We were meant to be pals. I think we spent other lifetimes together. I get that feeling with all of us guitar players who have known each other forever, the handful of us who came up together through the seventies, eighties, and nineties. Everybody knows everybody and there's a certain respect that we have for each other regardless of what style we play.

**Did you guys get together to jam?**

Not very often. Usually, I would play him recordings of unfinished rough mixes that I was working on, and he would do the same for me. I got to hear "Jump" in demo form way before it was considered for a record. He told me that David Lee Roth hated the song because it had synthesizers. The irony was that it became Van Halen's biggest record. The first time I heard it, I knew it was a fuckin' number one smash, and I told Ed that Roth was out of his mind. It turns out I was right that time!

Ed played me rough mixes of the *1984* album when I was hanging out at the pad just having a few beers or whatever, and I was going, "This is going to be the one." I thought the first album was the shit, but jeez, Ed really topped his game with *1984*. He was real proud of it. Al's playing was amazing. Everybody sounded great. It was one of the best albums they ever did.

**When Ed built the 5150 studio at his house, he really unleashed his creativity.**

Ed wanted to mess around the way *he* wanted to mess around. Ed was always tinkering like no one I've ever seen. I'm the kind of guy that if you give me a model to build I'll have a bunch of pieces left over. I'm an idiot. Ed was a genius. He was always soldering something or putting something together, making some sort of Frankenstein piece of gear. I was enamored by that, because it's so not me. His workshop was always open. That was the first thing you'd see when you'd walk into 5150. There was his workbench with all of his tools and projects. He was always taking a neck off of something and putting it on something else or swapping out pickups. He was always looking for something new, even if he got only one song out of it. That's why he was Eddie. He didn't do things the way everyone else does. Guitar lessons would have been the worst thing in the world for him, because the teacher would have told him he was doing things wrong. For Ed, doing things wrong was the right way to do things.

***The first record that the two of you ever did together was Michael Jackson's "Beat It." Was it your idea to get Eddie to play the solo on that song?***

No. That was entirely Michael's idea. A lot of people don't know that Michael was also a rocker. He loved Van Halen and he loved Toto. That's why he hired us to work on several songs on his record. Michael had a very wide musical palate. I knew Eddie, but I wasn't going to just give them his number. They had to go through the right channels. I wasn't Ed's agent or manager. Ed wasn't all that up on Quincy Jones and what he did. He was asking me, "Who is this Quincy dude?" I told him that he was a really heavy cat and that he should do it.

It was ironic that we both ended up playing on the same record together. Ed later called me up and said, "I just played on your record, 'Beat It.'" And I was going, "I know. We had to redo it because you cut up the tape!" He just started laughing.

***What is the story behind Ed cutting up the master tape?***

We recorded a version of the song at Westlake Recording Studios, which is where Michael recorded the entire album, and Ed recorded his solo later at Sunset Sound. Michael had already recorded five separate vocal tracks. They spent a lot of time working on his vocals, because they wanted it to sound as good as possible. Those finished first-generation vocals were on a twenty-four-track tape that we gave to Ed so he could record his solo. Either Ed or his engineer [Donn Landee] cut up that tape because Ed didn't want to record his solo over the original backing part where Quincy [Jones, producer] and Michael wanted him to play. He just edited the tape to create an entirely new section with chord changes that he liked better.

The problem is that back then we would record one track with SMPTE code [Society of Motion Picture and Television Engineers timecode] for synchronizing one twenty-four-track recorder with another twenty-four-track recorder. That allowed us to record more than just twenty-four tracks. When you cut the tape, the SMPTE code doesn't lock up to the master tape any more. Quincy called me and [drummer] Jeff Pocaro and told us to go to Sunset Sound and record all of our parts all over again, because he didn't want to lose Ed's solo or Michael's first-generation lead vocals. Jeff had to make an entirely new click track with drum sticks so he could play his drum part. He did that and nailed his drum track on the second take. Then I had to cram my guitar tracks onto it, and I also played bass.

We sent the tapes back to Quincy and he said, "It's too big sounding. It's too rock." I thought that since Eddie was on the track I'd better crank up some Marshalls and record quadruple rhythm tracks. Quincy explained that he wanted the song to get airplay on R&B radio as well as rock radio, so he asked me to play through my small Fender amps. I did it again like that, and that's the version that's on the record. I'm honored to be playing guitar and bass on "Beat It." It's one of the biggest records of all time.

### What did you think of Ed's solo?

That solo was like a collection of everything that Eddie ever did before crammed into twenty seconds—harmonics, tapping, whammy bar dives, superfast tremolo picking. To me it sounds like he just went through his solo a couple of times and that was the take. I don't think that a whole lot of thought went into it. He just played and was probably thinking, "I don't even know what I'm doing this for." I never knew Ed to labor over anything, so I think he was just goofing on it. But even when he was goofing, great things would come out of him.

### You later worked with Ed on a couple of your solo albums.

Ed always wanted to do interesting things, although his bandmates weren't real thrilled about him doing stuff outside of the band. That was still a bone of contention when I got him on my first solo album [*Lukather*, 1989], but Al is my friend, too, so it was cool. I didn't abuse my relationship with Ed. I wasn't going, "Ladies and gentlemen, Eddie Van Halen on MY album!" I would never take advantage of his name like that, and I promised him I never would. Our friendship meant more to me than anything else.

Ed wrote the riff for "Twist the Knife," which was something that he wrote for Van Halen ["I Want Some Action," originally recorded as a demo for *5150* but never released], but he gave it to me instead. He played bass on the track and I played guitar, but I had to set the guitar up the way he told me to. He went, "Look. You tune the guitar like this, and play it like this." I had to tune the guitar up a whole step and replace the guitar's low E string with an A bass string tuned to B. My guitar neck looked like a fuckin' bow and arrow, but it worked. I had to play all these false harmonics, and it took me a few seconds to get into Ed's head, the way he writes and plays and how he feels time, where he thinks the beat is. He did all this trick rhythm shit. It was just brilliant.

### How did you end up doing background vocals on For Unlawful Carnal Knowledge?

I just happened to drop by the studio. I'd often just drive up the hill and go right on in since I knew the code to Ed's security gate. I'd go over there and hang out for an hour or two. They were recording vocal tracks for the album, and Ted Templeman was there. Ted said, "We need a third voice. Lukather, get out there!" It wasn't a big thing. I didn't take any money for it. I sang a few oohs and aahs, and I got to be on a Van Halen record. That was good enough for me. People asked if I played guitar on that album. Of course not! Why should I play guitar on a Van Halen album when they've already got Eddie? Give me a break.

### In 2003 you and Ed recorded a jazz-fusion instrumental version of "Joy to the World" for your Christmas album, Santamental.

Al Schmitt and Elliot Scheiner are legendary Grammy-winning producers who are probably best known for their work with Steely Dan. They asked me to do a Christmas album, and I went, "What the fuck makes you think I'm Santa Claus? It's July!" But that's when we had to do it. So I had my keyboardist Jeff Babko do a bunch of these fusion arrangements of Christmas classics and had all of my guitar player buddies like Eddie, Slash, and Steve Vai come in to jam with me.

When Ed did that, he hadn't been playing for a while. He was going through a rough period where he just didn't want to do anything. I got him out of retirement. I told him, "Just come on down and do a stupid solo for me. It's just a jam." He agreed to do it as long as it was just him and me in the room. Elliot got Ed's sound and left the room. We recorded a couple of takes and that was that. He did it for me as a favor. He hadn't played for a while, but once he warmed up it was like he'd never stopped playing.

***Your first Music Man signature model guitar came out a few years after Ed's Music Man signature model. Did he convince you to work with them?***

When Music Man came out with Ed's guitar, they were courting me to work with them too. I went up to Ed's house while they were finishing up his guitar. They were choosing pickups. They were voting on the neck pickup and it was a tie, so they asked me to be the tie-breaker. That was a bigger responsibility than I wanted, but I offered my opinion and that's the one they went with. They gave me prototype number three—a purple one with gorgeous quilted maple—for my efforts, and I still have that guitar and cherish it to this day. I'm going to play it on my next tour.

I had my own deal with Valley Arts at the time, but that fell apart in 1993 shortly after they sold the company to the Koreans. The former head luthier at Valley Arts, Dudley Gimpel, had been working for Music Man for a few years, so it made sense for me to work with Music Man. Dudley designed Ed's guitar and he designed my Luke model, too, which is my favorite guitar.

**What do you remember the most about Ed?**

He always had a big smile, and he'd greet me with a hug and a kiss. It was fuckin' beautiful. We'd sit down and talk about *life*. We wouldn't talk about what kind of strings we use or boring guitar shit. We would cry on each other's shoulder and we laughed a lot. We shared so much, a lot of positive moments. It was the best memories ever. He was like a brother. He was Eddie—the greatest guitar player of all time. At least that's what I think. Nobody can argue that Ed wasn't one of the greatest of all time. That's a given.

# 6

# A TALE OF
# TWO SINGERS

*With the departure of David Lee Roth, Eddie
discovers that you can't always get what you want.
But with Sammy Hagar, he achieves a bit of much-
needed balance.*

---

" Dave used to say I wasn't happy
unless I was unhappy. That was a crock. "

---

I N ANCIENT CHINESE philosophy, yin and yang is a concept of
dualism describing how seemingly opposite or contrary forces
may actually be interconnected and interdependent in the natural
world. For example, heat cannot be understood without knowing what
cold feels like. Yin and yang forces can be thought of as complementary
(rather than opposing) forces that interact to form a dynamic system in
which the whole is greater than the assembled parts.

This dualism has long been a driving force in rock and roll. The Beatles
were a product of McCartney's boy-next-door charm and Lennon's rebel-
lious grit. The Rolling Stones would never have become legends without

Mick Jagger's calculation and Keith Richards's wild, street-smart instincts. Certainly, Van Halen would've never risen to the top without David Lee Roth's extroverted, show-biz razzmatazz and Edward Van Halen's introverted, obsessive-compulsive devotion to his instrument.

Ed and Dave were a dazzling team, but diametric opposites. They certainly understood each other's unique talents and how they complemented each other, but it didn't stop them from cursing the fates for locking them into an often-exasperating gravitational orbit—attracted yet repulsed—spinning around each other in the same circles year after year.

Anyone who spoke with either for any length of time would hear the same complaints, over and over again.

"I'm a musician. . . . Dave's a rock star," Ed would grouse.

"Ed's not happy unless he's unhappy," Dave would often tell the press.

It didn't help that both observations were to some extent true—and essential components of both Ed's and Dave's genius.

Since picking up the guitar at age twelve, Edward was never quite satisfied with his music. He was always searching for a better way to re-create the sonic explosions he heard in his head—"sound chasing," he called it. Although he was not a perfectionist in the traditional sense (a certain amount of rough-hewn messiness was baked into his aesthetic), he was rarely satisfied with his work, which pushed him to not only devising new playing techniques but also building his own instruments.

Some of this was due to his artistic temperament, but a great deal was the residue of deep-seated childhood insecurities caused by his critical mother, who often dismissed his guitar playing and called him a "nothing nut, just like your father." He was also psychologically wounded by the cruelty of the children who for years underestimated his intelligence in grade school because of his inability to speak English when he arrived in Pasadena from Holland.

During a 1984 interview with *Rolling Stone* magazine, he cautioned a writer that he wasn't "very good with words." When she argued that she found him to be highly articulate, he said, "I guess it's been too many goddamn years I've been told that I'm stupid."

Dave, on the other hand, was a breathtakingly witty motormouth who enjoyed every moment of the spotlight, had a blithe spirit and a laissez-faire attitude about his life. "The problem with self-improvement is knowing when to quit," he once quipped. Or perhaps more to the point, "I'm not conceited. Conceit is a fault and I have no faults."

Some of David's bravado was for the amusement of the press, but Ed, who was around Roth for months at a time, found his narcissism offensive, grating, the antithesis of his own sensibilities. It was only a matter of time before the creative sparks touched off by their conflicting personalities would combust into flames. Still, it was a surprise to both parties when it finally happened.

In 1985, after a grueling tour supporting Van Halen's mammoth *1984* album, the band took a break to spend time with their wives and recharge their creative batteries. Roth and producer Ted Templeman thought it wise to give Ed some space so the guitarist could recuperate and work at writing the next album. But Roth had no wife or family and had little desire to stop. Instead, he approached Templeman with the idea of recording a solo EP of cover songs that he liked but that had no place in Van Halen's universe.

"Dave and I both agreed about its parameters," Templeman said years later. "We'd avoid anything that sounded like hard rock. There would be no heavy guitar riffs or jungle drums. It was going to be a totally different musical ecosystem: all pop-vaudeville meets big band . . . it would be the [opposite] of Van Halen.

"At the time, I saw all of this as beneficial when it came to the future of Van Halen. I figured this would help Dave get this stuff out of his system and give him a clean slate from which to start the next Van Halen record. If I'd gotten even the slightest sense that he saw this as step one of David Lee Roth's post–Van Halen solo career, I wouldn't have done the record. I never, ever wanted to do anything to threaten the future of Van Halen. I can't emphasize this enough."[10]

Though it's often been blamed for driving a wedge between Dave and Edward, Roth's four-song solo EP, *Crazy from the Heat*, with its two hits, "California Girls" and "Just a Gigolo," was never the issue. Ed himself had indulged in several outside projects, including playing on Michael Jackson's "Beat It" and working on a soundtrack with engineer Donn Landee for a film entitled *The Wild Life*.

In a 1985 interview with journalist Steven Rosen, Ed actually spoke magnanimously about Roth's recording: "I think it's something he always wanted to do. It's great he's actually doing it. . . . I don't think he's out to prove anything. I know it will be good for him personally and his own self-satisfaction when it takes off in the way I expect it will. I seriously want the best for it, in the same way he'd want the best for me or Al or Mike if we did anything outside of the band."

What really created the turmoil was when CBS Studios offered Roth $10 million to write, direct, and star in a film tentatively called *Crazy from the Heat*. It wasn't an entirely nutty idea. Dave had codirected five very entertaining videos in heavy rotation on MTV—three for Van Halen and two for his solo project. And considering that Prince had just grossed $70 million on a $7.2 million budget with his movie *Purple Rain*, why wouldn't a film company want to take a modest gamble on an eccentric rock musician?

David's groan-inducing script, however, lacked the charm of his short-form videos (a draft can be readily found online), and the movie was never made. But while he was developing the project, he made it clear that the movie would take priority over the band. Naturally, Ed and Al were insulted. For the brothers, Van Halen was blood, and blood always came first. It was an idea that had been ingrained into them since they arrived in America.

As Ed once said, "All my energy goes into Van Halen; it's my family. I'm not going to leave my family until one of the members passes on."[11]

A series of uninspiring recording sessions with David led to more heated arguments, and according to Roth, "the chemistry had turned rotten." The singer especially despised Ed's recent synthesizer-driven demos that featured what Roth called "melancholy power ballads."

Ed's escalating alcohol and cocaine consumption also did little to diminish the rising tensions between the two, nor did the fact that they were wrestling with each other over the direction of the band. And with the group's entire recording facility now located in Ed's 5150 backyard studio, Roth understood he was losing the battle over the soul of Van Halen.

Their troubles finally came to a head in March 1985, during a meeting between the guitarist and the singer at Roth's mansion in Pasadena, where both aired their grievances. Their accounts of the evening differed wildly, but both admitted that tears were shed, and the upshot was that the name of the band was Van Halen . . . and Dave was out.

Replacing a front man as smart and charismatic as David Lee Roth was going to be no small task, and over the next few months panic ensued as Ed, Al, and Mike attempted to pick up the pieces of their shattered band. For a brief moment, Edward considered recording a one-off collaboration with The Who's Pete Townshend. When that didn't materialize, the guitarist suggested a couple of left-field ideas, including enlisting Patty Smyth of the pop-rock outfit Scandal to replace Roth, then Daryl Hall of Hall & Oates. He also advocated recording an album with several guest singers, including Joe Cocker and Phil Collins. Alex nixed all of those ideas, telling Ed he wanted something more solid, something that felt more like that familiar word, *family*.

One name that had been floating in the Van Halen cosmos since the earliest days of the band was singer-guitarist Sammy Hagar, who'd recently had a huge radio hit with his anthem to recklessness, "I Can't Drive 55." Van Halen producer Templeman had a long history with the singer, having produced Hagar in the early seventies when he was vocalist in the hard rock band Montrose. In fact, he had toyed with the idea of replacing Roth with Hagar on Van Halen's debut back in 1977, when he wasn't sure if David Lee Roth could cut it as a singer.

Oddly, it wasn't Templeman who suggested Hagar this time around, but an Italian car dealer who got Ed's wheels turning. Ed loved Lamborghinis and was a regular at Claudio Zampolli's auto shop. When Ed told Zampolli that Roth had quit the band, the dealer proposed Hagar, who was also a customer partial to fast cars.

Something felt right about the recommendation, and the guitarist called Sammy "right there from the shop." Three days later, Hagar came down to hang out and jam, and in twenty minutes the band finished "Summer Nights," a song that would later become a huge fan favorite.

At that moment in time, Sammy was a perfect choice for Van Halen—as a skilled and experienced front man with a terrific vocal range and a strong, radio-friendly voice, his learning curve would be minimal. He had an upbeat persona and blended well with the other band members, and most important to Ed, he was more of a musician than a spotlight-hungry "rock star." Though Sammy was no Eddie Van Halen, he was a top-notch guitarist and could speak Ed's language when necessary.

On the negative side, as a lyricist Hagar was no Bob Dylan . . . and he was no David Lee Roth. But he could crank out a perfectly workman-like chorus when called upon and emote convincingly on Ed's new pop-oriented ballads, and that was enough.

Although fans were divided on Hagar, those who didn't particularly like what he had to offer tolerated him because they loved Ed and the band. And his mainstream sensibility and party-hearty sentiments attracted an entirely new, broader audience to Van Halen.

The band's first album with the new singer, *5150*, rocketed to number one, driven by keyboard-dominated singles like "Why Can't This Be Love," "Dreams," and "Love Walks In." Four more albums, *OU812* (1988), *For Unlawful Carnal Knowledge* (1991), *Live: Right Here, Right Now* (1993), and *Balance* (1995) followed, and all handily achieved Platinum status.

**You seemed happy with the new band on *5150*.**
Dave used to say I wasn't happy unless I was unhappy. That was a crock. I was happy as hell while recording *5150* and we came up with great stuff.

**Did you or Dave pull the plug?**
He quit. We weren't getting along, but then again, we never did.

**How was it working with Sammy?**
Sammy and I were immediately in tune with each other. Dave and I were always at odds. We came from different backgrounds and our musical tastes were miles apart. Sometimes that works—the friction creates something interesting. And it did for a long time.

But Sammy and I were more alike, and it seemed to work better. There was some worry that *5150* would sound like a Sammy Hagar album, but I knew that wouldn't be the case. Al, Mike, and I had our own sound.

**You used Mick Jones of Foreigner to produce *5150*. What happened to Ted Templeman?**
Ted came to one rehearsal and we showed him about four or five tunes. He made notes and everything, but he had made a commitment to Dave and wasn't sure when he would have time for us.

It would've made sense for him to produce *5150*, given his past relationship with us and Sammy. And I didn't mind he was still working with Dave, but we wanted to get rolling. I was sick of sitting on my ass. It was funny. Dave said we wanted to sit on our butts and stay at home and not tour and not work. But I sat on my thumb waiting for him for eight months, then he quit, and I didn't want to wait any longer.

**Was building your studio any source of tension between you, Ted, and Dave?**
I guess it turned some people off. I built the studio for the benefit of all of us—for the family, for the band. But I guess certain people didn't look at it that way, because Ted sure didn't dig working up there. Even though he loved the sound of the place, I think he was worried that if I got pissed at him, I'd kick him out of the studio. (*laughs*) Though I would've never done that. If anything, that would be something Dave would've done.

**Before Sammy joined, you considered working with Pete Townshend.**
The thing is, I never thought Roth would quit. I thought he'd wake up. The things he said at our last meeting were so weird, though. He asked how long I thought recording the follow-up to *1984* would last. His attitude was, "Hey, man, I've got other things to do, how long is it going to take?" I told him to count on a year from starting point to album release—writing for a couple months, recording for three months, mastering, album covers, T-shirts, and all that.

Because he was trying to put together his movie, he suggested not doing an album and just cashing in on the summer circuit. And I said, "What? I don't want to go on tour without a record."

**5150 was your first number one album. Did you feel vindicated?**
It showed that music overpowers bullshit. Dave and I wrote a lot of good stuff and made a lot of good music together, but I guess the clowning and the show-biz part of it only helped so much. What's on that tape or piece of plastic is what counts. Bottom line. And our going to number one proved that. *5150* was a good record—a solid record. There's not a song on it I don't like.

**5150 was more radio-friendly than your previous albums. A little more polished.**

"Love Walks In" and "Dreams" started as piano tunes, which made them sound smoother, and I used an arpeggiator on "Why Can't This Be Love," which gave it a more uniform effect. Those songs were admittedly more pop friendly, but what's wrong with that? If more people like it, it's pop, right?

**How did you feel about *OU812*?**

I wanted to call it *Rock and Roll*. That album wasn't heavy metal or hard rock—it was just a good diverse rock and roll album. To me, "When It's Love" is just a classic tune. It's pretty, it's heavy, it's melodic, it has a sing-along chorus—it's a happening song. "Black & Blue" is a great slippery, grungy heavy funk song. And "Finish What Ya Started" was probably the most atypical thing you'd ever heard from us. It almost sounds like a Stones song.

**After you finished OU812, you were a guest on the Cinemax special *Les Paul & Friends: Live at the Brooklyn Academy of Music in New York*. How did that come about?**

I first met Les when we were inducted into the Hollywood RockWalk at the Sunset Boulevard Guitar Center in 1986. It was a hell of an honor to be inducted at the same time as Les because he's a real legend. I mean, it all started with him—the Les Paul guitar, multitrack recording. We got to talking and discovered that we both have a lot in common. We both always did things our own way and invented our own stuff to make music with because no one else would. We became instant friends and stayed in touch over the years.

One day Les called and asked me if I would play at this tribute concert in New York that was going to be filmed and broadcast later. There was no way I could say no. I mean, it's Les, right? He told me that I was the first person he invited, which was a total honor. Luckily, the Monsters of Rock tour was scheduled to finish a few weeks before they were going to tape the show, so I didn't have to change my schedule so I could do it.

That show was a blast! I played with Tony Levin (bass) and Jan Hammer (keyboards), and I got to meet David Gilmour and B. B. King, who later gave me one of his Lucille guitars.

*OU812* sounded like a continuation of *5150*, where *For Unlawful Carnal Knowledge* represented a dawn of a new era for you. You revamped your studio, built a new guitar with Music Man, hired a new producer, and it was a return to a heavier sound. Was that planned?

No, not at all. We started our last tour in 1988 and ended it in Japan in February of 1989. We consciously took a whole year off, during which I barely touched the guitar. I saw the band socially, but we didn't do any work. Then in the early part of 1990, we sat together and discussed what we wanted to accomplish, and everything just started falling into place. I don't want to spoil anybody's fantasies, but we rarely calculated anything. In general, Van Halen is a band that doesn't think that much. (*laughs*)

**What was the first order of business?**

Finding a producer. The name Andy Johns, who produced and engineered some of Led Zeppelin's records, came up. Coincidentally, I had just met him in a recording studio, so I invited him up and we had a meeting.

We needed to know whether we would get along with him on a personal level. Also, we wanted to see how he worked in the studio. All we knew was that he's made some great records. So, we called him. He answered his phone and said (*assumes a growling, pub-drenched English accent*), "Hey, mate, what do you want me to do? Come in and mess around a bit? No problem, but it's my birthday and I'm kind of hammered. Call me back tomorrow." He sounded like Dudley Moore in *Arthur*. And as it turned out, Andy was so rock and roll it was ridiculous. He really fit in.

At first, he insisted on a second engineer, but we had to nix that idea because 5150 was so small. So, he came by himself. We started miking up the drums, and by the end of the day we were convinced he was our man. He took control without being obnoxious.

**Did you have any music prepared at this point?**

Absolutely nothing! That was the next big problem. (*laughs*) I wasn't really prepared, because I thought it would take a while to find someone we wanted to work with. The guys were asking me, "Hey, Ed, you got any licks?" A little panicky, I said, "Hell no! Give me . . . uh . . . give me until tomorrow."

The first thing I came up with was a real headbanger called "Judgement Day." It's a pretty simple tune. I figured, "Gee, I haven't played guitar in a year. I can make it through this!" After that song was finished, we continued to jam in the studio, and slowly the tracks started to materialize.

The whole album was done one song at a time. We'd completely finish one track before moving on to the next one. That's why there are so many different textures on it. It wasn't done like our first albums, where we banged all the rhythm tracks out in a couple days. Interestingly, I think it's a more powerful rock and roll record than *OU812* or *5150*, despite the fact that it was conceived over a long period of time.

**What did Andy bring to the record?**
He brought rock and roll inspiration. More importantly, he was the first engineer to capture the sound of Van Halen's rhythm section. The bottom line is, if Al is happy, then I'm happy. It isn't hard to get a great guitar sound. It's much harder to get a fantastic acoustic drum sound—which Andy did. And that was the first time I really heard Mike on one of our records.

**You revamped your studio right before the album. What did you do?**
We installed a new, warm-sounding API console, which was custom-fitted for our relatively small room. It had thirty-six inputs and featured GML automation, which made it easier to mix the album. We also added a drum room that practically doubled the size of the studio. The additional room really helped Alex capture the sound he always wanted. In the past we had to resort to Simmons electronic drums because there was no way to isolate an acoustic kit when we wanted to play together—there just wasn't enough room. Playing together without having to compromise our sound was a dream come true. We really took our time on the actual recording process and made sure each one of us was happy with the sound of our instruments. In a way, it's the ideal Van Halen record.

**Did Andy make suggestions regarding the arrangements?**
Not really. Wait, let me rephrase that. What I really appreciated about Andy is that he gave me space when I needed to develop an idea.

**What happened to your regular engineer, Donn Landee?**
We weren't unhappy with Donn, but we had done eight records with him and we felt it would be nice to get a different spin on things. It wasn't a big deal.

**It was rather surprising that you brought Ted Templeman back for some of the album. What was his role?**

Ted came in to save the day towards the end of the album. None of us were very good at finishing things, so we asked Ted to help out. He was a very organized cat. I mean, you put Andy Johns, Sammy Hagar, Alex Van Halen, Mike Anthony, and me in a room together, and we'll piss up a rope for years, just having fun and experimenting. Ted was the one that said, "Enough is enough. What do you want, a double album? You'll be here for another year. Let's finish what we've got." He cracked the whip and pulled everything together. He also worked on a lot of the vocals with Sammy, while Andy and I worked on guitars and guitar overdubs.

**What did Andy think of Ted?**

There was definitely some tension. Not to rag on Andy—because we liked working with him—but he was an alcoholic and you could only really get two hours out of him before things would start going south. That was one of the reasons the album took so long to make and why we had to bring in Ted.

**There are a lot of overdubs on *For Unlawful Carnal Knowledge*, which was unusual for you. "Poundcake," for example, featured a complete wall of sound.**

It's just the way the album evolved. The original riff on "Poundcake" didn't excite anyone until Andy suggested I use some electric twelve-strings to flesh out the rhythm tracks. It turned out to be just the thing the song needed. Suddenly, the lyrics, the title, everything came into sharp focus. What you hear are two twelve-strings doubled under my usual dirty guitar.

Earlier, you asked what Andy Johns brought to this record. That was it—inspiration that comes from the sound elements. He would make a small suggestion, or move a knob or two, and our sound would change, goosing our creative juices.

**What kind of twelve-string did you use?**

It was a guitar developed by Roger Giffin, who worked out of Gibson's custom shop. We worked together on my Steinberger guitars. His custom twelve had these small Smith pickups that looked like something between a single-coil and a humbucker.

**On the solo to "Poundcake" you used the neck pickup. That was also unusual for you.**

Before I started *For Unlawful Carnal Knowledge*, I developed a neck pickup with Steve Blucher who worked with DiMarzio pickups for my new Ernie Ball/Music Man guitar, and it's all over the album. One of my major frustrations was that I never was able to find a neck and bridge pickup that sounded good together. I never used a neck pickup because they never sounded good with my setup. Steve and I worked hard to remedy that situation, and it was like, "All right! I got a new toy!"

**It also sounds like you dug your old wah-wah out of the closet. You used it quite a bit.**

People always ask me what I was thinking. I wasn't thinking! It was pretty spontaneous. A wah-wah happened to be floating around the studio. I plugged it in, and that was that. I used it because it was handy.

**You've had a studio in your backyard for almost half of your career. How studio savvy are you?**

I know how to run the shit, believe it or not. Actually, this is kind of a touchy subject. In the old days, Donn Landee kind of monopolized 5150. He was the only one who really knew how to run anything. It was his gig, so he was very protective and didn't want anyone else touching the knobs. During the recording of *Knowledge*, Andy was just the opposite. He showed me how to run the console and seemed more than happy to receive my input. It was a real relief to finally know my way around, because I could go in and record ideas at any given time. I actually got to the point where I could punch myself in with my toes! I think my wife also punched me in on a couple of things. It was like, "Honey, when I count to four, push record!" My setup was so simple—two Shure SM-57s on a Marshall cabinet—one directly in the middle and one angled from the side.

At one point, Andy complained that he wasn't hearing enough bottom. So, I said, "Okay, okay, then put another mike on the speaker." That's the way we solve problems in the studio. A lot of it was just common sense.

*For Unlawful Carnal Knowledge* **was probably the most sonically adventurous of your career. "Spanked" is a good example.**

We didn't set out to make the album experimental, it just naturally evolved that way. The guitar-like bass line on "Spanked" was a total fluke. One day Andy walked in with a Danelectro six-string bass, and I thought, "Ooooh, that's neat." I plugged it into my Marshall amp and it sounded wild. It just seemed appropriate for the main lick in "Spanked."

**But you were using a new guitar and were in the process of developing a new amp, at some point you must have consciously wanted to experiment with new sounds.**

I wasn't after a different sound—I was just trying to find the epitome of what I've always heard in my head. The only reason I co-designed the new Music Man guitar was that Sterling Ball had been hounding me to do it for over a year. He was after my ass! Fender wanted me, too! At one point, all these guitar companies came out of the woodwork because I wasn't working with Kramer anymore. I went with Sterling because his company did a fine job with my 5150 strings. I was confident that he would do good work.

At first, I really wasn't sure if I wanted to put my name on a guitar. The initial step was to see if I could come up with a body shape that I liked. Once I got over that hump, it just snowballed. But to get back to your point, I wasn't searching for something different. I just have a natural curiosity that varies from day to day. If I started the album today, I'd probably approach it in a completely different manner.

**In the beginning of 1991, you were briefly using a Soldano amp on stage. Then you started developing an amp with Peavey. You seemed pretty restless. Your legendary Marshall, which you used on all of your albums, always sounded incredible. Why change?**

I'm not sure whether my taste changed or the amp changed, but I think my Marshall started to fade—it didn't sound like it used to. Even Donn Landee started noticing it on *OU812*. It was time to start looking elsewhere.

**It must've been frightening to rely on that old Marshall, knowing it could've blown at any minute.**

And believe me, it did! Many times.

# EDDIE'S ODDITIES

**GUITAR:** Custom 1988 Gibson Les Paul Standard
with Floyd Rose vibrato
**USED:** Gift from Les Paul Tribute concert

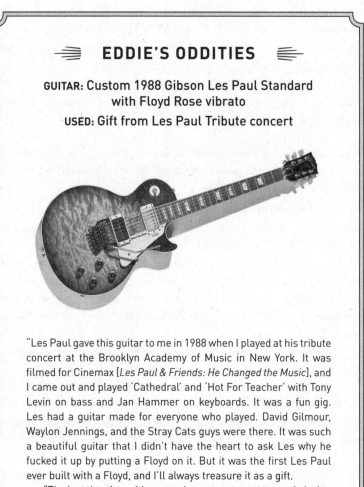

"Les Paul gave this guitar to me in 1988 when I played at his tribute concert at the Brooklyn Academy of Music in New York. It was filmed for Cinemax [*Les Paul & Friends: He Changed the Music*], and I came out and played 'Cathedral' and 'Hot For Teacher' with Tony Levin on bass and Jan Hammer on keyboards. It was a fun gig. Les had a guitar made for everyone who played. David Gilmour, Waylon Jennings, and the Stray Cats guys were there. It was such a beautiful guitar that I didn't have the heart to ask Les why he fucked it up by putting a Floyd on it. But it was the first Les Paul ever built with a Floyd, and I'll always treasure it as a gift.

"The last time I saw him was when we were on tour and playing a show at the Meadowlands in New Jersey [November 3, 2007]. Les came into the tune-up room before the show, and I introduced him to Wolfgang. He said, 'Show me how you do that finger stuff [tapping].' He almost tried it, but then he went, 'Nah, I can't do it.' Wolfgang said, 'It's easy. See I can do it.' That was a special moment—me, my son, and Les in the tune-up room."

**It was always rumored to be heavily modified . . .**

That was all bullshit, man! The guys in the band used to say, "Don't tell anybody what you use." I took their advice, but I never lied *that* blatantly. (*chuckles slyly*) Basically, I just let people believe what they wanted to believe. The only thing I ever did was use a Variac to lower the voltage to about 89 volts, so I could turn the amp up without blowing it up. It's been retubed, but basically, it's just a stock amp.

The bottom line is I really think that every guitar sound comes from the player's fingers. I must've told this story on countless occasions. One time, Ted Nugent wanted to play through my "magic box"—until he found out I didn't have one. When he played through my rig, it still sounded like Ted.

**Have you ever put solos together from different takes in the studio?**

Hell, yes! I admit it, I'm not proud. "Jump" for example, was punched in. You can hear that there are two distinct parts to that solo. I can't even remember what I played originally. All I remember is the recorded, pieced-together version that everybody knows.

**Let's talk about some of the songs on *For Unlawful Carnal Knowledge*. The solo on "Judgement Day" sounds premeditated.**

Yeah, it wasn't a wing-it thing. It was definitely something I set out to do. It's a double-handed thing that I used to do in my live guitar solo. I just took part of it and inserted it. The actual body of the solo is a kind of surf thing I came up with.

**How many takes do you usually do?**

No more than three.

**Do you keep them all?**

No, and that scared the hell out of Andy Johns. I'd say, "Man, I can beat that take. Just record over it." Andy would always look at me very suspiciously and say, "Ohhh, Eddie, I don't know . . ." But really, I never worried about it because a solo ain't gonna make or break a tune. A solo should just highlight a song.

**"Spanked" really stomps.**

It's actually kind of a joke tune. I mean, c'mon, it's about getting spanked! Let me tell you where the title came from. Anyone who has ever spent any time in 5150 complains about the placement of our monitor speakers. They're strange because the room used to be a racquetball court—it wasn't designed to be a recording studio. So, Andy Johns walked in for the first time and said, "Hey, mate, your speakers sound kind of *spanked*." Spanked! That killed me. When something is beat to shit, it's "spanked." We quickly adopted that into our vocabulary, and Sammy wrote a song about it. I think it's the funniest song on the album, but nobody seems to get it. It's such an odd combination of heavy music and goofball lyrics. A week ago, Mo Ostin, the big cheese from Warner Bros. came up here. He listened to that track with a puzzled look on his face, stroking his chin and saying things like, "Gee guys, that's, er . . . nice."

**"Spanked" and "Pleasure Dome" have a Zeppelin influence.**

It's funny you should mention those songs together. Al really helped to shape both tunes. He's a total Zeppelin freak, so that's not surprising. I don't mean to downplay Andy's influence, but I think Alex had more to do with the Zeppelin-esque touches. He's a very musical guy—he's not just a drummer. In my book he's the baddest! He was the one that suggested using the EBow at the beginning of "Spanked." And "Pleasure Dome" would not be on the album if not for Al. At one point it was just three disjointed riffs. He helped me bridge them together.

**You and Alex have always worked closely together. Are there any areas you don't mesh?**

I'm always screwing around with time, because I never count. The solo in "Poundcake," for example, goes four bars, another four bars, then two bars. Al kept insisting it wasn't finished. He likes to count, and I never do. I'm strictly feel.

**"Right Now" has a gospel feel.**

I can hear Joe Cocker singing that one. I wrote that music before Sammy was in the band. If there was any other vocalist I'd like to make a record with, it would be Joe. That song has that classic "Feelin' Alright" groove.

**What about "316"?**

That was also something I had for quite a while. I played it to introduce my solo segment, and I also played it to put my son to sleep at night. The guys dug it and wanted to put it on the record. I decided to call it "316" because that's Wolf's birthday. I used a Gibson Chet Atkins acoustic solid body steel-string guitar and ran it directly into the board and processed it with an Eventide Harmonizer.

**"Top of the World" features the riff you used in the fade-out to "Jump."**

Wow, you noticed that? I almost didn't put that on the record because everything else seemed so new and fresh. Andy forced me to put it in. He kept saying, "I love that song. You have to put it on the record." I used my "Hot For Teacher" Gibson Flying V and my Marshall on that tune, which was cool. But, to be honest, we had five other tunes that I would've preferred to use that didn't make it on the album.

**"Pleasure Dome" features one of the best solos of the album.**

It's an overdub, but I just winged it.

**By the time you recorded *Balance*, your playing had progressed in an interesting manner. How would you compare it to the first album?**

In a funny way, a lot had changed yet at the same time nothing had. Sometimes I look at my playing and I go, "God! I sure haven't gotten any better." (*laughs*) But by the time we were recording *Balance*, it wasn't about "getting better." Once I got to the point where I could play pretty much whatever I heard in my head, then you tend to play whatever thought is in your head. How much faster can you play? How much faster do you need to play? But I've changed a bit. It's funny, because every now and then I listen to old tapes—somebody will send me an old bootleg tape of us at the Whisky or whatever and I'll go, "Wow. I don't really play any better, do I?" (*laughs*) You just get your point across however you can.

**So, you're able to play whatever you hear in your head?**

Yeah. That's when I kind of realized that I know what I'm doing or that I've reached a point where I'm happy with my playing, meaning whatever pops into mind I'm able to execute.

**Your tapping technique wasn't as prominent on *Balance*.**

That's because I didn't actually do a piece like "Eruption" or "Spanish Fly" or anything like that. Over the years it has just become part of my playing to the point where it's just something I do. There's probably more than you think.

**There weren't too many long lead breaks on the album either.**

Over the years I've come to look at solos more as little pieces within the songs. It's just a way to make the overall picture better. On the first record, it was like, "All right! I get to solo!" and I'd blaze without thinking. Now I try to plan my solos a little more except there are still songs like "Feelin'," which is more old style, total spontaneous, whatever comes up, reckless abandon.

**How did you choose Bruce Fairbairn [Aerosmith, Rush] to produce *Balance*?**

I prefer having an outside ear. We met with a handful of producers, but we liked Bruce's vibe. He was very professional. There was a mutual respect there and he didn't try to sell himself. He just asked what we were up to. I played him a few things and one thing led to another and before we knew it, we were doing a record. He was great to work with.

It's really difficult to say what a producer does. Bruce definitely made us work harder and faster. This was the quickest record we've made in a long time. It took us four months. But it was a joy to work with the guy. I'm always one who goes, "We can do better than that," and he'd say, "Nah. This one has a vibe. It's cool." So, I trusted him and in hindsight I'd listen back and go, "Oh yeah! I might've been a little sloppy, but it's got a vibe."

**You quit drinking during the *Balance* sessions. Did it make the recording process more difficult?**

I was sober most of the record, which really weirded me out. It took me a while for me to get used to playing without the help of the alcohol. In the past, if I recorded something that sounded too stiff, I'd have a few drinks to loosen up. When I drink I don't think about what I'm playing. It's like, "Oh, I made a mistake, big fucking deal." My inhibitions are lower when I drink, so I just play stuff without thinking about it too much or getting embarrassed or nervous.

I'd been doing that so long it was hard for me to feel comfortable playing while I was sober. But I had to get used to it, because I'd been drinking too long and it was a problem. I'm an alcoholic. I can't stop after just a couple of drinks. It's like "Fuck you! I'll drink till I go to sleep." I also become quite a prick when I get drunk. I don't mean violent. I just get real obnoxious.

**Your father gave you your first drink, and he used to drink a lot while he played music. Did you pick that habit up from him?**

I don't think my drinking is genetic. It's more a product of the environment that I grew up in. I was nervous before I had to play gigs with my dad, and one day when I was twelve, he gave me a shot of vodka to calm my nerves. It worked. My dad got me into drinking and smoking, and my mom would even buy me cigarettes, so it just became a habit. I would only drink to get drunk—to get a buzz. And I'd do it to calm my nerves. Unlike a lot of people, I don't drink for recreation. I drank more when I was writing, recording, or even just playing. I drank in the studio when I was working. But I didn't drink when I was at the house or relaxing at the beach on weekends with Val and Wolfie.

**By 1995, you had been working with Sammy longer than you did with David Lee Roth.**

I think it showed on *Balance*. This album was everything rolled into one. It had a rawness that was there on our first record and it had the polished quality of hopefully all the years we've been doing it. I was proud of it.

**As much as you liked *Balance*, cracks were beginning to form between you and Sammy. You weren't happy with his lyrics for "Amsterdam."**

I didn't like that the lyrics were about smoking pot. My brother and I actually came from Amsterdam, but we didn't smoke pot. I didn't want people to think that we're into that, and I wanted him to come up with something more serious or deeper. But it wasn't my job to write lyrics, so I really didn't complain about it, especially since he was the one singing it. He didn't always like everything that I played either. You can't please everyone all of the time, so you just figure out how to make things work. But, yeah, I wasn't happy with some of his writing.

**Do you have a lot of ideas on tape?**

Tons of tapes. I've got so many tapes. I'm too lazy to go through them to see what's on them. One of these days I'll get around to it. Whenever we start a record, I go, "God, I've got all this stuff," but then I'll write something new and I'll get more excited about that.

**Is there ever the possibility that you'll make a solo instrumental record?**

Nah, I don't see the point. Ninety percent of the reason most people do solo records is because they can't get out their ideas in the band. Every Van Halen record to me is a solo record. I usually get to do what I want.

**Was the instrumental "Baluchitherium" meant to be a response to players like Steve Vai and Joe Satriani?**

Not really. I never really listened or paid much attention to that stuff. "Baluchitherium" didn't start out to be an instrumental—it was a bit of an accident. We had the song for a while, but we could never agree on a vocal melody. Bruce finally said, "Let's see if it holds up without vocals." We all said, "Yeah. Why not?" So, we just left it. I try to make all the music I write hold up instrumentally. It ain't just a bunch of barre chord shit. There's always something going on melodically.

**Yeah, your rhythm playing is usually as interesting as your lead work.**

It's always been that way, because I'm a very rhythmic player. Alex and I are sort of a unit. Normally in a band, you would think that the bass player and drummer are the rhythm section, but in this band it's more Alex and me. The bass is more a subsonic rumble that you play over.

That's nothing against Mike, it's just how Alex and I developed. We never had a bass player in the very beginning, so it would be just Alex and me. I played so fucking loud you wouldn't have been able to hear a bassist anyway.

**Where did the name "Baluchitherium" come from?**

The working title was "Heavy Groove." After we decided to make it an instrumental, I was left with what the fuck do you call it. It sounded huge to me—this big drum sound. So, my wife says, "Well, how about this?"

And I go, "What the fuck does that mean?" She goes, "It's the biggest mammal to ever roam the planet."

**How did you get that monstrous bass sound?**

It's actually Mike playing bass and me doubling his part with a Music Man six-string bass. Bruce wanted me to do something silly at the end, so I went, "Okay, you've got silly coming." I started making a bunch of funny prehistoric-sounding noises. It started sounding like a zoo, so I decided to see if I could get my dog, Sherman, on the track, too. We duct-taped a hot dog to a microphone and we wouldn't let him get it, and he started howling "Aww roo!" You can actually hear it on the track.

**Your playing on "Big Fat Money" was unusual.**

I was just playing around, and a regular solo didn't seem to fit. Bruce goes, "Hey, you got an old Gibson 335 laying around?" and I go, "Sure." He says, "Try something a little jazzy." I played it in one take quietly through my Marshall and put a slap echo on it. It sounds tripped out. I wasn't sure it would fit. I took a while to get used to that one because it's not typical me at all. I was just noodling along with it and I go, "Something like this?" and he recorded it. He went, "Yeah! That's it! Done!" Great! I go, "Oh. Okay. Next."

**A Gibson 335 used to be your favorite guitar.**

It was back in the early days because it was easy to play. Thin neck, low strings.

**In the early days, you used to tune your guitar down approximately a half step, but when Sammy joined the band you started tuning to concert pitch.**

You know what's funny, a lot of people imitated that, but what they didn't understand was the reason we used to do it was because our singer had a limited range.

There's a reason why an A vibrates at 440. Why do you want to change that? You get a truer tone. I guess it sounds a little heavier if you tune down. But you get some problems—the bass guitar strings start flapping and they don't vibrate correctly.

**What amps did you use on *Balance*?**
I used the old 100-watt Marshall that I've done all the records with. I just added the 5150 to the arsenal because it did things that the Marshall wouldn't do and vice versa. The 5150 had more of a high-gain sound.

**"Strung Out" sounded like a tribute to the avant-garde composer John Cage.**
That track was really old, actually. Back in '82 or '83, Valerie and I rented Marvin Hamlisch's beach house out in Malibu. Everything was white—white piano, white carpet. We had to leave a huge deposit for cleaning the place. I got drunk one night—actually more than one night—and I started dickin' around on this piano. I don't know what possessed me to do this, but I went in the kitchen and grabbed forks and knives and started scraping the strings on the inside of the piano to create all these different sounds. In the process, I wasted his fuckin' piano. But I just let a tape roll and I recorded it all.

One day, Bruce asked me if I could come up with some kind of intro for the ballad "Not Enough," and I went, "Well, I've got some pretty twisted shit that you might like." I played him the tape and he said, "This is great!" So, we ended up using it. It sounds like a terrible B-level horror soundtrack, but it was all in fun.

**I was curious about a bonus track on the album called "Crossing Over."**
If you balance to the left, you hear my original demo for the song—the guitar, pad drums, and I'm even singin' on it. It's a demo song that I wrote for a friend of mine who committed suicide. On the right we added Al playing drums and Sammy sang. We tried to put it together, but it didn't quite jive, so we left it off.

**Your guitar action is pretty low.**
It's as low as I can get it. (*laughs*) Why make it hard? I put it as low as it can go without buzzin'. I love the way the neck feels. The sweat and oil have soaked in over the years. That's why I prefer a nonfinished piece of wood. After a good year of playin', nothing tops it.

**You don't keep your fingerboard too clean either.**

I told my tech that I'd wring his neck if he cleaned my neck when he refretted it. He's refretted it a few times.

**There's a lot of dirt all over the guitar.**

It gets a lot of use.

**What was one of the highest points of your career?**

I thought I arrived as a player when I could pretty much play whatever I heard on the radio or whatever I heard in my mind. I went, "Hey, I'm getting there."

I'm kind of a hack golfer. If I've got nothing to do, I'll go play a round of golf. One day I was playing out in Pasadena with these two old guys. I was playing terrible because I'm not very good at it. It's just for fun. This old-timer says, "Damn! A bad day on the golf course is better than any good day at work."

I started thinking, "Wow. This poor guy." Because, with me, I would rather be here in 5150 playin' than getting pissed off trying to hit this little fuckin' white ball. To sum it all up, I'm so lucky and blessed to love what I'm doing and to have other people like it is like a home run. Every time I walk onstage is like a high point. You'd have to be numb or dead to not get excited about twenty thousand people screaming. That will always get you up. The only thing I hate is doing videos.

**It's amazing that you and your brother have gotten along so well for so long.**

He's not just my brother, he's my best friend. We do everything together. We're buddies. We argue about things, but we're tight. A lot of it has to do with coming over to America and not having any friends. We had each other. It was great. And it's still that way. We know each other better than anyone else.

**So, you can't get away with anything.**

Actually, we both get away with a lot of shit. (*laughs*)

**You've called yourself basically a blues player, but what you play doesn't sound much like the blues.**

No, but it's all blues scales. It's just these notes. (*plays a minor pentatonic scale*) I don't know what that is, but that's the notes you use in blues. You've got twelve fuckin' notes and you just mix them up as you want. I don't have the blues, so I don't play the blues. (*laughs*) I'm a pretty happy guy.

**So, you're no Eric Clapton.**

Well, I don't think Clapton's got the blues, either. But really, I don't go outside of blues scales all that much. I don't do anything that weird. I don't know what it is I do. It's just rock and roll, which is based on blues.

To me, it's harder to write something simple than to make it complicated. Billy Gibbons calls me up every now and then when he's in town and goes, "So, Eddie, did you find that fourth chord yet?" I go, "Nope." I hope I never do. There's a reason why I-IV-V works. But it's hard to write something new with it.

**How do you confront your own legacy? Do you worry about repeating yourself?**

Not really. Change is a natural part of my evolution as a player. It just happens, because everybody changes over a period of time. It's a very unconscious thing.

Every time I walk into the studio, it seems like the first time. It's like I've never written a song before. I'm just as scared. Someone asked me the other day what I thought I had learned about making music after all these years, and I said, "Nothing." I'm scared shitless all the time. I'm really insecure that way. That's why I don't go out. That's why you never see me at the Rainbow or at parties. I have a hard time dealing with people. . . . I can't play the game. The only way I can do that is to get shitfaced drunk, and then I make an ass out of myself.

# MUSICAL INTERLUDE

*A conversation with the former*
*David Lee Roth guitarist* **Steve Vai**

---

Van Halen albums were like atomic explosions on which Eddie Van Halen laid to waste all notions of what a guitar could do. Even if they weren't interested in the kind of hard rock his band played, most guitarists were forced to come to grips with what amounted to his reinvention of the instrument, including how they'd incorporate his ideas into their own playing.

One great guitarist of that era who had to deal with what Eddie brought to the table was the young virtuoso Steve Vai, a highly innovative player who would go on to become a six-string superstar himself.

In the interview below, Vai unhesitatingly acknowledges that he was a direct beneficiary of many of Van Halen's innovations, though unlike many guitarists of the time who mimicked Eddie, he wasn't remotely his clone, as was borne out by his own brilliant success. Vai was only twenty years old when, in 1980, he joined the legendary composer and guitarist Frank Zappa's band. He remained with Zappa for approximately five years before embarking on a solo career that saw him release eight groundbreaking solo albums and win three Grammys—a remarkable achievement for an instrumentalist.

On the other hand, the degree to which he understood Edward's playing was made clear in 1985, when Steve famously joined David Lee Roth's first post–Van Halen band, playing guitar with the singer on two of his solo albums, *Eat 'Em and Smile* (1986) and *Skyscraper* (1988). Roth performed many Van Halen songs on tour, and Vai was required to play Eddie's parts or at least approximate them to a degree that did them justice. That he was able to do this flawlessly conclusively demonstrated his understanding of Ed's sound and techniques.

***Do you remember hearing Edward for the first time?***

It was like a monolith appeared on the planet. Eddie Van Halen's impact was very sudden. I was attending the Berklee College of Music when the first Van Halen record came out. My tone sucked, man. I was just interested in chops. I could play fast and pick all sorts of fast notes, but I spent precious little time on my sound. So, when I heard the tone Ed produced, I realized I needed to raise my own bar. It's a very select group of people that have really brought the electric guitar to a different level. As far as I'm concerned, Jimi Hendrix did it and Edward did it.

***What do you think his legacy will be?***

As great of a guitar player as he was, I think he'll be remembered more for his songs. History tends to forget those that originated playing techniques. For example, so much of what we do today came from Les Paul, but nobody remembers that. And when most young kids grab a whammy bar or tap, they probably have no clue those ideas came from Edward, because those techniques went through a refining process and were filtered through many other players. Same with his tone. Those sorts of contributions tend to go into this huge washing machine of riffs that get processed by newer players . . . many times more proficiently.

But songs are another matter. When we think of Jimi Hendrix, yes, his guitar playing is important, but the first thing you think about are his songs. Songs carry something special because of the combination of people involved. Whether it's the Beatles or Van Halen, it's that chemistry that is impossible to replicate and it's just nectar to the world.

***Well, you bring up an interesting point, which is exactly what we wanted to discuss. We were curious how Ed's various ideas and techniques have been absorbed into the "washing machine" of guitar culture.***

The thing that struck me the most about Edward was his simplicity. There was such an innocence and clarity in what he did—the way he gravitated to practical ideas and was so in the moment. He was similar to Frank Zappa in that sense. Ed had this great immediate energy—"Anytime, anywhere, for no reason at all except I want it now." His idea to put a humbucker on a Stratocaster seems like such a simple idea, but it was innovative.

I think it's important to understand, however, that he wasn't trying to change the guitar, he was just in pursuit of sound that he was hearing in his head. I mean, you can analyze it in terms of what pickups he was using or that he was using a power soak, but really his tone was manifested as the result of a particular way that he was hearing it in his mind. He was striving for something and didn't stop until he found it. I was at his studio once and he pointed to a Marshall head and said, "I've recorded every single Van Halen song through that head except for two songs." I thought that was interesting. He found the perfect amp to give him what he needed to hear.

**When did you discover tapping?**

I actually heard Frank do it first. I was probably around fourteen years old when I noticed it on his solo on "Inca Roads." Frank did it sparingly and used a pick instead of his finger, but I thought it was cool. I remember experimenting with that idea when I was attending Berklee during my teens, but I was approaching it in a very caveman-like way. It wasn't refined. Then when my friends and I heard Edward, we just fell apart. All my fellow guitarists were like, "Now *that's* tapping!" It was obvious that he took the idea to a whole new level and we were stunned. I immediately understood the larger implications of what you could do with it.

**What did the technique mean to you?**

I'm a contrarian by nature. I knew if I was going to explore this "tapping thing," I'd need to put my own stamp on it. But that's just my way. Even if it's something elemental like the blues. When I was younger, I'd think, okay, playing the blues is fun, but let me put my own spin on it.

So, when I was at Berklee and I heard Edward, I immediately knew I wanted to start refining my tapping and slowly, slowly, through the next years I developed my own approach.

*I think that's what Ed was hoping for. He didn't mind when others used his ideas, as long as they did their own thing with it.*

When I replaced Yngwie Malmsteen in the band Alcatrazz in 1985, there was a song that had this crazy passage in it. I just couldn't play it like Yngwie, so I cheated by tapping it using two fingers on my right hand. That ended up being a launching pad for me to explore all sorts of bizarre—or at least what I thought was kind of bizarre—tapping techniques. But, that said, I don't know if I've ever heard anybody tap quite as cleanly and with as much integrity as Edward.

*What does tapping allow you, or any other guitarist, to do that wouldn't be possible any other way?*

It added a completely new dimension to the guitar, because now you have a new opportunity to create intervals, chord voicings, and linear riffs that just could not be done any other way.

*Could you explain how your approach is different from Ed's?*

His approach is more linear—he tends to use it to produce a string of notes on one string, then he'll move to the next string. I very rarely did that. I also often tap using multiple fingers on the fretboard, where Ed, I believe, used mostly just his index finger.

*One of Ed's other contributions to the guitar was popularizing the locking Floyd Rose vibrato bar, which allows players to use the whammy bar without going out of tune.*

Well, it was important to me because I'm a whammy bar fanatic. One of the biggest attractions to me about the guitar was the fact that it had a whammy bar. I mean, you can hear it in my playing— my concerts are like whammy bar clinics—and it was impossible to keep a guitar in tune with a whammy bar until the Floyd Rose system. I remember getting an early version, but it was difficult to tune until Floyd started incorporating the fine tuners.

*The fine tuners were actually Ed's contribution. That was his idea.*

I didn't know that! Once the fine tuners came along, the guitar became almost a different instrument for me. It was a tool that I embraced hard. I had always imagined the idea of creating melodies with just the bar, but couldn't do it because before the Floyd, my guitar would always go out of tune. Once I had that piece of guitar hardware, I was able to bend notes, create chords, and resolve melodies in entirely new ways.

*You created your own variation on the locking system.*

Yeah. The original locking system would only allow you to depress the whammy bar, which only lowered the pitch. I wanted to be able to bend notes upwards, as well. The problem was, the wood underneath the tailpiece prevented you from pulling the bar up, so I literally took a hammer and a screwdriver and chiseled the wood out. The next thing you know, I'm pulling up and notes are going higher.

*When David Lee Roth left Van Halen, he chose you to be his guitarist. On your first tour with him, almost half of your set was Van Halen songs. You had to learn a bunch of Eddie's guitar parts. What was your takeaway?*

Yeah, it was actually a lot of fun. I mean, who wouldn't want to play those songs? I'm a weird bird. I grew up as a teenager in the seventies, and half of me was really into rock, like Zeppelin, Queen, Hendrix, and Kiss. But, by the same token, I enjoyed listening to a lot of experimental music and avant-garde contemporary classical music. That's why it was great playing with Frank Zappa, because he did both. But after leaving Frank, it was just pure fun to indulge in my rock and roll side and play with Dave, including the whole back catalog of Van Halen material.

My musical approach to writing songs is so wildly different than Edward's, so it was a nice opportunity for me to see guitar songs constructed in such a full-bodied way. They were simple, but yet they demanded to be played in a very particular way. I mean, if you play "Panama," yeah, the chord changes are not that difficult, but to make them sound like the way Ed played them, that was a big boy's game. It was challenging to get all the nuances right.

**Did you socialize with Ed much?**

On occasion. He invited me to the studio one time and started playing some things he had recorded on his own. I remember saying, "That's amazing, what are you going to do with that? You gotta do something with that—why don't you do a solo album?" And he said, "Well, I don't really see myself as a solo artist, but I see my songs without the vocals as being perfectly constructed instrumentals." I'm paraphrasing, but the gist was, even without the vocals, the guitar parts could stand up on their own merits. And as a person that played some of them, I totally agree.

Each of Ed's songs were just like these beautifully composed pieces that arrived on a silver platter with all the edges nice and neat. You can play a Van Halen song on the guitar from beginning to the end and they are perfect. It's like being a pianist and being given a beautiful piece by Liszt. That was the thing. Ed wrote guitar parts that were so well designed they could stand on their own. They were like perfectly written stories, where every sentence satisfied you but left you wanting more.

**Give us a good Ed story.**

The thing I loved about Ed was his reckless perfection. That's why his guitars looked so beautifully beat to shit. They were heavily abused, but they worked. I remember jamming with him once at Frank's. We were just passing around this guitar, but the E string was buzzing, right? If it was me, I would've said, "Well, we shouldn't be playing this guitar, the E string is buzzing." But Ed just looked around the room and found this long screwdriver with a very thin tip. And he just wedged it under the nut and cranked it up a little until the E stopped buzzing. Now, there's this giant screwdriver sticking out of the headstock, but there's no buzz, so he just keeps playing and continues to pass it around. I'm like, "Well, there's Edward—by any means necessary."

*Considering what a creative dynamo Ed was, it's shocking how meager his output was during the last twenty years of his life. It took him over a decade to regain his footing after the failure of* **Van Halen III** *in 1998.*

Here's my take. As an artist, dealing with rejection can be very difficult, and it can almost be like going through the stages of great loss—there's grief, disbelief, anger—all of these intense emotions. So, it was like a dent. He was so successful for so long that when the album didn't work, it was a loss like none other, because he'd never experienced anything like that before. But the final stage of grief is acceptance—that's the relief of suffering—and I think Ed embraced a good portion of that before he left us.

(*left to right*: Michael Anthony, Edward Van Halen, David Lee Roth) Ed plays a modified Stratocaster with a humbucking pickup—the precursor to his legendary Frankenstein—at the Starwood nightclub in late 1976. ©*Kevin Estrada / Kevin Estrada Archives*

Holding the Frankenstein with its original black and white finish backstage at the Day on the Green festival in Oakland, California, July 23, 1978. ©*Getty Images*

(*left to right*: David Lee Roth, Michael Anthony, Edward Van Halen) Ed and Michael often performed a "four-handed bass" solo during the 1979 World Vacation tour. The black and yellow "bumblebee" Charvel seen here was Ed's main guitar on the tour. ©*Mark "WEISSGUY" Weiss*

(*left to right*: Edward Van Halen, Michael Anthony, David Lee Roth, Alex Van Halen) America's number-one party band breaks out the balloons in 1981. ©*Mark "WEISSGUY" Weiss*

At his Coldwater Canyon home in 1981. Guitars include (*left to right*) an early 60s Fender Stratocaster, his custom "Circles," "Frankenstein," and "Rude" guitars, a David Petschulat mini Les Paul, a 1959 Gibson Les Paul Standard, and Gibson EDS-1275 doubleneck later used to record "Secrets." © *Almay Images*

With wife Valerie Bertinelli hanging out backstage at Nassau Coliseum during the band's massive *1984* tour. ©*Mark "WEISSGUY" Weiss*

A fluke of scheduling found Van Halen in Dallas, Texas, on July 14, 1984, at the same time Michael Jackson was on the Victory Tour with his brothers. The two couldn't pass up the opportunity to perform "Beat It" in front of an audience. ©*Getty Images*

With his hero, guitarist and inventor Les Paul, backstage at the Les Paul Tribute Concert at the Brooklyn Academy of Music, Brooklyn, New York, August 19, 1988. ©*Getty Images*

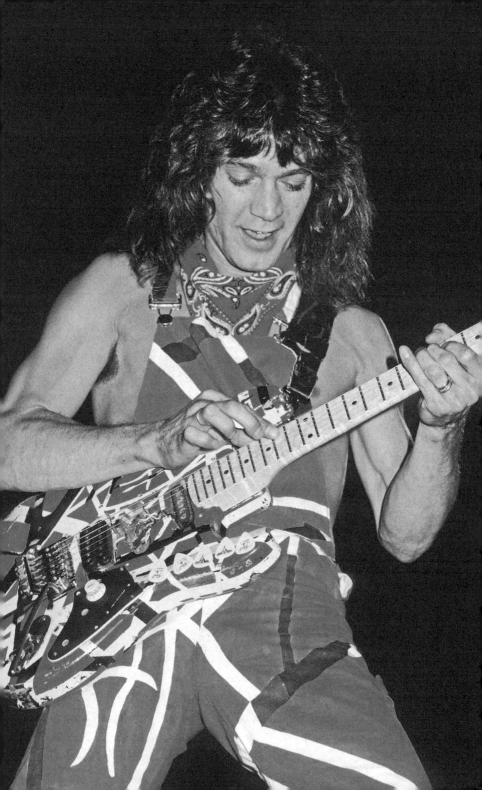

(*facing page*) Demonstrating his signature "tapping" technique.  © *Mark "WEISSGUY" Weiss*

Vocalist Sammy Hagar and Eddie Van Halen literally at each other's throats in a 1988 photo taken for *Circus Magazine*.  ©*Mark "WEISSGUY" Weiss*

At 5150 in 1991. Ed holds the "Hot for Teacher" 1958 Gibson Flying V; on floor (*left to right*) 1959 Gibson Les Paul Standard and Music Man EVH signature models; on stands (*left to right*) the "Top Jimmy" Ripley stereo guitar, Steinberger Les Paul, Frankenstein, Music Man EVH, Music Man StingRay bass, 1958 Gibson Les Paul Standard, custom Music Man doubleneck, 50s Gibson Les Paul Jr. Ed's original Marshall amplifier head is in the top right corner.

*©Larry DiMarzio*

Edward and drummer Alex Van Halen were not only brothers, but also best friends.
Here they are during a 1994 Van Halen Golf Tournament in Los Angeles, California.
©*Getty Images*

Playing his favorite
Music Man EVH guitar on the
Balance (a.k.a. Ambulance) tour
at San Jose Arena, May 14, 1995.
©Chris Gill

With Van Halen's third singer, Gary Cherone. "We were in rehearsals discussing the
setlist, but my mind was on the upcoming tour," explained Cherone, who looks pensive.
©Tracey Glynn Photography

The 2004 Van Halen tour found Ed at one of his lowest points. His increased struggles with substance abuse and contentious relations with bandmates Sammy Hagar and Michael Anthony made for markedly erratic performances. ©*Getty Images*

Noticeably healthier, Ed attends an *Esquire* party in New York with second wife Janie Liszewski, September 17, 2013. ©*Getty Images*

(*below*) Performing face-to-face with son Wolfgang Van Halen during the 2015 *Billboard* Music Awards on May 17, 2015. ©*Getty Images*

At the beach in Malibu, California, July 12, 2013. Ed's very first electric guitar was a Teisco Del Rey WG-4L, exactly like the one seen here, which Ed bought decades after he sold the original. ©*Kevin Scanlon*

With his favorite Wolfgang guitar on his final tour at Sleep Train Amphitheatre, Chula Vista, California, September 30, 2015. ©*Getty Images*

Eddie Van Halen mural at the Hollywood Guitar Center by painter Robert Vargas. ©*Getty Images*

# 7

# IN AND OUT

*Sammy gets on the wrong side of Eddie and Alex.*
*And so does Dave. Again.*

---

" I just started thinking,
hey man, let's write something *real*. "

---

WHEN *BALANCE* WAS released on January 24, 1995, it went straight to number one on the Billboard 200 and achieved Triple Platinum status three months later, continuing Van Halen's remarkable streak of ten hit studio albums.

As Ed did his usual round of interviews with the press, he spoke enthusiastically about the music, its producer Bruce Fairbairn, and his newfound sobriety. But the unsettling imagery on the album's cover told a different story.

Looking anything but "balanced," the artwork featured conjoined twins fighting with each other while sitting on an off-kilter seesaw in a desolate, postapocalyptic landscape. Intentionally or otherwise, the album cover spoke volumes about the band, because behind the scenes Van Halen were literally tearing themselves to bits.

To put it bluntly, Sammy Hagar—like David Lee Roth a decade earlier—had fallen out of favor with Edward. It was a surprising turn of events because Ed and Sam often spoke glowingly of each other, and it was thought that they were the best of friends. But over the last year much had changed for the guitarist, causing him to reevaluate his life, music, and friendships.

During the recording of *Balance*, Ed made an earnest attempt to deal with the destructive nature of his alcoholism and drug use. He had failed several times throughout the years—even spending time at the world-renowned Betty Ford Clinic—but with the help of a renowned psychotherapist, Sat-Kaur Khalsa, he was able to cut down on his drinking. It was an inarguably positive step for the guitarist, but it put him on edge at a time when he was also battling chronic hip pain—the result of what was soon to be diagnosed as avascular necrosis.

His therapy and physical problems also made him more introspective than usual. He realized that he was no longer a kid and was becoming disenchanted with the group's "goofball party band" reputation. And though he often claimed that he didn't pay much attention to musical trends, the angsty hard rock of Seattle bands like Nirvana, Soundgarden, and Alice in Chains had struck a nerve in him. He related to the naked honesty of their lyrics, admired their lack of rock star pretense, and wondered if it was a valid pathway for his band.

Some of the material on *Balance* reflected that influence, particularly the grim album opener, "The Seventh Seal," and the melancholy "Feelin'." But it wasn't enough for Ed, who began harboring a not-so-secret disdain for the sunnier side of Hagar's lyrics on songs like the pro-cannabis anthem "Amsterdam" and the avaricious "Big Fat Money."

"We had this perception [of] just playing good-time music, and a large part of that was Sam," said the guitarist. "People would throw bras onstage and he would wear them and dance around . . . that kind of shit. And to me, that's not what it's about. I was getting older, and I wanted to mature."

In fairness to Hagar, not all of the lyrics on *Balance* were juvenile. He had recently weathered a difficult divorce, and his serious side came to the fore in songs like the bittersweet "Can't Stop Lovin' You," which was about the deterioration of his marriage, and "Don't Tell Me (What Love Can Do)," which was inspired by the death of Nirvana's front man Kurt Cobain. But those tunes just weren't who Hagar was, and his heart wasn't really in them. Like Roth, Hagar liked to have fun and had little interest in transforming Van Halen into a moody alternative rock band.

"I loved 'Don't Tell Me (What Love Can Do)', but, man, it was dark," said Hagar. "That song didn't take us anywhere, and I know why now. It wasn't what Van Halen fans wanted. It showed the darkness of Van Halen and it was basically the end of the band."[12]

Although that might sound a bit melodramatic, it was essentially true. After *Balance* was released, Sammy would leave the band, and Van Halen would record only two more studio albums over the next twenty years. It was a shocking turn of events for one of the world's most successful and productive bands.

TO SOME DEGREE, VAN HALEN had been lucky. Over the previous two decades they had enjoyed relatively smooth sailing. The group had dodged a huge bullet when David Lee Roth left in 1985 by recovering quite nicely with the addition of Hagar. Unfortunately, ten years later, the band was back on shaky ground.

At the heart of Van Halen's problems were the genuine artistic differences between Sammy and Ed, but those might've been sorted out over time if it weren't for a simultaneous dumpster fire of health issues, personal problems, business quarrels, and ongoing substance abuse.

Their issues came to a head in 1996, a year after the release of *Balance*, but one could trace the disintegration of "Van Hagar" to the death of their manager Ed Leffler from thyroid cancer in October 1993. Leffler had managed Hagar's solo career, and when Sammy joined Van Halen in 1985, he assumed control of the band's business affairs, replacing their former manager Noel Monk.

For the next decade, the fiercely protective Leffler did an undeniably terrific job steering the band's career to greater heights, and the foursome grew to trust him implicitly. "He was like a father to us, a fifth member," said Hagar. "When he died, the thing that went through my mind was how vulnerable we were because we trusted him so much. He made it so we didn't have to think about certain things. He kept the vultures, the wolves, and the thieves away so we were free to just have fun, fun, fun. The only responsibility we had was to make good records."[13]

Leffler also had an uncanny ability to keep the peace in the band and maintain a healthy balance of power between Sammy and the Van Halen brothers. And he was adept at providing a reassuring, fatherly hand with Edward, who struggled with alcohol, drugs, and the pressures of stardom.

During the months following Leffler's death, the band was rumored to have received overtures from most of the music industry's top managers, including Doc McGhee, best known for working with Kiss and Bon Jovi, and Tim Collins, who managed Aerosmith, but found it difficult to replace Leffler because he'd provided them with so much personal support. Eventually, though, they were desperate for help, and Eddie later recalled just how bad things had gotten.

"We were managing ourselves," he said, "and I was going nuts because I was getting the bullshit phone calls Leffler must have gotten that we never heard about, like 'Hey, Eddie, would you like to host *Star Search?*' I was sitting around with Tim Collins. This was probably one of the last nights that I drank . . . but I was guzzling a bottle of wine down, and finally I said to Tim, 'I'll be right back.' I walked down to the house, grabbed my Norelco shaver and just shaved my head. Cut [my hair] completely off. I looked like an Auschwitz victim. I guess everything in my life all came to a head, literally. I was losing it. I was so frustrated and pissed off that I just didn't know what else to do."[14]

To Hagar's dismay, the Van Halen brothers and Mike Anthony eventually decided to ask Alex's brother-in-law, Ray Danniels, to guide the band. Danniels was the respected manager of Canadian rock superstars Rush and the moderately successful Boston band Extreme, but he wasn't regarded as a top-tier manager. Hagar felt the band could do better, and he also harbored some fears that Danniels would favor the Van Halen brothers in future business dealings as a result of his family ties to Alex. Hagar's displeasure became more evident when he bumped heads with Danniels over specifics of his management contract, and though the issues were resolved, the incident foreshadowed things to come.

Meanwhile, Geffen Records, which had Hagar under contract as a solo artist, began pressuring the singer to allow them to release a greatest hits collection of his pre–Van Halen material. Leffler had been doing his best to convince Sammy to hold off on the album out of concern that it would conflict with Van Halen, but with Leffler gone, it was difficult for Hagar to tell Geffen no. Ultimately, the singer knew there was no avoiding the contractually obligated release, so instead of fighting with the record company, he decided to make the best of it.

At that time, Sam was going through a difficult separation with Betsy Berardi, his wife of twenty-six years. He figured if he was going to have to release a "best of" album, he might as well use its proceeds to help pay for his divorce. Geffen sweetened the deal by offering Hagar more money if he contributed two new songs, so all in all, the singer stood to make a million dollars from the deal. But first Sam needed to clear everything with the Van Halens.

Initially, the brothers were fine with the idea, understanding that Sammy needed the cash for his divorce, but when they discovered that Hagar planned to use two songs that had been originally presented to Van Halen (which they'd rejected), they were upset, accusing the singer of planning to go solo like Roth. Without Leffler in the mix to reassure them otherwise, Ed and Al felt betrayed. Hagar ignored the brothers' concerns and went ahead with the Geffen deal, figuring that what he saw as their paranoia would subside when they saw how little it would affect Van Halen. Two years later, however, his 1994 *Unboxed* collection would come back to haunt him.

Tensions within the band abated somewhat as Van Halen hit the road from March to November 1995 to support the *Balance* album, but the nine-month tour had its own set of problems. Both Alex and Eddie were having physical issues, and over the course of what they'd jokingly refer to as the "Ambulance" tour, Alex was required to wear a neck brace to play through three ruptured discs in his vertebrae, and Eddie's hip pain only intensified, forcing him to walk with a cane.

"I was hobbling," Ed said. "It was from years of hopping around onstage and drinking, not feeling what I was doing to myself. I was almost seven months sober, so the pain was a lot worse."

Despite their substantial medical problems, the band pushed through the strenuous 138-date tour with remarkably few hiccups. But as it came to a close, a series of skirmishes between Sammy and the Van Halen brothers once again lit the bonfire of animosity that had been smoldering during their time on the road.

It started innocuously enough. After Hagar's divorce from his wife was finalized, he announced plans to marry his then-pregnant girlfriend Kari Karte, who was expecting in April. The couple planned to have their baby via natural childbirth in Maui, and Sam said he would come back to Los Angeles and work on the new album in June, after he had some time to bond with his new family. In the meantime, he recommended that the brothers attend to their various physical ailments so everyone could return refreshed and ready to go.

It sounded reasonable, but unbeknownst to Hagar, manager Ray Danniels had already scheduled two new major projects for the band. The first was to record two songs for a soundtrack to an upcoming blockbuster movie, *Twister*, and the other was the band's first greatest hits package, which would also require some new music. Hagar went ballistic.

"I told him point-blank we needed a break from each other," Hagar told *Guitar World* magazine. "The brothers were supposed to take care of their physical ailments, and my wife was pregnant. We were all at wits' end. Eddie was walking around with a cane [and] on painkillers because his hip hurt so badly; Alex had a neck brace on. He had to see a chiropractor on a weekly basis, and a massage therapist came over to his house every day to rub down his head and neck just so he could get out of bed."

Danniels did his best to explain the financial benefits of the *Twister* soundtrack and how it would keep the band's profile elevated while they worked on their next album. Sammy wasn't happy but relented and composed lyrics for two new songs, "Humans Being" and "Between Us Two."

The brothers expressed dislike for both and asked Hagar to revise them. To add salt to the wound, they also rejected the singer's request to record his vocals from Hawaii, where he and his wife had arranged for a natural delivery of the baby. After multiple trips from Maui to Eddie's 5150 studio in Los Angeles, Sammy decided to move with his wife back to his San Francisco home to be near her. Upon completion of the two songs, Hagar was about to head back to the Bay Area when Eddie announced that they needed to extend "Humans Being." Hagar wrote another two verses and recorded them in about an hour and a half with producer Bruce Fairbairn, before departing for his flight. When attempts to bring Sammy back to rework "Between Us Two" were unsuccessful, Alex and Eddie jettisoned the track and recorded an instrumental entitled "Respect the Wind" instead.

If the *Twister* soundtrack kicked up a considerable amount of dust, then Van Halen's *Best Of—Volume 1* blew the band to bits. Danniels had brought up the idea of releasing a greatest hits package several times

since becoming their manager, and every time Hagar vehemently opposed the idea. The singer felt that having all of their best songs in one
package would hurt the band's back catalog, which continued to sell
in respectable numbers, and he also had issues with having his songs
lumped in with the group's David Lee Roth–era music.

"I didn't want to do a greatest hits package, period," Hagar said. "If
Eddie, Alex, and Ray were going to insist on doing one anyway, I wanted
them to put out a record that only covered the David Lee Roth era. If
they had to do just one, I told them to do the old stuff because that
way we wouldn't have to be attached to it. My second choice, and I had
to swallow hard to say this, was to put out two separate greatest hits
volumes—one covering the Roth years, the other just our stuff, and let
the fans make the choice."[15]

The Van Halen brothers argued vociferously that they had every right
to issue the album in any format they pleased. After all, Hagar had just released his *second* "best of" compilation the previous year, so why couldn't
they also take advantage of their past success? In their minds, this was
just another instance of Hagar being a self-centered "solo artist" and not
a team player.

While the project was being fiercely debated, Eddie reached out to
superstar producer-songwriter Glen Ballard, who'd worked with Michael
Jackson and Alanis Morissette, with the idea of revisiting "Between Us
Two," the unfinished song from the *Twister* soundtrack. Once again expressing dissatisfaction with Hagar's lyrics, the guitarist asked Ballard to
rewrite them. While Hagar agreed to entertain a collaboration, he ultimately rejected Ballard's lyrics and refused to sing them. But what really
angered the vocalist was Eddie's informing him that they planned to use
the song for the "best of" compilation instead of their next album.

Although the timeline is fuzzy, depending on whom you ask, Eddie
claimed that after the Ballard session, Hagar quit, insisting he "was fucking frustrated" and wanted to return to being a solo artist.

Certainly, the final nail in the coffin came when Eddie decided to
reach out to former lead singer David Lee Roth to collaborate on some
tracks for the *Best Of—Volume 1*.

"Dave happened to call me around the time Sammy quit, because
Warner Bros. notified him that the greatest hits was going to come out,
and he had some questions about the packaging," said Eddie. "We were on

# EDDIE'S ODDITIES

### GUITAR: Custom Steinberger Les Paul
### USED: "Me Wise Magic"
### (*Best Of—Volume 1*) and others

Ed was one of only a handful of guitarists who ever truly mastered the revolutionary Steinberger TransTrem vibrato, an engineering marvel that maintains consistent pitch intervals of each string when the vibrato bar is used, allowing guitarists to raise or lower chords in tune and instantly lock into a variety of preset transposed tunings. Van Halen used the TransTrem to great effect on several songs, including "Summer Nights," "Get Up," "Pleasure Dome," "Me Wise Magic," and "Fire in the Hole."

"I used this Les Paul on 'Me Wise Magic,'" Ed said. "Ned Steinberger put the TransTrem on it. We worked together on the TransTrem design and he asked my opinion. I was trying to get him to make things simpler. He was such an engineer that he would overengineer things. It was very kind of him to make a special guitar just for me. I used a regular Steinberger guitar on 'Summer Nights,' but it was hard for me to play because the body is so thin and small. I ragged and moaned so much about it that Ned made me that guitar. It's very fat sounding. Everything on that guitar is unique. The tuners are really different."

the phone about forty-five minutes, and we apologized for things we had said back in high school. It was probably one of the best conversations I ever had with him.

"I decided to drive over to his house, and we had a great time bull-shitting as friends. We hung out for about three hours and smoked some cigars. It was only about two weeks later when I realized that the only new track that we had for the greatest hits was 'Humans Being.' That's when I came up with the crazy idea of having Dave sing on a couple of new songs. I was very clear that he was not in the band—that it was just a project. So, Glen Ballard and I sat down with Dave, and I okayed with him all this new material I had, and eventually we narrowed [things] down to this pop song, 'Me Wise Magic,' and a shuffle, 'Can't Get This Stuff No More.'

"During the process, Dave and I were really becoming good friends. In my heart I really wanted to believe that he had changed a bit. It was a struggle to find any music that inspired him and that he could connect to, but we worked and worked, and he actually thanked me for hanging in there with him."[16]

The recording sessions with Roth went well, but the aftermath—like everything else during that period—was an unmitigated disaster. At the September 4, 1996, MTV Video Music Awards, the band appeared on-stage with Roth for the first time in a decade to drum up a little publicity for their two-song reunion, and the audience went nuts.

But Ed and David appeared to almost come to blows when the guitarist took offense to Roth's grandstanding onstage during Beck's acceptance speech for Best Male Video. The bad blood continued to flow backstage, when Roth shushed Edward for talking to the media about an upcoming hip-replacement surgery.

Whatever chance there was for a reunion with Roth was dashed that evening, and shortly thereafter, the band hired Gary Cherone, the former lead singer of Extreme, also managed by Danniels.

**What was at the heart of the disagreement between you and Sammy?**
There are a bunch of reasons. I don't want to be a prick about it. I'm a very insecure person, which is why I'm an alcoholic. I have a hard time dealing with people and I hate confrontation. But I'd been having a hard time dealing with Sam since I quit drinking on October 2, 1994. In many

ways he was just like Roth. Sam and Roth are both Libras . . . they both think their shit don't stink. They're also insecure people, but they act like they aren't.

**So, was it just chemistry?**

Some of it. For example, I think music should evolve naturally and shouldn't be contrived. It should be honest. I would never sit down and say, "Hey, let's try to write something different." But Sammy would walk in and say, "Hey, let's update our sound and write some dance music," and try to get me to go to some dance club. He and Roth just come from a different place than I do.

**You've complained about his lyrics in the past. Was that part of the problem?**

Yeah, that was also part of it. I wasn't sober before, so I never even really paid attention to the lyrics, so I let a lot go. But "Amsterdam" was a good example of my difficulties with Sammy. I felt the music called for something completely different.

I didn't want Sam to be my puppet, but I hated the words to "Amsterdam" because they were all about smoking pot—they were just stupid. It was about the limit for me lyrically. I'm sorry that I'm maturing and growing. Lyrics like "I Can't Drive 55" meant something at the time when we were younger, but those days were over.

There was a song on *Balance* called "Feelin'" and one of the best lines in the song was, "If I were you and you were me, which one would you rather be" . . . and that was something *I* wrote. It's cool to get people off in a party way, but not all the time. I just started thinking, hey man, let's write something *real*.

**What did you like about Sammy in the beginning?**

When Sammy joined the band, I was so excited because he could actually sing, and the other guy couldn't. You can't goofball your way through a song like "Dreams" or "Love Walks In."

**Did you consider collaborating or finding a collaborator? Not everything he wrote was bad.**

Yeah, that was starting to happen. The way we had always done things is that everyone has their own domain. I didn't necessarily want to write the lyrics. If I wrote the words, it wouldn't be a band anymore—Van Halen would become one-dimensional and not four people.

But I think I was looking to have our music make more of an emotional connection with people, because music doesn't get any deeper than that. The goofball partying thing takes you away from achieving that.

**So, when did everything come to a head?**

Probably when we began working on the soundtrack to the movie *Twister*, after the *Balance* tour. It got so bad that I actually started drinking again.

Alex had called up the director, Jan de Bont, to ask him how closely he wanted the lyrics of the song that became "Humans Being" to be related to the movie. De Bont just said, "You have a pretty free rein—just don't write about tornadoes. I don't want it to be literal. I want it to be reflective of the emotions of the characters." So, we put him in contact with Sam.

De Bont called after, sounding worried. He said, "I told Sammy what I wanted, but he insisted that I fax him tornado-related jargon." Al and I weren't that concerned, but what did Sammy come back with? Lyrics filled with total tornado stuff.

We had several band meetings with Sammy where we told him that if he wanted to continue with Van Halen, he would have to be more of a team player and that might involve collaborating on a lyrical level. He said, "No problem."

So, after the *Twister* premier we began working on "Between Us Two" with Glen Ballard. Everyone thought it had amazing potential. Sammy called Mike one Sunday afternoon and said, "I heard that Glen has some great ideas for the song. I'm really excited." Then he called me that evening to give me his fax number so I could send over Glen's lyrics, and suddenly, he started yelling and screaming at me, saying, "This is a fucking insult! I ain't gonna sing someone else's bullshit!"

I was totally startled. I said, "Wait a minute, we discussed this at length on two occasions." Finally, I said, "Okay, forget the new lyrics, but at least come down, take another pass at the performance, and change a few lines."

The next day he showed up like nothing had ever happened—like he hadn't yelled or screamed at me. Did he think I was some idiot who didn't remember what had happened the night before? I'm sober now, dude. Glen and I were sitting there, working on the song, and the opening line was something like, "I want to see you / I want to know who you are"— kind of a Pink Floyd *Dark Side of the Moon* vibe. Then Sammy decided to change it to some shit like, "I can't see your diamond ring / through your shining star."

I was like, "Sam, please, Glen's got some great lyrics right here, just go with them." His only reply was, "If I thought those lyrics were better, I would sing them. Besides, I have an eight o'clock plane to catch." Glen and I were dumbfounded. Then Glen asked me, "How long has this been going on?" I said, "Longer than I'd care to mention." So, that was the last straw.

I called Sammy a bunch of times, and when he finally returned my call, I said, "Sam, if you want to make another album or do another tour, you've got to be a team player." I went over everything with him like eleven times, and he finally said, "Yeah, goddamn it, I'm fucking frustrated. I want to go back to being a solo artist." I said, "Thank you for being honest." We ended hanging up like everything was cool because it was all out in the open. He'd admitted that he wanted to do solo stuff. And I said, "Well, you can't be in a band and do that, too, so see ya." I didn't fire him. He just quit.

**You also had issues with Sam and *Best Of—Volume 1*.**
Yeah, Sammy was dead against our greatest hits package because he was afraid it would lead to comparisons between him and David Lee Roth. I said, "Wait a minute, Sammy. This band has been putting out records for twenty years and never put out a 'best of' set, but you already have two of them [*Best of Sammy Hagar* (1992) and *Unboxed* (1994)]." It just goes to show that, in his mind, he was always a solo artist. Once a solo artist, always a solo artist. He was only into being in Van Halen for the prestige of it.

**Fans were excited when it looked like you were going to make a new record with Dave. What happened with that?**

Everything went to pieces at the MTV Video Awards. After we went out onstage to present the award to Beck, we started doing some interviews there, and I was just telling the truth. I said, "If we do a tour, we'll have to write and record a new album. But before any of that can happen, I have hip replacement scheduled for December 16, and that's going to put me out of commission for at least four to six months."

After doing a couple interviews, Dave's attitude changed. I asked him what was wrong, and he said, "Well, what's with this hip thing? Would you stop talking about it?" I said, "Okay, no problem. In the next interview I won't say a thing about my hip." I guess he didn't like the tone of my voice. He turned to me and said, "You motherfucker, don't ever talk to me like that again." I thought he had changed, but two minutes onstage and a half-assed standing ovation and he turned right back into the Dave I hated.

# MUSICAL INTERLUDE

*A conversation with*
*Van Halen manager* **Ray Danniels**

---

During the course of their career, Van Halen had five managers—Marshall Berle, Noel Monk, Ed Leffler, Ray Danniels, and Irving Azoff—all very different from each other. A nephew of comedian Milton Berle, Marshall Berle, who at various times worked as an agent for the Beach Boys, Creedence Clearwater Revival, Ratt, and other bands, helped Van Halen get their first record deal but couldn't give them the day-to-day commitment they needed and desired.

He was fired in favor of the group's tour manager, Noel Monk, a dedicated peer who steered the band's ship from 1979 to 1985, its most decadent years on the road. Monk was famously "one of the boys" even as he took care of business, and he wrote about his exploits with the band in his very entertaining 2017 book *Runnin' with the Devil*.

When David Lee Roth exited Van Halen, Monk went with him. New singer Sammy Hagar recommended his personal manager, the older Ed Leffler, who got the job and became a beloved mentor and father figure to the entire band until 1993, when he died of thyroid cancer at age fifty-seven.

Replacing him was Ray Danniels, a Canadian music executive, record producer, and manager whose sister-in-law, Kelly Carter, was married to Alex Van Halen. He rose to prominence in the seventies as manager of the Rock and Roll Hall of Fame band Rush, and during his time with Van Halen, he also served the same function with Extreme and King's X.

Danniels, who was with the band in some of their most tumultuous years, was the only manager to work with all three Van Halen singers—Hagar, Roth, and Gary Cherone. His time with them was relatively brief, from 1994 to 2000, but he was on hand to witness and experience some of the most trying episodes in the band's history, including Hagar's departure, Roth's chaotic reunion appearance with the band on MTV, and the hiring of singer Gary Cherone.

After Danniels left, Alex looked after the Van Halen empire until he was eventually replaced by Eagles' manager Irving Azoff in 2004. In the following interview, Danniels recalls his controversial time with Van Halen and clarifies some of the misconceptions and mysteries surrounding his years with the band.

**When did your journey with Van Halen begin?**

I met Alex while he was dating my wife's sister, Kelly. I got her tickets to see Van Halen at Maple Leaf Gardens in Canada and, somehow, she met Al. They eventually got married and the rest was history.

**When was the idea of having you manage the band first presented?**

It wasn't long after their previous manager Ed Leffler passed away, and just before *Balance*, the last album with Sammy.

**You already had a lot on your hands. You were managing Rush and some other bands. Did you have any reservations about taking on a band as big as Van Halen?**

I was up for the challenge. I thought it made sense. The guys in Rush were okay with it. There were no issues there. If anything, they encouraged it. So, it all made sense.

**What was your first impression of the guys?**

They were the polar opposite of Rush. The Rush guys were like the Three Musketeers, all for one, one for all. Van Halen was not like that. There always seemed to be stuff going on, but it was functional.

In the beginning, I wasn't trying to deal with the personalities. I was more focused on how to make all of their deals better, because they weren't particularly good. Al had brought me in, and Ed endorsed it.

*I got the impression that Al was more involved on the business side of things. Was he your go-between with the band?*

Both Al and Sam were very aware of the business side. Ed didn't really care. He was focused on the music. I mean, he cared. When somebody says a musician doesn't care, it doesn't mean they don't care. It just means it's not their principal concern.

Ed knew Al had his eye on the ball. He knew Sam had an element of being a businessman to his personality. I don't think anyone ever asked Michael all that many questions. I don't say that in a bad way or disparagingly. It's just that . . . when you have strong personalities in a band, somebody needs to lay back.

*When did you know managing Van Halen wasn't going to be a piece of cake?*

Pretty early. How do I explain this? Everything about them was a little difficult. I had the support of the two brothers, and Michael was okay with me. Sammy was somewhat opposed to me but understood that he had chosen Leffler and now the brothers were going to pick their guy. As far as I was concerned, I was going to try to be *everybody's* manager.

Very quickly, I knew there were two camps and that it was not going to be easy, and everything was made a little more difficult because I was based in Toronto. They were in Los Angeles with an LA record company and had previously had an LA manager. I was a foreigner, literally and metaphorically.

There was an element of "Who's this guy? Why is he here?" But it worked out. As time went on, I was accepted and, for a while, everything was okay.

*Did you have a vision beyond dealing just with their day-to-day business?*

My goal was to straighten out the business side of Van Halen. I changed agencies, redid the record deal, redid the publishing deal, dealt with the fact that there was a clause in the contract where they would eventually have to give Warner Bros. a "best of" record.

I was dealing with all of that. I was not thinking in terms of, "Oh, geez, how great this would be if David Lee Roth came back," or, "How great this would be if whatever, whatever." That wasn't in my headspace at the time.

However, there was a lot of pressure about getting David back in the fold. There were an awful lot of people that were obsessed with how big the band would be if they reunited with David, but that wasn't where I was.

*You were just trying to get the lay of the land.*

One hundred percent, yes.

*After you got settled in, what was your view of the band?*

I realized it was essentially Eddie's band. He was the primary reason that people came to see them. He was the superstar in the band. It was a unique situation for a band to have had two very different singers, both equally successful. But I think it was because people came to see Ed—he was the main attraction.

Not that David Lee Roth wasn't absolutely terrific. He was what they needed in the beginning and was perfect for the MTV era. Sammy had a different set of skills, but he was also essential when the band needed to grow. But Eddie Van Halen was the brand . . . and of course, Al as well, because it was a package deal. They were brothers. They were as close as two people could be.

*Was the fact that Ed was the star a problem for Sammy?*

Maybe, but Sam had been pretty much in control where he wanted to be in control. My sense was that Sam did not think he was going to be in Van Halen for the rest of his life. He had a solo career that had done well. He saw joining Van Halen as a boost to his brand. I think, in his mind, he didn't know if he was going to be with them for one, two, or three records. But they were so successful together, how could he not do it again and again and again?

*It must've been complicated for everyone when you entered the picture. Ed Leffler not only was Sammy's longtime manager but also became a father figure to Ed and Al.*

Ed Leffler was older than these guys, and I think he was a father figure to them in a very, very good way. You're right, it would've been hard for anybody to step into a management position.

Ed Leffler's passing disrupted the band. Whoever else came in— unless it had been somebody that Sam picked or knew—would've found it difficult to gain Sammy's trust.

*During this period, Ed was working toward sobriety. Were you involved in helping him achieve that?*

No. Of course, I was in favor of it. I think he was in the process of recognizing that he had a problem, and he wanted to clean up. Al had gotten sober. But, yeah. I don't know. That wasn't really my job.

Keep in mind, too, I would only be in LA one week out of a month, and then went back to Toronto, where I had four kids and a family. I didn't want to move to LA. But I don't think Ed wanted that from me or anyone else. I think that was between him and Valerie.

He was certainly cleaner than he had been when I began managing the band. He was making an effort to be cleaner. I didn't have a lot of experience with substance abuse. I never had to deal with those issues with Rush or the other acts that I'd worked with. It was all new to me.

*You've been accused of splintering the band.*

When I came in, it was already a divided camp. But I think that was normal for the brothers, because they were a divided camp with David. I don't think they ever had somebody that they truly got along with other than the two-year period with Gary Cherone.

They respected Sammy. They liked Sammy. Sammy respected them. But they were very, very different, with different objectives, work ethics, and commitments. Eddie worked 24/7 on his music. Sammy was more grown up and wanted a life beyond being up all night in a recording studio.

*It seemed like Ed wanted everyone in the studio at all hours.*

That was what Ed liked to do. He was in his comfort zone in his studio. It was totally his thing. Sam wasn't interested in working that way—he didn't want to be leaving at three a.m.

There was a Peter Pan element to Ed. He never really had to grow up. He was a rock star. He was like Elvis Presley—there were always people around him taking care of everything. I think Sam was much more of a grown-up. He wanted success and was driven to have success, but he wanted a life and a lifestyle beyond being a guy in a band.

Ed, on the other hand, was happy to have his relationship with Valerie and Wolfgang, but his focus was on his guitar and his music. That was his life.

*That was a pattern that started from the time he was twelve, when he would just go into his room and spend all day playing the guitar. His studio, 5150, was sort of an extension of his bedroom that he had in his parents' house.*

I think you're right with that. But he wasn't the only artist like that.

*I have a hard time thinking of any other artist that was so dedicated to his studio and guitar.*

When I said that, I was thinking of Prince, who I didn't know but who was rumored to be the same kind of person. Everything he did revolved around music, his Paisley Park studio, and touring. He lived it. Ed was the same kind of person.

*You were working with the band when David Lee Roth came back into the picture.*

I think I'm the only manager that worked with all three singers. Well, I had seen how the band functioned with Sam. I had seen what happened when David came back just to do the greatest hits and the little MTV thing. Then, of course, I was there for the cycle with Gary.

*You mentioned earlier that there were some outside forces encouraging the Roth reunion.*

I don't know if anyone would've said that to Al or to Ed, but fuck, everyone was all over me about it. As soon as it was rumored that the band was having problems with Sam, I started hearing from promoters, the record company, agents, and a million other people how big it would be if David came back.

*1984* had been their biggest record. David had left when they were as big as they were ever going to get—arguably the biggest band in America at that time. People saw the potential to make a lot of money.

*How involved were you in getting Dave back into the studio?*

I wasn't involved. That was all Ed. I believe Ed made the call to David. I don't think Al loved the idea, but we were trying to get two new songs, for a "best of" album, and Sam was against releasing one.

*How did you feel about Dave returning?*

It didn't really matter what I thought. It was Ed's studio at Ed's home, or Ed's bedroom, living room, whatever you want to call it. Ed was in control of it.

If Ed wanted somebody to come and make music with the band, they just had to come. It wasn't like we had to go book a studio or get a budget or do any of the things that most bands at their level would have to do. It was like, boom, Ed has his full studio, and he made his records there. He had a full-time engineer and a guitar roadie—he was set up. So, all he had to do was make a call and get David to go there and make Al aware of it.

At first, Al's reaction was, "We're not re-forming with him—let's just do these two songs." I think Al made it clear to David, but I don't think David was really listening.

*David didn't really want to listen.*

Well, David's career wasn't doing as well. He made a little bit of noise early on, but he needed the reunion more than they did. I'm sure he was eager to get back to that level of success. And if it had worked, and the magic had been there, the whole story might've been different. A reunion would've been incredibly successful and all that. But the magic wasn't there. They didn't fall in love again— if they'd ever been in love.

*Were you at the MTV show when Ed and David fell out? Did you go, "Uh-oh."*

Yes. It was just . . . none of it was fun. It was just chaotic, but for some people in the room, it seemed normal. It wasn't normal for me. There was enormous pressure from MTV to push the band and Dave together for the show. There was also enormous pressure from the label to do it.

*How about you? Did you want the reunion?*

There was no great plan on my part to get David back. I was quite happy with the level of success they had with Sam. I had heard too many stories about how they didn't get along with Dave to think that he was going to come back and it would suddenly be great. The other side of that coin was, "Well, the guy's been gone for ten years, maybe he's learned something, maybe he's changed."

*That almost never happens.*

Never happens. Never happens. Never happens.

I haven't looked at the MTV footage since that night. I just remember it being something I wished we hadn't done. But there was no easy way to get out of it. Everybody wanted them to do it. It was very difficult in those days to say no to both your label and MTV—especially when they were pressuring you at the same time. My recollection is of the chaos that was going on behind the scenes and trying to keep a handle on that. It was not fun.

*On paper, the idea of getting Gary Cherone in the band was a good one. Extreme was sort of a mini Van Halen, and his voice actually had a similar timbre and range to Sammy's. You were his manager at the time. Did you feel it was obvious to recommend him?*

I wanted Gary to get an audition, but I would have been happier had we auditioned two, three, or even five people. I would have opened it up and tried to find whoever was the best, but it was Ed's decision.

I thought that Gary should've had a legitimate shot at it. My biggest hope was that whoever they chose, they were going to pick somebody that they were going to get along with. I was tired of wearing a referee's jersey.

What I did know was that Gary was a skilled songwriter, a great stage performer, and had a great work ethic. If Ed wanted somebody to stay past seven p.m., that was Gary Cherone. He had also come out of a band where the guitar player was the dominant force, so he was used to somebody like Ed. Gary was the ultimate team player and that's not something you can say about every lead singer.

*How was their chemistry?*

If Ed liked you, he fell in love with you and there was a honeymoon period, and that's what happened. That's part of why Ed didn't want to try somebody else. But keep in mind, when they picked Sammy, they only tried Sammy, they didn't try three other guys, four other guys. It was the same deal.

*That's not quite true. Ed toyed around with a few other options before they hired Sammy. I know he was interested in doing a record with multiple guest singers.*

Yes. And he talked about that before Gary. That came up again, but Al wasn't into it.

*How was the honeymoon period with Gary?*

Ed loved him and Al was okay with him—or appeared to be okay with him. Nobody asked Michael.

*Whose idea was it to use Mike Post as the producer of* **Van Halen III?** *It was an unusual choice. He was famous for writing television theme show music, not producing rock bands.*

I didn't know Mike Post. Eddie knew and liked the guy and decided it was a good idea. I know it didn't come from the label. Once Ted Templeman was gone, Van Halen had very little connection with the label. They did what they wanted to do. Ed called the shots.

*Mike Anthony intimated that at this point, Ed was basically just looking for a "yes man" so he could do whatever it is that he wanted to do.*

I think that's fair. *Van Halen III* was essentially an Edward Van Halen solo album. He no longer had a singer that was going to fight him or disagree with him. And so, Ed was going to do what he wanted to do the way he wanted to do it. And Al would go along with things because Ed had his role and Al had his role.

If you took Mike Post out of it and you had put in a more experienced producer, maybe the record would've been different. I don't know.

*It's clear that Ed was not a fan of lead singers. Why didn't he just do a solo instrumental album?*

I don't think anyone would have encouraged him to do that. And if it wasn't within him to really want to do that, then it wasn't going to happen. He'd go from being Eddie Van Halen to Jeff Beck, and I don't think that interested him. All the guitar players would love it and he'd still have a career, but that's not quite the same as being in Van Halen.

*You felt that he still desired to have that big-time recognition.*

Well, I think to him, that was a given. He'd always been successful. He wanted the band to be successful. Eddie never wanted to fail. When he talked about the band becoming more credible or less of a "party band," he never added, "And I, of course, will sell less records because of that." That wasn't part of the plan.

By the same token, he wasn't saying, "And I want to do this because we'll then sell more records." That wasn't on the radar with him, it was just what he wanted to do. And I think that there was somewhat of an assumption that he would be successful because he'd always been successful.

It's like Michael Jordan or Wayne Gretzky or any great athlete who's never had a bad season. Their thinking is, "Of course I'm going to do well. Of course we'll make it to the playoffs. We may not always be number one, but we'll always be there—we're contenders." I think that was just a general assumption, and not in an egotistical way.

If you want to stretch the comparison, some athletes will move down in the ranks, get less ice time or court time, and stick around as long as they can. And there's other guys that are a certain age and they see the writing on the wall and leave while they're on top. In music, it's not so easy to do that because they don't force you out because you're thirty-eight.

**When Ed took total control of Van Halen III, *was there any pushback?***

No. Al was generally supportive of Ed. Occasionally, you could tell Al had his reservations about some of Ed's decisions, but he was supportive and protective of his brother. If you took on one of those guys, you had to take on both, they were very much like that.

But Al was not a cheerleader-type guy. He was a realist. His attitude was usually something like, "We'll wait and see. If this is successful, great. If it's not, well, then we'll talk about it. Won't we?"

Al liked Gary. Al knew that Gary was a decent guy. Gary is fucking Joe Biden, okay? He just oozes integrity and decency. And had *Van Halen III* sold well, we would've been sitting here talking about the twentieth anniversary of Gary Cherone with Van Halen. He had the right aptitude to get along with Ed and Al. He had the work ethic, and Gary's not a troublemaker.

If Gary was touched by your music, he was very affected by it. He had that ability to be a fan. Whether it was for Queen, Van

Halen, or whatever else he was into. Gary was definitely excited by people's talent—he's the least narcissistic guy in the music business.

**Ed was very invested in Van Halen III. He felt it was some of his best work. He must've been gutted when it didn't do well.**

He wasn't happy.

**Was there any sense before it was released that the album wasn't going to do well?**

Nobody tells the artist that they don't think an album is great. When you're a big-name act, people generally tell you what they think you want to hear. Or they don't say anything, and the artist often doesn't notice the silence. And that's a big part of why you have a manager. The manager tries to filter some of that and gives the message to the artist, hopefully without trying to do the conquer and divide thing and turn the artist against people.

I knew that there was a lot of disappointment when they didn't reunite with David. And I knew that there were some people that didn't think *Van Halen III* was going to be great. Ed wasn't one of them.

The first week it came out, it sold like 460,000 or 480,000 and that was terrific. And then, the next week it didn't do so well. When MTV didn't pick up the video, I knew there was trouble. But that wasn't the issue, it was just a symptom. The reality was that the word of mouth from fans wasn't good because the falloff was pretty dramatic.

**What did you think of the album?**

I was hoping it would be successful.

**I mean, when you listened to it . . .**

In all honesty, I was caught up in Eddie's enthusiasm for it and Gary's hopefulness, but I wasn't getting that feedback from everybody else. People were just telling me, "Why don't they just get David back?"

*What was the obsession with Dave about?*

The businesspeople thought that if Van Halen could sell 75 percent of what they sold with David using Sammy, then what would happen if you had David back? They felt the band could return to the level they were at when they recorded *1984*, right? Van Halen would go back to being the biggest band in America again. But the music world isn't that predictable, and they would discover that less than a decade later when Dave returned. *1984* was a moment in time and combination of many factors.

I don't think people gave Sammy Hagar the credit he deserved for how good he was, and how he made Van Halen a different band. Sam was a big part of why those records sold.

If you want to be Led Zeppelin and you don't sing, you have to find your Robert Plant. And that's what Van Halen is, the American version of Led Zeppelin, and Sammy was a great singer. I thought he was a much better singer than David Lee Roth was. On the other hand, I think David Lee Roth's lyrics were just fucking right place, right time, and very witty.

**Van Halen III** *had some amazing moments. It certainly isn't as bad as it's been made out to be.*

I agree. There's some great music on it! But here's the question: Has anybody ever replaced a singer for the third time and had success?

*I don't think so. It's a difficult feat. This doesn't get discussed, but there was a certain amount of fan fatigue surrounding Van Halen. You had serious David fans and serious Sammy fans, and both of those camps were upset when Gary was hired. Don't get me wrong, Ed was the central figure, but those guys had their fans as well. There was just too much commotion. It was annoying for fans.*

You're right. To go test that a third time after they'd already brought David out for two songs on the "best of" record and then here we were again. They needed to do something brilliant, and that's not what happened. Gary, however, was really good live and his version of some of the catalog songs were arguably the best they had ever been performed live. And the response was good, but that didn't mean people were going to buy the current record.

It was a lot to put on Gary's shoulders. Both singers were hard to follow because both of them were stars, and both of them had their era.

I don't know what would've happened if Sammy never entered the picture. Who knows? Would they have kept it up or did David depart at exactly the right time? In retrospect, bringing in Sam, who had better musical chops and was a better singer, was probably not a bad move. It actually proved to be a good thing.

**Do you think, no matter who the singer was, Van Halen's decline was inevitable?**

Perhaps. Had they stayed with Sam I doubt if their next record would have done as well as *Balance*. Eventually, most veteran bands don't sell as many records as they once did. They may still sell as many tickets because they're still playing "Jump" live, but there's an inevitable slow attrition when a band gets older and the fans get older. People will still make an effort to go see you, but they won't necessarily make an effort to go to Walmart or Peaches or whatever record stores there were at the time and buy the record.

You already had a divided fan base where everybody had picked the era they liked best. There were some people that liked both eras, but most gravitated to one over the other.

**However, as you mentioned at the beginning of this conversation, Eddie was the main attraction. When Sammy came on board after David, a lot of people hung in because they wanted to see what Ed was doing.**

Yes. Eddie Van Halen was the Great American Guitar Hero. You have to go back to Jimi Hendrix to find anyone else at that level. He was incredibly good-looking and likable. He had the painted guitars, the fucking sneakers—whatever it was—Van Halen was mostly about Eddie Van Halen.

***Both you and Gary left around the same time. What happened?***

I don't think it's anything that Gary did. It was simply because the album wasn't successful, so Ed and Al pulled the plug.

When you've always been successful, and suddenly, you're not successful, it gets magnified, especially when you live in LA and you're surrounded by the music business.

Some bands would've shrugged it off and made another record, thinking, "We've got the benefit of a hundred shows or whatever we did under our belt. It'll be better. We'll do whatever, we'll bring in a better producer, a different producer, a cowriter." Whatever it is. There was none of that. They just got beat at the box office and Gary was out.

And I can't tell you if they recorded another album with Gary whether it would've been any better or more successful. They'd already been one of the very few bands on the planet that managed to change singers and still be hugely successful. Maybe there just wasn't a chance in hell that they could've gone with a third guy, let alone a fourth guy.

When they started recording again with Gary, I think they realized it wasn't going to be different. I don't know whether Al threw in the towel or Ed wasn't in love anymore. I don't know what it was.

***Over the last twenty years, Van Halen recorded only two studio albums. Considering how much music Ed had on file, that's preposterous.***

Well, it's preposterous and dysfunctional. Candidly, I had redone a record deal for them. They could have made another four or five records and Warner Bros. would have paid a small fortune for them. And it wasn't an option. It was a firm deal. But this is back at the height of the record business. They could've made a record every eighteen months and kept delivering them. This was not a situation where someone was going to pay them less for the next record or not pick up an option because they hadn't sold enough copies. It was an incredible deal.

I didn't know if things were going to work out with David, or if they were going to work with Gary Cherone again. I didn't know if

Steven Tyler or David Coverdale was going to join the band. I had no idea, but Warner Bros. weren't going to let the band go.

*Was there pressure from the label to get rid of Gary, or was it ultimately just a band decision?*

No, I can't say that there was any pressure. These were all Ed and Al's decisions. People assumed that I had more to do with Gary Cherone being the singer than I did. Gary was my client in Extreme. I liked and respected him, but I didn't force him on the band.

Ed had just fallen in love and that's all there was to it. If at that moment in time, Paul McCartney or Robert Plant called and said, "I really want to join fucking Van Halen," I don't think he would have auditioned them because Ed had made his mind up.

One time Ed said to me that he wished his parents had had three boys instead of two boys because "dammit, we would've made him a singer." That's a difficult hurdle for any singer to overcome. But still, the guys liked Gary.

*So, when did you decide to leave?*

They were unhappy, and I was unhappy, too. Everything was becoming so dysfunctional, and I wasn't the guy that was going to be able to go there and be a cheerleader. And then it started to get carved in stone that I had put Gary Cherone in the band, which, as I have told you, was not true.

But as crazy as my time was with the band, it was a real honor to work with them, and I think I did well by them. I had an advantage over a lot of managers at the time because I owned my own label. Rush had recorded for me. I owned the publishing company. I knew where every nickel, dime, and penny was hidden. And I had been a booking agent and I booked Rush when we were kids and when I was managing them. So that was the part that I really understood and understood well. I just hadn't taken any courses in psychology or therapy or addiction or any of the things that would have been helpful at times with this band. And those skills weren't needed, with Rush or anyone else I'd worked with.

If they had wanted to try a fourth singer, I probably would have been there for it. If they'd wanted to try it again with Gary, I certainly would have been there for it. But things were falling apart.

Rush had had records that were much bigger than other records, and they didn't need to blame anyone for it. They were very much of the mind that, "This is our record, we made it, we stand behind it. And if people like it and buy it, great, if they don't, hey, it's still our record."

They never broke up because they went from a record with "Tom Sawyer" that sold 3 million copies down to 1.2 million to 800,000. They kept it going. And so that was what I was used to. And eventually Rush recorded another record that did big numbers again. And if you stay in the game and you're really good live, people will always come to see you, especially if you have a good manager and a good agent and they know the difference between Monday night in Toledo and Saturday night.

*What are your final impressions of Ed?*

He was as close to Elvis Presley as anybody I was ever going to meet. He was always surrounded and protected by his crew. You've got a bit of Elvis, you got a bit of Prince, you got a bit of whatever.

He was not a fully functioning human being. Today, more than ever, addiction is recognized as an illness. God only knows what he was prescribed on top of the alcohol issue when he had his hip surgery and cancer surgery.

Ed and Al came by their drinking honestly. I'm sure it was inherited. I met the dad, and he was a lovely guy. He was funny. He was personable. He was a lot like Ed. They were incredibly functional for the amount of alcohol they drank. It would've killed most people.

Drinking a case of beer was maintenance for them. They would get through the day with beer, then move to wine at night, and then they'd move to hard liquor after that. It was like, fuck . . . I'd never seen anything like it. Other than being a rock star, there's not very many jobs in the world that you could ever hold on to and get away with that.

ᨆ

# 8

# WHO THE FUCK IS EDDIE VAN HALEN?

*With Sammy and Dave out of the picture, Ed Van Halen records the most progressive and personal album of his career.*

*" Everything comes to me when I'm sitting on the pot. "*

I N MARCH 1998, a scruffy figure with a Keith Richards slouch and a cigarette firmly screwed between his lips scowled from the cover of *Guitar World* magazine. Emblazoned on his black thrift-store T-shirt was the question in all capitals: WHO THE FUCK IS EDDIE VAN HALEN? Without his usual million-dollar smile, you had to look twice, but the man wearing the shirt was none other than the guitarist himself. The question was meant to be ironic—he was poking a little fun at his guitar hero status—but it was also genuine.

After years of navigating through a haze of alcohol and answering to a succession of domineering figures like his mother, various producers, two flamboyant front men, and even his own brother, Alex—Edward was determined to break free, to find out who he really was.

The title of the band's eleventh album, *Van Halen III*, suggested that it was a third and completely new chapter for Ed and the band. And it was. The guitarist called *III* "the most important album of my life. For the first time, I was able to let go and let the music happen through me."

Featuring two instrumentals, several extended guitar intros and solo breaks, and no song under five and a half minutes long (with one hitting the eight-minute mark), it was the album Ed always wanted to make. In addition to letting his ax run wild, he coproduced, cowrote lyrics, played bass on all but three tracks and even drums on a few others. This was his show, and the album's last song—and grand finale—told the whole story: "How Many Say I," a dramatic ballad featuring Eddie on lead vocals for the first time ever and his own acoustic piano accompaniment.

Part of Ed's renaissance can be attributed to his sessions with Sat-Kaur Khalsa, a psychotherapist who combined traditional therapy with a deeply spiritual approach. Her words carried significant weight with him, and during this period he spoke somewhat manically and peppered his conversations with the kind of phrases one usually hears in therapy. In an extraordinary chat with journalist Vic Garbarini (excerpted below), Ed talked with an almost religious fervor about the significance of his counseling.

That wasn't all. He was also ecstatic about the band's new singer, Gary Cherone, one-time front man of the then-defunct Boston-based band Extreme, a group that had enjoyed some success in the early 1990s, most notably with the hit single "More Than Words." In Cherone, Ed believed he'd found a vocalist, lyricist, and musical partner that he could finally respect and trust.

"It's like I've been waiting for Gary for twenty years," he said. "He'd hand me the lyrics from something like 'From Afar,' and boom: I'd write the music, the melody, and was able to sing it back to him. I'd call him up and say, 'Gar, check this out—is this what you had in mind?' And he'd say, 'Fuck me, Van, you did it again.' And it went on like that. I've been making music for thirty-seven or thirty-eight years and never has somebody handed me lyrics to work with. This record is the biggest milestone in my life because the lyrics came first, then the music. I finally had something to bounce off."

Truthfully, Ed desperately needed a change. His playing had become a little less inspired with each Hagar album. Without David Lee Roth's manic intensity and improvisational goofiness to drive him, Eddie's playing had become more predictable and a lot less fun. Layers of watery, effected rhythm tracks replaced the dangerous sharp edges heard on earlier albums, and his imaginative battery of whiz-bang sound effects that once functioned as commentary on Roth's larger-than-life persona and cartoon energy had diminished to a rather tired series of whammy bar dives that often functioned as a ho-hum period to many of his recent licks.

Cherone's energy and support gave Ed a much-needed creative lift, but ironically, the album Ed considered to be his greatest triumph would be rejected by most critics and fans, barely achieving five hundred thousand in sales—far from the three million copies of *Balance*, their previous studio album.

The new record did have its flaws. Many of the songs had too many disconnected parts and not enough hooks to keep the listener interested. The production was also spectacularly uneven, with Cherone's vocals mixed so that it was right in the listener's face or almost submerged. And even Ed's lead guitar is noticeably out of tune at the 2:40 mark of the album's single "Without You." The drums and bass lacked the presence they had on *For Unlawful Carnal Knowledge* . . . or even their first album. In Ed's unbridled excitement and haste, it seemed like much of the album's lengthy sixty-five minutes had been left unpolished.

Still, it wasn't quite the disaster publications like *Rolling Stone* and the *Chicago Tribune* claimed it to be. Those that have dismissed the album as self-indulgent missed some of the most creative playing of Eddie's career—meaning some of the greatest electric guitar playing ever. Had it appeared on another album, his slide work on "Ballot or the Bullet," for example, would've been hailed as masterly, as would the wonderfully elastic flange solo on "Dirty Water Dog."

The album's poor reception shattered the guitarist's self-confidence, sending him into a downward spiral that would last for years. It took more than a decade before he would recover, record new material, and become Eddie Van Halen again.

**In most older cultures, you don't become a master musician until you hit forty, the age you are now.**

That's interesting, because now that I think of it, everything that prepared me for this record started when I hit forty, about three years ago. That's when I got sober. I've smoked a few times, had a glass of wine every now and then, but that was when I really started to get clear. And I started seeing this therapist, a Sikh woman, and that changed my life.

**Was there a moment or incident when the walls came down and your consciousness opened up?**

There was, yeah. I started playing guitar, drinking, and smoking at the age of twelve. Here I am forty years old, almost three years ago, and she says, "I'm not giving up on you!" Because I had fought her tooth and nail, man. I said, "There's no way—I need a couple of beers to loosen up before I play." So finally, about a year ago last summer, she said, "Just give me twelve hours to work with you." I said, "Okay." So she comes out from Santa Fe, New Mexico, and says, "Are you ready?"

I said, "Yeah, I guess . . . this is *weird*." So, we do all kinds of mind-balancing things for a half-hour straight, and she tells me to sit down. I thanked her, because I was about to drop. She goes, "Close your eyes and just breathe. Now go to that 'room' you go to after you drink. Go to that place, that *feeling* that you have after you drink."

A couple minutes go by. She goes, "Are you there yet?" I go, "No." She goes, "Go to that room." Suddenly, this whole new feeling comes flooding in. I said, "I think I'm there!" She said, "Keep your eyes closed." She handed me a guitar. And I immediately wrote three songs. It took her an hour, not twelve hours.

She told me, "You don't understand, Ed, you've been blocking the light." She was right, and now I can't stop the light coming through, and I don't want to stop it. (*laughs*)

**So, all your life you thought that drinking and worrying and stress would make that energy come, but it was actually blocking you.**

I was numbing myself because I couldn't deal with things. I was hitting the brake when I thought I was hitting the gas. And now it's wide open. Because that ego, all those neuroses and worries and fears, just aren't there.

I was watching myself do *III*. And I was playing and thinking, "Ed, this is coming from that place of being—it's you, not the old 'you.'"

**Many people think ego just means pride. It's also your fear and everything artificial.**

Yeah, that's what I mean. That false outer shell we build up of pride and fear and anxiety and insecurity. That need to control. People are born pure: no racism, no hate—your ego learns all that through fear. Then, when you manage to let go of that stuff, you find your real self is free of all that. And your creativity isn't blocked anymore. You realize you have a direct line to music and god or the universe or whatever you want to call it. You're home, man. I mean, I know I still have a long way to go . . .

**That's a big step.**

And it sure hit me like a ton of bricks. I saw that what my therapist was saying was so right. For years I was getting in my own way, blocking the light. She also said that once you get clear, you're going to start attracting people with that kind of light and clarity. And now I've got Gary Cherone who's coming from the same place.

**You wrote most of the lyrics to your first single "Without You."**

I wrote the first two verses and the chorus, and Gary wrote the third. We wrote the A section the first day after blasting through four Roth-era tunes and four Sammy tunes to warm up. But you're going to think I'm crazy if I told you where I wrote it. I went to the bathroom, and I could still hear the drum loop through the wall. Fragments started coming to me, "Hey, you, wake up, get yourself together . . . there must be some kind of way we can make it right, but I can't do it without you. You've got to give more than you take." And people will probably take that as being about a relationship, but it's not.

It's about the fact that we're all living on the planet, and in order to keep the light alive for our children, we've got to get it together. "I can't do it without you." I certainly can't do it on my own. I picked up this book on Buddhism in Japan and it was so to the point of what we're talking about: all things are impermanent. Ego isn't real. "You" own nothing. If you surround yourself with impure people, you wind up with impure toxic thoughts. Greed and being out of touch with what's real in ourselves is the basis for so much of what we've screwed up. Humans have only been around for a short period of time and look what we've done to this planet just in the last hundred years. It's like we're sawing off the limb we're sitting on. That's basically what "Without You" is about.

It's funny. I don't know if I was born or conceived in the bathroom, but everything comes to me when I'm sitting on the pot. I've got to show you the bathroom in the house. It's turned into a full-blown studio. It started out where I'd sit on the pot and play. Now, I've had the urinal removed, set up a whole rack system: I've got a recordable CD, a TASCAM DA-88, and a mixer. Actually, I wrote the whole record there. If it was a solo album, I'd have to call it *Straight from the Pot*. (*laughs*)

You are literally relieving yourself of your toxins, and then new stuff can come in. I mean, where do ideas and music come from? They're given. The key is to stop thinking and let it happen. I thank God every night that I can keep my chops up so that when I get handed this stuff, I can execute it on the guitar to the best of my ability. I can't sit down and intentionally contrive a song. I won't mention any bands' names, but I can't do the same record, the same thing, over and over. It isn't about money. It's about letting go. The music really does have the power to heal.

**The guitar solos on *Van Halen III* sound very fresh and free. If they could talk, what would they say?**

That's a good question. They'd say, "I'm not afraid to fall on my face. There are mistakes, there's slop, there's whatever—but it's real emotion. It's human. It's really me at my most vulnerable. It was not planned." And most of them are live, first takes. Actually, I don't remember playing the guitar. I was looking at the big picture.

The chords are a series of movements, but I don't know what made me think of doing them—because I wasn't *thinking*. The less I thought, the better. It's like explaining a color to somebody—how do you do that? It just came through because that's what the songs called for. On a song like "Once," the melody that I came up with when I saw the lyrics had certain rhythm, an emphasis on the one. It was what it was. I decided I couldn't build on it vocally, so I built musically and rhythmically underneath the melody. Every time around I added something, layering it up until it slowly builds into a complete piece. But again, I didn't think it through.

# EDDIE'S ODDITIES

**GUITAR:** 1958 Gretsch 6120 Chet Atkins
**USED:** "Once" (*Van Halen III*)

Ed's personal guitar collection numbered well into hundreds of instruments, and he often experimented with them while he was working at 5150 Studios. However, it wasn't until he recorded *Van Halen III* that the public heard a good variety of them put to use, sometimes even during the course of a single song. In addition to his regular stable of homemade custom and signature guitars, Ed used a Coral electric sitar, a metal-body National acoustic resonator guitar, and a vintage Gretsch 6120 Chet Atkins on the album, among various other oddities.

"I used this Gretsch on the song 'Once' on *Van Halen III*," said Ed. "You can hear it at the end of the song where Gary Cherone and I do a trade-off. It's very bluesy sounding. Gretsch guitars have a unique sound. The pickups do not sound at all like Gibson humbuckers. The first time I ever plugged it in I thought that it sounded even more like Clapton than Clapton did himself. The Bigsby made the licks really tasty.

"It's too bad that *Van Halen III* didn't sell really well because fans didn't accept Gary in the band. I probably did some of my best playing on that album. Some of the riffs are great, like on 'Fire in the Hole.' At the end it goes into a completely different thing. Al was asking, 'Why are there so many parts?' I just liked them."

**Like riding a bicycle. Think about it too much, you fall on your ass.**

That's perfectly put. If you start thinking too much, you're not letting the creative power that's in control do its thing. Or like sex—if you worry about your performance, you're lost.

**The last few Van Halen albums didn't have that much harmonic movement.**

It also depends on the dynamic of the people you've been working with. "Wham, bam, Amsterdam" wasn't my fault! Blame the music on me, but not the other stuff.

**So, you've taken charge of the music this time ...**

What I did was I took charge of myself, my own life. And that freaked people out who used to control me. Because so many people love to control others. Look at history. The point is, control yourself and don't get out of control, rather than trying to control other people.

**Controlled you through intimidation? Guilt tripping?**

Oh yeah. Then I realized there's really no such thing as guilt. Fuck guilt! It serves no purpose. Why beat yourself up more about something you did wrong? Everybody makes mistakes. Are you going to carry guilt around with you for the rest of your life? It's pointless. In fact, in reality, there's no such thing as ego. It's just a man-made thing.

**Describe the old, intimidated Ed.**

One thing I've really learned is that I'm actually a very shy, nervous person and that I used to be very easily intimidated. That's why I used to drink. It was like, "Okay, just give us the riffs, Ed ... you stupid ... shut the fuck up!" You know what I mean? And I've learned not to be afraid of being afraid. I named the studio here 5150 because that's the police code for escaped mental patients. What I'm saying is that, at the time, I thought I was a nut. But now I realize I'm not—everyone else is! (*laughs*)

**Does it bother you that so many people are still harping on the Roth/ Hagar stuff?**

At this point it really doesn't. They ask me if I've read Dave's book. Why bother? I know the guy better than he probably knows himself. One

Japanese journalist said it was like "fiction comedy." I thought, that's kind of the way he is.

He's an intelligent, well-read guy. But it's like he can't connect the dots somehow. He's like a disgruntled postal worker. . . . I didn't mean to say that.

**Do you have the confidence to just walk away from people who intimidate or want to control you?**

That's what happened with Dave. I just wanted to give him another shot on those two songs on the "best of" album. The idea was not for him to be in the band again, but to try and help him get out of the Vegas trip he was in. Let him establish himself as a rock and roll singer again so he could put together a new band and do his own thing. But he was never back in this band. Then he basically spit in my face. And I said, "Okay, I thought we were friends, forget it." Then this incestuous thing in the media and on the internet snowballed.

**Looking back, do you regret getting dragged into that media battle with Sammy and Dave?**

That's where I made the mistake over a year ago—when both Roth and Sammy were just slinging shit at us. I got on MTV and said, "I'll take a lie detector test. Both those guys are lying. They're both full of shit." Then what does Sammy do? He does a video with a monkey taking a lie detector test. And people ask, "Doesn't that bother you?" I actually thought the monkey was kinda cute! (*laughs*)

**On a more positive note, what did you enjoy most about working with Gary?**

He was very much like me—very normal. People think he's a prick because he's quiet.

**When you were a kid, was music the only way you could communicate with that deeper part of yourself?**

Yeah, that was the one thing that nobody could take away from me.

**Your father was a musician and he had issues with alcohol. Were you close to him?**

He was a happy guy. He wasn't an angry drunk. He worked his ass off. Both my parents showed us that you could make something out of nothing if you put your mind to it. The funny thing is, my mom was the one pushing us. And my dad, who was the musician, didn't push us at all.

**One thing that burns musicians out in this culture is the idea that rock has to be about youthful energy. When you hit forty, you may be looking for deeper stuff.**

It's all contrived. Even when I was in my twenties, or my teens, I knew music was about much more than that. But I dressed up funny and did all that stuff because it would've looked pretty silly with one guy up front dressed like that and me in the back being normal. So, I played the game, so to speak. But I knew what music was really about ever since my earliest memory of hearing my dad downstairs in his music room, holding just one note on his clarinet for as long as he could. I'm serious. He wouldn't just sit there pissing up a rope. He was going for the tone—*the* tone.

**Are you excited about performing this new music live?**

I'm nervous about doing my best to execute what I was given. About giving that same intensity and vibe onstage that I captured on record.

**Wouldn't you approach playing it live the same way you did recording it—by letting go and allowing yourself to be in that "room" of creative flow?**

That's what I was going to get to. Since my therapist said, "Go to that room," I haven't been able to get out of that room, which is a blast! So much so, Valerie has started saying, "When are you going to see that therapist again? When are you going to get out of that damn room and get in the bedroom?" (*laughs*) But I swear to God, I just can't stop—it just keeps coming.

**They say there's an inner faucet you can eventually use to balance the flow.**

I know, but after forty years of being in pain, of feeling beaten down, I want to stay wet! It's like, give me a couple of years of just letting it flow.

# MUSICAL INTERLUDE

*A conversation with*
Van Halen III *vocalist* **Gary Cherone**

---

In 1996, after Sammy Hagar left Van Halen and their reunion with David Lee Roth fizzled, the group wasted no time announcing the name of a new singer. Whereas a half dozen famous names were rumored to be in contention—including Ozzy Osbourne, Aerosmith's Steven Tyler, and Whitesnake's David Coverdale—it was Gary Cherone, who'd made a name for himself as lead singer in the Boston-based hard rock band Extreme, who took up residence in Edward's guest house in November 1996.

When the announcement was made, those unfamiliar with Cherone scratched their heads. But his selection made a great deal of sense. Extreme was something of a "mini Van Halen," featuring a hot-shot guitarist named Nuno Bettencourt who modeled himself after Eddie and songs that straddled a similar line between hard rock and radio-friendly pop, like the hits "More Than Words," "Get the Funk Out," and "Hole Hearted."

Cherone was also an ideal mashup of Van Halen's two previous singers, combining the vocal range and technique of Hagar with the onstage showmanship of Roth. He also had much to offer of his own, including a 24/7 work ethic that must have especially excited Ed.

Perhaps even more important to Eddie was that Cherone was a genuinely "good dude" who both took his role seriously and knew when to check his ego at the door. All his life, the guitarist had been searching for a singer who'd be a true collaborator—say, a Robert Plant to his Jimmy Page. Roth was too independent—too much his own man—to be a supportive bandmate and true team player. And Hagar, who liked to draw a strict line between his professional and personal life, had no real interest in maintaining the unorthodox late-night hours at 5150 that Ed desired . . . and often demanded.

Cherone, unlike Hagar, devoted himself entirely to the band, and unlike his predecessors, encouraged Edward to expand his guitar horizons and allow himself to try ideas that had been percolating in his mind for years. The guitarist had reached a musical dead end with Hagar and Roth, and Cherone's support and constant supply of new lyrics inspired him to write and play with his old enthusiasm and inventive fire. Their partnership was like nirvana for Ed, and the duo spent the next year writing and recording a new studio album in 5150.

*Van Halen III* represented a creative reawakening for Edward, and it came at a perfect time. He was as clean and sober as he'd been at any time since he was a teenager, and his work with his therapist had transformed him psychologically. He was on an artistic high, and fresh ideas came pouring out of him like water from a busted main.

Tragically for Eddie, Van Halen fans hated the record. It wasn't entirely Gary's or Ed's fault. For many of those fans, the rejection had less to do with the music than with who wasn't on the record: both Sammy and Dave had legions of devotees, and for Van Halen to turn their back on both was simply unacceptable to many.

Add the exile of two very popular singers and the "un–Van Halen-ish" songs on the album—an eclectic collection that included two eight-minute ballads, a sitar solo, and Ed's crooning over a solo piano accompaniment—and you had the potential for a debacle from the outset.

The rejection, however, shook Ed to his core, and it was unfortunate, because it can be argued that given some time, Cherone could've produced more Van Halen–eseque material and Eddie could have found a way to find a balance between his new material and the older, beloved approach in a way that would have been accepted on a new album. Instead, as we shall see, *III*'s failure knocked him out of commission for years.

During the course of the next twenty years, Edward would record only one more studio album: *A Different Kind of Truth*, in 2012, featuring the return of David Lee Roth as vocalist. It was a solid album, but it literally was a retreat to the past. Built around songs written in the seventies, it had only the slightest hint of the daring innovation of *III*, and in that respect, it was the opposite of the classic records he'd made with Roth, which were forward-looking, innovative, and chance-taking.

*Van Halen III* sold only a fraction of the number of the group's previous albums, and one can only assume the guitarist's self-confidence in his grand new vision had been smashed to bits.

In this bittersweet interview, Gary Cherone looks back at *Van Halen III* and speculates on what might have been.

### Were you a fan of Van Halen before you joined?

The first Van Halen album was a watershed moment. It was like Before Christ and After Christ. They brought in a new era.

### Were Van Halen familiar with your first band, Extreme?

I don't think they ever listened to Extreme. After I joined the band, I walked into 5150 one day and they were watching one of our old videos and laughing. Alex said, "Are you gonna do those moves in our band?" I said what moves? And Alex would do a hilarious imitation of me.

### Were you concerned about singing the band's catalog live?

When I auditioned for the band, I had to sing a few songs from the Dave era, and three from the Sammy era. I wasn't worried about the Dave stuff, but Sammy has an incredible range. I was like, "Damn, this shit is above my pay grade."

### What did you think of Dave?

He influenced a generation. You can go down the line, from Jon Bon Jovi to Vince Neil, and you see Dave in all of them. He was the Master of Ceremonies for an entire generation. His tool was that distinctive two-tone scream of his, which was completely different from Roger Daltrey, Steven Tyler, or anybody, really.

***How did you feel when Ray Danniels arranged for you to audition with them?***

I laughed—auditioning for Van Halen sounded so surreal to me. It certainly wasn't a difficult decision, but I didn't know how seriously to take it because the rumor was that Dave was back in the band. I figured I'd go and sing "Jump," be dismissed, and then have a good story to tell everyone later. I wasn't thinking that way out of insecurity—I know I can sing. The whole thing just seemed so random. But then I got on the phone with Eddie and we hit it off right away.

He sent me a song called "That's Why I Love You," and I did a demo and sent it to him. He liked it, so I flew out to California the following weekend. I went to 5150 directly from the airport, and as soon as I got there, Eddie came out and said, "You want to sing?" I still had my bag in my hand, and I said, "Can I take a piss?" So, I went to the bathroom, said a prayer, and thought, "Just don't embarrass yourself."

***What did you sing?***

I started with "Panama" and I flew through the Dave stuff. Then I sang the first two Sammy songs, but hesitated when we got to "Don't Tell Me (What Love Can Do)." I looked at Mike and said, "Yo, Mike, you gotta help me with the high notes on this one—it's brutal." But luckily, my voice opened up and it sounded fine. Eddie was smiling, we were laughing, and everything was very casual.

My first observation was these guys are deaf because it was *loud* in their rehearsal space. But the volume sorta helped, because the vocals were very up front, and they had a nice delay on it. I was like, "Man, this is a cakewalk." The next thing they said was, "Wanna write a song?" So, we wrote some lyrics on the spot and we came up with a melody. I mean, I had just *met* these guys. It was a trip.

***Van Halen, as a whole, are good at making people feel comfortable.***

Yeah, Eddie knows how he affects people, and he's disarming almost to a fault. Alex is more aloof until you enter the circle. He's more guarded. And everyone loves Michael. You have all your food groups in Van Halen, and that's why it worked.

**So how did you get the gig?**

On my second day there, Ed and I were standing around outside the studio while he was smoking a cigarette. We had just written "Without You," and he nonchalantly said, "Hey, man, want to join the band?" I was stunned. I think I said, "Did you talk to the guys?" He said, "Oh yeah, yeah, no, I haven't talked to them yet, but yeah, I'll talk to them." I said, "Of course I'll join the band, Eddie." I mean, do you want to join Van Halen? Can you answer that any other way?

**What was Eddie's relationship to alcohol at this point?**

Ed was working at his sobriety. He wasn't really drinking. He was seeing his therapist and as far as his creativity goes, it was like the floodgates were open. I would bring in lyrics and he'd be excited about that, because no one had ever given him words to write to before. I think that's why *Van Halen III* was so eclectic—he was really uninhibited during that period. He wanted to try new things.

**You were a much different lyricist than Sammy or Dave.**

I was actually a little apprehensive about writing for Van Halen. I knew my approach was more cerebral, but I discovered it wasn't a concern. I think Ed wanted something different.

I would hand him a lyric and we'd sit at a piano or with an acoustic guitar and have a great time. We were like kids, and the writing process made us closer. Everything we worked on seemed very fresh. In a way, part of me wishes the record company would've released one of the sprawling, seven-minute tracks like "Once" or "Year to the Day" as the first single instead of "Without You," which was a more traditional-sounding Van Halen song. It would've signaled a real departure, like when they released "Why Can't This Be Love," their first single with Sammy.

"Once" was so different for the band. It was influenced by Peter Gabriel's *So*, one of the few contemporary records Ed ever listened to. I thought it was brilliant. Lyrically, it was a door for me—I had somewhere to go that wasn't old Van Halen or Extreme. It was a turning point for Eddie as well, and it bonded us.

*This is a contrarian view, but I felt* **Van Halen III** *was an important album.* **Balance** *was successful, but musically there wasn't anything new on it. On* III, *Ed was trying new things and creatively stretched out more than on any record since* **Fair Warning.**

Absolutely. Our writing process was a blessing and a curse. It was a blessing as an artist because we were exploring so much new territory. But it was curse because it alienated the band's fan base.

*How do you feel about the album?*

One of my criticisms is that the album had an engineer and not a producer. Mike Post didn't provide enough structure or guidance. Sonically, it's a tough record to listen to. Arrangement wise, some things are a little too long. If we had an experienced producer, I think the record would have sounded better and the arrangements would have been a little tighter, because I truly believe there are some gems on the album.

*Ed would complain about how Ted Templeman would rein him in. It feels like he hired Post to be more of a facilitator.*

I'd agree. But I think the record would've been better if we had a stronger overseer. A producer might've heard "Josephina" and said, "Yeah, okay. Let's just put that over on the side—we need a rocker."

*Ed's playing was very different on* III. *The songs were longer, but the solos on "Fire in the Hole" and "Once" were refreshingly minimalist.*

Yeah, they were more in the vein of "Runnin' with the Devil." However, the solo on "Ballot or the Bullet" is as imaginative as anything he ever played.

***Why did Ed sing "How Many Say I"?***

That was a lyric I gave him. He read it late one night, and he was inspired. He asked Valerie permission to get up and go to the piano. It was like three in the morning and Eddie's voice was scraggly and tired, but he just recorded himself banging away at the piano and singing this song.

The next morning, he played it for me and all I could think of was Tom Waits or Roger Waters. I told him I loved it, and that I wanted him to sing it. He was criticized for it, but I think it's one of the best moments on the record. It's the only time in the entire Van Halen catalog you really hear Eddie's voice, and whether you like it or not, that was the artist right there. I loved it. I loved his singing.

***What was it like to work with him in the studio?***

Much of the time I was just an observer and I'd just let him do his thing. On many occasions, I'd walk in and see he'd have every guitar on the ground, and I'd ask what he was doing, and he'd say, "I got the sound in my head, I got the sound in my head." I learned to know when he was on a mission and back off, and I just felt privileged to watch.

***Did he contribute to the lyrics?***

A bit. I think Ed and Al both contributed to the chorus of "Without You." I have one funny memory. We were working on a song called "Pursuit of Happiness" that didn't make it on the album, and I showed Eddie the lyrics. He looked them over and said, "What does 'lament' mean?" I said, "It's like a cry." He said, "Well, why don't you just say 'cry'?" I was like, "Well, it doesn't rhyme with the line that precedes it."

***Your manager Ray Danniels said that Ed loved you. He said if Paul McCartney or Robert Plant had called and said they wanted to replace you, Ed would've sent them away.***

That's probably true. We bonded quick. It's funny, he liked to kiss people, and when you're in his inner circle, he kissed you on the lips. In the beginning, Eddie would come to kiss me hello or goodbye, and I would move my cheek and hug him. But on the third day, I went to give him my cheek and he grabbed my head and said, "No, this is how we do it here." And he put the kiss on my lips.

**What was it like to tour with the band?**

It was fun, but you had a lot of people in the audience that were loyal to both Sammy and Dave. And many people thought Dave was coming back, so it was difficult for me to win them over. I'd hear people shout things like, "Cherone sucks more than words!" and all that. But Ed would always defend the decision. Sometimes I think it would've been better to just do a greatest hits tour first, and get to know the band, the catalog, and their fans before recording an album.

**But then you would've been indoctrinated and not have attempted something like "Once."**

True. There were a lot of reasons why the album came out the way it did. Between Ed being sober, a producer who was more of an engineer, and a new singer with a different perspective—all of those things made Ed less inhibited and contributed to the eclectic nature of the album.

**It's been said that Ed was consumed by his work. Was that your impression?**

Eddie was singularly focused. He was inspired. I'll always remember my first weekend at the guesthouse. It was like ten a.m., he was still in his pajamas, he's got a guitar, he's in the golf cart, he's got no shirt on, and he's beeping. I'm opening up the door and he's like, "Ready to work?" And I'm like, "Yeah, yeah, let me put a bowl of cereal down." He was obsessed. That's all he did. He even had a pedalboard under the toilet in his private bathroom in case he was inspired. It was a reflection of his brain. There was so much going on.

I mean, this is my dime-store psychology here, but I think much of his drinking was to just get some peace. I think his brain worked differently than ours—than us mere mortals. I truly believe that it was always racing. Like he always said, in his humble way, "I don't know where it comes from. Where does a song, where does a melody come from? It comes from somewhere else." And he was always trying to get it out.

It was always coming to him, so he had to get it out. It didn't matter where he was. There was a demo that didn't make the record where he created an entire intro out of playing an electric bass with a bow.

It was funny, Eddie sometimes rambled, or he'd repeat himself. Maybe that was because of his years spent drinking. I remember saying to our tour manager Scotty Ross, "Hey, Scotty, Eddie just told me a story, and he's telling it to me again—what's up with that?" He said, "Oh yeah, he's just circling the airport. Just remind him that he already told you."

But the point is, when he put on his guitar and was noodling, he actually spoke clearer. Swear to God. Whatever the synapses were that connected his fingers to his brain, they were so strong that when he played, he spoke with more clarity. I'm not exaggerating.

*One thing about Ed's later work that I think makes it more difficult to process is that throughout any given song his rhythm parts continuously change and evolve. It's exciting from a musical perspective, but I think that's unsettling to the average listener.*

Yeah. I mean, you're nailing it. And like we said with *III*, it meandered. I think it's because of his brain—he always had so many ideas. And that's why he needed a strong producer. Listen, there's no rules to playing rock and roll stuff, but I think you're onto something in a sense that he didn't like repeating himself and he started losing the plot when it came to writing a pop song.

You're not Pink Floyd, you're Van Halen—you should give your audience a verse, a chorus, and a middle eight. But that was his prerogative. But the consequences are that not everyone was going to jump on that bandwagon with you, you're going to lose people along the way.

*As much as he wanted to do things his own way, Ed seemed like he desired input. He expressed his anger to me several times when he felt Sammy and Mike weren't as invested in the music. What was your experience?*

Yeah. It was something you had to feel out. I usually knew when I could be in the room, because he would ask me my opinion. For example, Mike Post and I would be sitting at the recording console while he did three or four takes, and he'd ask us, "Which one do you like?" Often it was hard to respond, because they'd all be really good and completely different, but you would toss out your opinion. But then there were other times he wouldn't look up, so you knew he was in a zone. I had the luxury of living there, so it was easier for me to be available when he wanted an outside opinion. But I remember Sammy saying to me a few years back, "You lived there? What were you? Crazy?"

It was sorta funny because Eddie would knock on my door at two a.m. sometimes when he had an idea he wanted to try out, so he had access to me. He didn't have that with the other guys, and when inspiration struck and they weren't around, he would get frustrated. I don't blame them. Why should they have to be at Ed's beck and call?

I remember after the record, we came back, and I said, "Hey, Ed, man, I'm thinking of looking for my own place and moving down the street so you and Valerie can have your privacy." And he was hurt. And I'm like, "No, no, no. I didn't mean . . . Eddie, you're so generous. I love it here. I'm only thinking of Valerie and the family."

I did eventually move out, but only ten minutes away. I'd get my coffee and go up there. But I remember him being hurt, and it was like, "Is it me? Why . . ." Maybe I was the closest thing Ed ever had to a real collaborator on a consistent basis, and maybe that's why the album went down the road it went down.

*Did Ed ever open up to you about his struggles with alcohol?*

At the beginning in working the process, he was open about it and he was on top of it. Meaning, he was controlling it. And it's probably again that small period of time where the stars aligned, because, if it wasn't, I don't think it would have worked with me. I don't think we could have got through making a record if he was drinking.

Ironically, it was Alex who was having some substance problems at that time. I was only in the band for two weeks when they held an intervention for Alex. All of his close friends and associates were there . . . and me. I didn't really know him very well yet, but everybody was asked to talk. The crazy thing was the intervention was organized so the first people that had to speak were his most recent acquaintances. And who's the new guy? I had to talk to first!

It was pretty intense. Like I said, Alex was great—but a little intimidating. He would horse around and take my arm like a little kid and twist it, and ask, "Does this hurt?" Or pinch me on the neck on this tension point and say, "Does this hurt?" And I'd be, "Alex! Yes, yes, it hurts!" It could be funny, but when he was a little buzzed, it could also be scary.

So, there we all were, and he comes in and figures out what is going on right away. I was first, so I had to get up and say, "You don't know me, but . . ." It was terrifying. I got through my little thing and it goes through everyone and finishes with Eddie. Although Ed was clean at the time, Al knows about his history, and I was wondering how it was all going to go down. But Eddie was great and kind.

If I learned anything while I was with them, for the Van Halens, it's all about family. It's all about the brothers. They would kill for each other. After the tour, when Ed started abusing alcohol again, Alex tried to get him back on track. It went back and forth. And that's what happened towards the end of my time with the band. It just got to be very dysfunctional.

When you were in the circle, you got the kiss on the mouth. When you're out, you're either hated—like some of the ex-members—or you just lose touch. When I left, we were still on good terms, but we went our own ways.

*Up until* **Van Halen III,** *Ed had never experienced failure in his career. How did it affect him when the album that he was so clearly invested in was not well received?*

It's always difficult. When I was in Extreme, we had a hit record with *Pornograffitti*. We thought our following record was ten times better, and it didn't do nearly as well. I remember it was pretty disappointing. But if you're Eddie Van Halen, who had been on an upward trajectory for twenty years, it had to have hurt.

That affects you as an artist when people don't understand something you put your heart and soul into. But that's art. Someone paints a painting and people don't get it, then they don't get it. But I know from personal experience how difficult that is. Unfortunately, we never talked about the failure of *VH III* amongst ourselves, and we probably should have. We just started writing new stuff.

I don't know the cycle of an alcoholic, but I don't think it was the lack of success of *III* that started Ed drinking again. I think it was a combination of lots of stuff. Personal. Family. Being a guy that needs that escape from his own brain. . . . All those compounding things hitting him all at once.

Surgery? He was such a great performer. It had to have been a source of worry. Cancer? Did that give him another reason to drink? Sure. Even though I was out of the loop when Ed was having problems in 2004, it crossed my mind that he might become a casualty.

*Do you think he suffered from insecurity?*

Eddie had his insecurities, but it never occurred to me that he had any self-doubt about his playing. He was aware of what people expected of him. And again, there's only a few people you can think of—maybe Jimmy Page—who suffered from that burden. He was alone with that expectation on his shoulders.

Like you said, *VH III* could've been an opportunity or a turning point. He could've expanded his horizons as an artist. Because it wasn't, he was almost forced to take a step backwards and just play the Sammy catalog on the 2004 tour. That meant he was being restrained. I wonder if his drinking was a form of rebellion—lashing out against the people who would only accept him in his old "Johnny Bravo" suit.

*That sounds reasonable. As* **VH III** *demonstrated, he had more dimensions as a musician.*

You're taking a broader perspective and looking at him as a musician. I mean, the popular perception was Eddie Van Halen, Guitar God. That's a narrow description of the guy. He truly was a composer.

*Did you ever reconnect with Ed?*

Yes, but it took a while. There was no way to really connect with him in the early 2000s because of the condition he was in. But sometime in 2015 or 2016, I saw his interview at the Smithsonian, and I was really moved by it. I wrote him a letter and he sent me a beautiful response. He said something to the effect of "Hey, Gary, I think of you often—every time I drive by the guesthouse." We exchanged numbers and met socially a few times after that.

*It was rumored that he was thinking of putting together a tour with you, Dave, and Sammy.*

The first time I went back to his house, we picked up right where we left off. At one point in the conversation, he brought up the idea of doing a tour with everybody . . . Sam, Dave, Mike, and me. He said that his manager, Irving Azoff, was awesome and was pushing for it. So, I asked him if he really thought he was going to do it. He started throwing a few jabs, like "Ah, look at Dave . . . and fucking Sammy just wants to sell tequila." So, I joked and said, "If things don't work out, I know a singer who'll work for cheap." He laughed and said, "Hey, man, stranger things have happened." That was the extent of the conversation.

*Did you know the extent of his health issues?*

Yeah, he was open. There were a couple times we couldn't get together because he was recovering from chemotherapy, and times when he was lethargic because he had been through a treatment, but he was always positive.

He would tell me about his treatments in Germany and say, "I'm kicking its ass." But on other occasions the news wouldn't be as good. "They got rid of the cancer and now it's a little bit of a pea," or "Shit, Gary, it came back." But he was always honest, very open, and incredibly optimistic. He'd always say he was gonna kick cancer's ass.

I'd always be supportive. But there were times when I saw him, and you could see it on his face that he was drained.

# 9

# THE LOST YEARS

*A series of personal, professional, and health-related calamities leave Eddie Van Halen in a dangerous state.*

---

" I came home and on the six o'clock news Dan Rather was saying, 'Up next, Eddie Van Halen has cancer.' "

---

I N THE EARLY 2000s, Van Halen went silent. There were no tours, no videos, no signs of new music on the horizon. Edward's name occasionally appeared in the press, but rarely was the news good. Frankly, it was a hellacious period for the guitarist. Almost absurdly so. In addition to wrestling with serious health issues, his band was in shambles, he split with his wife, and he was spotted looking unkempt and behaving erratically. He was a mess—but given his personal issues, it was understandable.

Eddie's troubles had been mounting for some time. *Van Halen III*, his 1998 pet project with singer Gary Cherone, was the band's only major commercial failure in twenty years—and it was a big one. The critics were merciless, with *Rolling Stone* giving the album only two out of five stars, while the usually friendly *Billboard* magazine declared it "a wasted opportunity to breathe life into a now-tired formula."

The rejection crushed Ed. He felt that the record represented some of his best work ever and was stunned when it wasn't well received. But Tom Sinclair, in a piece in *Entertainment Weekly*, grasped the album's significance: "Judging from the renewed intensity of Eddie's guitar playing throughout much of *III*, having a merely competent, relatively ego-free singer seems to have reinvigorated his muse."

The band made a valiant attempt to rebound the following year by recording some promising new material with two rather intriguing producers, Pat Leonard, who had worked extensively with Madonna and Pink Floyd's Roger Waters, and Danny Kortchmar, a respected session guitarist best known for his sleek productions on albums by Don Henley and Bon Jovi. Cherone later described one unreleased song, "Left for Dead," as one of the most up-tempo rockers Van Halen had ever committed to tape, and "You Wear It Well" was said to have "a stellar tapping intro that sounded like an extraterrestrial on acid."

The album was derailed, however, when the singer unexpectedly quit the band in November 1999. He later told *Rolling Stone* magazine, "I wasn't in a great place, mentally. I had some things going on in my personal life that affected me. When we broke up, it was mutual." Cherone's exit was quickly followed by that of manager Ray Danniels, who returned to devoting himself full-time to Rush.

With Cherone and Danniels gone, Ed decided to take advantage of the lull to consider his next move, and he proceeded to have his hip-replacement surgery, something he'd been putting off for more than five years. The operation took place on November 16, 1999, at Saint John's Health Center in Santa Monica, and was performed by Dr. John R. Moreland, a surgeon to stars like actresses Liza Minnelli and Elizabeth Taylor.

In Eddie's ever-increasing need to assert control over every situation, he insisted that he remain conscious during the arduous procedure "in case something went wrong," requesting an epidural instead of general anesthesia. He also demanded that the entire operation be recorded in high-definition audio.

Wife Valerie Bertinelli later reported with some amusement that Eddie took his original hip bone home with him, put it in a plastic bag, attached a note that read MY HIP BONE—DO NOT COOK—and popped it in the freezer.

The operation was deemed a success, and it looked like Ed would soon be able to jump again, when another health scare came his way. A few weeks after his surgery, the guitarist was at the dentist for a routine checkup when it was discovered that he had some unusual scar tissue on his tongue.

A specialist at UCLA Medical Center had it biopsied and discovered that Eddie had squamous cell carcinoma—a fairly common form of skin cancer. Although it wasn't life-threatening, the doctor explained that this type of cancer could be aggressive and had the potential to spread to other parts of the body. After removing the cancer—and part of Ed's tongue—he warned the guitarist in no uncertain terms that he was never to smoke again, and that if he did, the cancer would undoubtedly return.

In May of 2000, Eddie began undergoing additional cancer treatments at MD Anderson Cancer Center in Houston. Although he did his best to keep his illness a secret, the news leaked, and the media began reporting on Eddie's health issues.

"The hospital used me for publicity," he complained bitterly. "I came home and on the six o'clock news Dan Rather was saying, 'Up next, Eddie Van Halen has cancer.' Two commercials go by and he keeps mentioning it. I was having an out-of-body experience. I was yelling at the television, 'You're gonna use my name to promote your facility?'"

Having already lost part of his tongue to the disease and frustrated with his medical care, Ed and Val flew to New York to meet with Dr. Steven McClain, a specialist in alternative cancer treatment. In her memoir about this period, *Losing It*, Bertinelli wrote that she was skeptical of the doctor, that he "seemed like a quack."

But McClain impressed the guitarist with his holistic ideas and experimental research, and Ed continued consulting with him for the next several years, eventually partnering with him on a successful dermatopathology laboratory.

As his cancer treatment became widespread public knowledge, Ed was keeping another big secret. Shortly after Cherone left, the band once again reached out to David Lee Roth and, according to the singer, they "wrote three astonishing tunes." But, alas, yet again, a genuine reunion failed to take root.

In a surprisingly candid interview with his golf instructor, Ron Del Barrio, for *Maximum Golf* magazine, Ed voiced his disappointment. "Everything looked pretty positive about getting together, but before you knew it, attorneys were involved," he said. "It made cancer seem like a tiny zit on my ass. Everything seemed to fall apart after these guys got involved. I mean, we used to do it on a handshake. At this point, I don't have a clue what's going on.

"I write and play music for a living. I'm not a businessman. It seems like all attorneys ever do is stir up trouble. They create problems that never existed and ream you for half your money, then they try to fix what they started and nail you for whatever money you got left. I don't see how these guys sleep at night. But what the hell are we talking about? This is *Maximum Golf*, not *Maximum Dirt*, right? So, let's get back to my suck-butt swing."

But if 2000 was difficult, the next two years were absolutely brutal. In January 2001, Van Halen severed their twenty-three-year relationship with Warner Bros., and Ed and Al found themselves floating without a label or management for the first time in two decades. That same month, Edward discovered that his cancer had returned, and it shook him to his core. At Valerie's insistence, he went to Cedars-Sinai hospital in Los Angeles for the chemotherapy treatments he had long resisted, and on April 26 he released a message on the official Van Halen website:

"I'm sorry for having waited so long to address this issue personally," he wrote. "But cancer can be a very unique and private matter to deal with. So, I think it's about time to tell you where I'm at. I was examined by three oncologists and three head and neck surgeons at Cedars-Sinai just before spring break and I was told that I'm healthier than ever and beating cancer. Although it's hard to say when, there's a good chance I will be cancer-free in the near future. I just want to thank all of you for your concern and support."

To some degree, the recurrence was no surprise. Despite numerous warnings from doctors and his wife, the forty-six-year-old guitarist continued to smoke, drink, and do cocaine, finding it almost impossible to break the cycle of addiction that had started in his teens.

Desperate, Val and Alex staged an intervention in October, but it did little good. Completely frustrated by Ed's unwillingness to change his ways and concerned at how his behavior was affecting their ten-year-old son, Wolfgang, she filed for separation.

With his family, health, and band spiraling out of control, Ed plummeted into the abyss. Then he received some much-needed good news: the chemo treatments had successfully eliminated his cancer, and he was given a clean bill of health. But without Valerie there to keep him in check, he immediately returned to his bad habits.

In addition to smoking, he began drinking red wine straight out of the bottle, staining and rotting his teeth and destroying his once-famous smile in the process. He also insisted on wearing a pair of dilapidated combat boots with holes in their toes, and his entire wardrobe began looking like he did his shopping at the Salvation Army.

Those in the press who took note of his appearance dismissed it as "eccentric" rock star behavior, failing, unfortunately, to see the truth. Edward was in deep psychological trouble. The two things he took pride in and depended on—his family and his band—had evaporated. He was alone, terrified, and filled with self-loathing for his inability to kick his destructive habits.

He sequestered himself for days on end in the familiar cocoon-like comfort of his studio. Located just yards away from his house, it was his refuge, no doubt reminding him of his teen bedroom, where he would practice his guitar for hours when his parents argued or when things got difficult in school. Playing the guitar was the only thing he could truly control, and he endlessly noodled and recorded hundreds of hours of ideas for his own gratification. He had named his recording facility "5150" after the California law code for people who are determined to be unstable or "crazy," but the joke seemed less funny as time progressed.

Ed's world was collapsing by the minute when Irving Azoff, Sammy Hagar's new manager, came to the rescue. He encouraged Sam to reach out to Alex Van Halen, with whom he maintained a cordial relationship, to see how things were going. Azoff, who legendarily managed acts like the Eagles, Maroon 5, No Doubt, and Bon Jovi, was canny enough to see an opportunity for his client. With both Cherone and Roth out of the picture, the executive wondered if there might be an opportunity to stage a potentially lucrative Van Hagar reunion.

Alex responded positively to Sammy's overture. He knew his brother was in a difficult place and felt that recording with Hagar might be just the thing to help him get back on track. "[I thought it would be] therapeutic for what Ed was going through with his health," Al told *USA Today*. "In times of doubt and when you're depressed, you tend to go to what gives you comfort, and that's music."

Hagar was excited to get back to work with Ed, Al, and Mike. A decade had passed since their split, and he hoped that both sides had matured, that they could return to their platinum glory days. It had been years since Hagar had had any direct contact with Ed, however, and he was shocked at what he saw.

"I had been waiting at 5150 for more than an hour when Eddie finally showed up," Sam recalled. "He looked like he hadn't bathed in a week. He certainly hadn't changed his clothes in at least that long. He wasn't wearing a shirt. He had a giant overcoat and army pants, tattered and ripped at the cuffs, held up with a piece of rope. I'd never seen him so skinny in my life. He was missing a number of teeth and the ones he had left were black. His boots were so worn out he had gaffer's tape wrapped around them, and his big toe stuck out. He walked up to me, hunched over like a little old man, a cigarette in his mouth. He had a third of his tongue removed because of cancer and he spoke with a slight lisp."[17]

Despite Ed's condition, Hagar forged ahead. Sure, the guitarist was acting strangely, but he was still functioning creatively at an extraordinarily high level. The singer was blown away by the literally hundreds of songs and demos Edward had produced. The hope was to record a new album and then tour, but after an arduous three months in the studio, producer Glen Ballard was only able to coax three completed tracks out of the band. Sammy had knocked out all three of his vocals in a single afternoon, but Ed was being unnervingly picky about his guitar parts. Unlike the old days, where he would be content to play his guitar parts in one or two takes, he had begun experimenting with recording multiple layers and overdubs, sometimes taking weeks to finish a song. One of the new tunes, entitled "Learning to See," was a particularly complex piece of music featuring six or seven different parts.

Ed had always been a dedicated musician, but in 2004 his diligence took on a feverish new intensity. According to those around him at 5150 during that period, the guitarist would spend eighteen to twenty hours a day in the studio, return to his home, crash on a mattress, wake up four hours later, light a cigarette, and walk back to the studio.

Tensions mounted, however, when Edward demanded the same commitment from those around him. Even if his fellow band members had finished their parts, Ed expected them to be in the studio while he experimented for hours on end.

Hagar and Anthony, however, were having none of it. "It took three months for Ed to do the guitar parts to three songs and a couple of solos," Sammy said in his autobiography, *Red: My Uncensored Life in Rock*. "I went in and knocked out my vocals on all three songs in two hours. [Michael] came in and we did all the backgrounds in another two hours. They spent the next three months doing Eddie's guitars."

Although it was hard to fault the guitarist for pursuing excellence, his relentless experimentation slowed the band's productivity to a snail's pace. Because the three new tracks took so long to complete, the idea of making a new album was jettisoned in favor of releasing another greatest hits collection entitled *The Best of Both Worlds*, with the trio of new Hagar tracks included to incentivize sales. The rest of the album contained a mixture of sixteen Roth-era studio tracks, fourteen from Hagar's stint in Van Halen, and three more concert recordings with Sam on vocals, from 1993's *Live: Right Here, Right Now*. Conspicuously, no tracks from the Cherone era were included.

On the plus side, the new tracks on *The Best of Both Worlds* all featured some brilliantly ambitious guitar playing. "It's About Time" contained dozens of tricky syncopations and doubled down on the progressive approach of *Van Halen III* but benefited from Hagar's arena-sized chorus, which prevented the song from hurtling into outer space as much of the Cherone-era material had.

Edward's playing was also terrific on "Learning to See," which showcased a series of flawlessly performed cascading harmonics during the verses and one of his most wildly psychedelic solos ever. Over a chugging detuned rhythm guitar, the guitarist unleashed a stunning display of echoing shrieks, tremolo-picked runs, and wah-wah-effected licks that exploded like fireworks before dissolving into the song's chorus.

Of the three songs, "Up for Breakfast" was the most conventional, with Sammy bellowing sophomoric sexual double-entendres as if it were

1985. But it also highlighted what made Ed's latter-day work so brilliant . . . and difficult. Each verse in the song featured a dizzying number of rhythmic variations, and though these were fascinating in their own way, one wished he would've landed on one or two ideas and stayed with them. To guitar players, the song was a brilliant exploration of Ed's restless imagination, but for your average rock fan, there was simply too much to digest.

"It's About Time" and "Up for Breakfast" were released as singles, but like the songs on *Van Halen III*, neither managed to connect and both failed to break into the Billboard Top 100.

Still, it was a promising start to what could've been the next chapter in the band's career. Unfortunately, Ed's erratic behavior, grouchy demeanor, and inconsistent playing during the band's eighty-stop tour to promote the album annoyed Sammy to the point where no amount of money or success seemed worth the hassle.

"Whenever he came out onstage with no shirt on and his hair tied up, samurai-style, he seemed fucked up," wrote Sammy in his book *RED: My Uncensored Life in Rock.* "That was his little signal. He would come out first with his hair down, then go back to change guitars or after Alex's drum solo and come back with his hair up. I'd look at Mike and we'd roll our eyes—here we go again."

Many dark myths and legends about Eddie's behavior in that rough period have cropped up over the years. Some of the reports of his deteriorating mental state were true, but many were exaggerated.

We spent a few days interviewing Ed at 5150 at that time and also watched the band rehearse. And it was clear to me that though there was legitimate reason for concern over his well-being, he was hardly on his last legs, physically or mentally.

Yes, Ed's teeth were bad, he had a bottle of cheap Smoking Loon Cabernet wine with him for much of our time together, and he wore those by-then infamous boots with the holes in them. His speech was intense, irregular—normal at one moment and then abruptly shifting to a conspiratorial whisper the next. But for the most part he was lucid and appeared happy to be able to share his ups and downs with someone he believed understood him as a musician and a person. He had a lot on his mind and spoke at length, often for twenty minutes at a time without interruption.

# EDDIE'S ODDITIES

### GUITAR: 1961 Fender Telecaster
### USED: "Learning to See" (*The Best of Both Worlds*)

Ed owned a variety of vintage Fender Stratocasters and Telecasters, many of which were used in the studio. Examples include a late-fifties Strat that Ed used to record "Cathedral" on *Diver Down* and a Telecaster Custom that he played on "Runaround" from *For Unlawful Carnal Knowledge*. "I decided to go for a different sound on 'Runaround,'" Ed recalled. "I just wanted that twang, and the Tele was perfect."

However, there was one instance when Ed wanted to use a Tele that ended up being less than perfect. "I tried using my '61 Tele when we recorded 'Learning to See' for the *Best of Both Worlds* greatest hits compilation," he said. "I just wanted to use it for a simple three-chord overdub on the verses. When we were recording that, it was humid and had been raining for two straight weeks. I couldn't keep the guitar in tune. I was so upset that I took the guitar outside in the rain and threw it up in the air as hard as I could. Then I just left it out there in the rain for at least an hour. When I picked it up again, it was still exactly as out of tune as it was before I threw it. That guitar is a brick shit house. It had a big dent in the side from where it hit the concrete, but tuning-wise it didn't budge.

"That blew my mind. It pissed me off so much that I ended up using three Airline guitars instead. I tuned each guitar in separate open tunings to the chords that I needed, and I C-clamped each body to the seat of separate wooden stools. I set the stools in a half circle in front of me so I could just reach over and strum the guitar for the appropriate chord. Everybody thought I was nuts, but it worked. I remember the look on [producer] Glen Ballard's face when he walked into the studio and saw what I was doing. He said, 'Only you would think of doing something like that.' I had to do whatever it took to get the song done."

Some of his stories regarding his health care seemed quite far-fetched at the time, but most of them later checked out to be fairly accurate. In the conversation below, Ed provided a glimpse into what was going through his mind during those difficult days.

**You were out of the picture for quite a while.**
Well, a lot happened to me. I had hip-replacement surgery, I beat cancer, and my marriage ended. Those were all important and difficult events and I needed time to deal with them. There was nothing really mysterious about any of it, but all three of those things were extremely personal, and I didn't feel the need to share them with the public. But I never stopped making music. I worked through those issues, and I discovered there was a light at the end of the tunnel. And it wasn't an oncoming train. It changed my life forever, but there's nothing that can keep me down. Whatever stands before me, I will deal with it.

**How would you describe Van Halen at this moment?**
Van Halen is something that is very difficult to explain, pigeonhole or put your finger on. I look at it as this creature that just won't go away, because we just are. My brother Alex always says, "You don't work music, you play it," but it takes a lot of hard work to be able to play it. The reason I have never done a solo project is that takes a team, and the team we have now is more powerful, soulful, and more fun, with a depth that nobody can deny. I'm proud to be part of it, I'll tell you.

But without my brother, who is the key, I would not be. He is and has been there for me since before I was born. We fight, argue—we even argue about agreeing on things—but there is a bond and unconditional love that very few people ever experience in their lifetime. I do accept and own my power. Without me, there also is no Van Halen, because it starts with me.

We are not a rock band. We are a rock and roll band. Alex is the rock—I'm the roll. He inspires me in a way I can't even begin to describe. I don't think he even knows. I'm probably the most blessed person on this planet.

**After *Van Halen III*, the band was quiet between 1999 and 2004. What happened?**

A lot. Those years were a hell of a trip. The three songs we recorded for *The Best of Both Worlds*, "It's About Time," "Learning to See," and "Up for Breakfast," reflected that. After my health problems, it was huge to have Mike and Sammy back in my life. I think we grew up a bit. I know I did. And we were tighter, deeper, funnier, and more of a team than ever before. Van Halen was back.

**What else changed?**

I accepted my God-given power for the first time in my life. I was in therapy for many years, and my therapist kept telling me, "Focus on yourself, focus on yourself, focus on yourself." I finally got the hint. Now, when I go onstage, if people start chanting, "Eddie, Eddie, Eddie," like they have in the past, I'm not going to try to silence them because the lead singer doesn't dig it. Instead, I'm going to say "thank you." That's called owning your power; it's not abusing it.

The whole time I was growing up, my mom used to call me a "nothing nut, just like your father." When you grow up that way, it's not conducive for self-esteem. That's why I try to go all-out for my son, because positive support is what counts. I don't believe in punishment. I rarely told him, "Don't do this." Instead, I tried to make him think about the consequences of his actions and allowed him to make his own decisions. For example, if he talked back to me, I'd tell him, "If you treat someone else the way you're treating me, you'll get your ass kicked." He once asked, "What's that like?" And I responded, "You'll see." That's how you learn. Either listen or learn the hard way, but you will learn.

**How did you assert yourself musically?**

For the first time, I took real control in the studio. With the support and encouragement of our producer, Glen Ballard, and my best friend, Matt [Bruck, Van Halen associate], I basically engineered, mixed, and mastered all the new songs on *The Best of Both Worlds*. Throughout my career, I've relied on someone else to record my sound, and I can't say that I've ever been really happy with the end result. I never really understood why no one could capture the sounds I made on tape, but I never complained because professional engineers always intimidated me. But on those three songs I did most of the work myself, and I think I got pretty close.

**What did you do differently?**
In a nutshell: I eliminated as much as I could between the source and the tape. I recorded with no EQ from the board, and when I mixed the songs I simply adjusted levels. I got the sound I wanted on tape, so there was no need for any further compression or EQ. I'm all about making things simple. It's like my guitar: it has one knob. I don't know why you would need any more than that. Simple works for me. I really don't understand why engineers always want to make things so goddamn complicated. Job security, maybe?

I've got an SSL [Solid State Logic] board, but as far as I'm concerned, it's a million-dollar piece of shit. I've disabled it as much as I can, but it's incapable of being simple. I'd use my vintage Urei board, but I got talked into buying this, so I'm doing my best to make it work like an old analog machine. I don't know how to run it and I don't give a shit. I don't need state-of-the-art. I follow my heart.

**State-of-the-heart.**
That's a good way of putting it. I don't intellectualize my emotions, because you can't. I just am. Like in "Learning to See," the song says, "I can't pretend to be anything but me. I don't give a damn if you don't like who I am." If you got your eyes wide open and you can't see, then close your eyes and look within. You want inner peace, then look inward. That's how I kicked cancer's ass: I talked to it. I told the fucker the party was over. It's all about how you think.

**What's the trick to good engineering?**
Just using your ear, man. Remove the *g* from *gear*, and what do you have? Everything started falling into place with my music when I started taking more control over it. I had a studio engineer who I allowed to live in my house and use my studio for three and a half years, but I finally came to grips with the fact that he never really delivered the goods, so I let him go. He always did what *he* wanted to do, not what *I* wanted him to do.

**What happened after he left? Was it daunting to teach yourself how to use an SSL board?**

Have you ever seen the SSL manual? It's as thick as a phone book! I can't stand reading manuals, so I didn't bother. I thought, How hard could it be? So, of course, the next day, no matter how hard I tried, I couldn't do the simplest thing: get signal from my two overhead mics onto Track 1 and Track 2. I tried everything, but all I got was silence.

I was sort of embarrassed and I thought I was a total idiot. I was so frustrated that I literally started crying. Finally, as a last resort, I decided to replace the overheads with a couple of Shure SM57s, my workhorse mics. Immediately, I got a signal. And then it hit me: It wasn't my fault at all. My former engineer had been recording with two broken mics! Unbelievable.

That's just a snapshot of what it took for me to take control. I finally realized that all I really needed was me and Matt. We ran the whole place anyway; we didn't really need anyone else. We knew it would be hard and the hours would be long to learn how to run every aspect of the studio, but in the end we would get the clearest translation of our music, and that's exactly what happened. It took a little bit to get going, because I just wanted to play guitar, but within five months of experimentation we were getting things out of the studio that we had never gotten before. I learned how to use the SSL the way *I* need to use it.

I hate to admit that it has taken me close to fifty years to figure out how to take control of my life, but everything happens for a reason. I had to understand what life was all about before I could run my own studio. All in God's time, I guess.

**Did you also engineer Al's drums?**

Yes, I did. I used a combination of six mics on his kit: two overheads, two placed on the floor a couple feet away from his kit, and two farther away. Al gave me the biggest compliment he's ever paid me in his life by saying his drums have never sounded so good on tape. Again, there was no science involved. I just used my ear.

Everything was recorded using natural ambience. The only effect I used was an AMS delay on some of the guitar parts. I've always had an unorthodox but very simple approach to things, and when I have the courage of my convictions, it usually works. EQ is designed to subtract sound, not add it. When you use too much of it, you end up with Velveeta-cheese processed shit, so I decided not to use it at all.

**You mentioned that you also took charge of mastering the new songs. What did that entail?**

The most important thing I requested was that we not use any compression on the radio mixes. I figured music always gets compressed when it's played on the radio, so why compress it twice? Glen Ballard supported me on the idea, so we'll see how it goes. That was a huge breakthrough for me. It's something I've always wanted to try, and I'll always be grateful to Glen for supporting my decision to try it. I also asked Glen to give me three different versions of the master to choose from, and he did that, too. In fact, he thought it was a pretty good idea to try. I don't suffer from my mistakes—I grow. If I fall down the steps, I can always pick myself back up. You're not living unless you make some mistakes. That's the only way you grow.

**What brought Sammy Hagar back to the band?**

He called, we had a couple of good conversations, and he was back in. It was as simple as that. Usually, when bands break up and get back together, things are never quite the same. But I thought there was a chance because we were communicating a lot better. When Sam left the first time, he said a few things I didn't like, but we ended up talking about it and cleared it up. That's the way it's supposed to work. I gave him a hug and kiss today and told him that I loved him.

**What was the source of the problem?**

I've discovered that because I'm so unorthodox, sometimes just being me—this little fucking Dutch boy that learns from his mistakes—intimidates people. But I'm not out to prove jack shit. I just do what comes naturally, and it scares people.

**Isn't that part of asserting yourself?**

Yes, and I'm getting more comfortable expressing myself. In the past, I thought I was in control of my life, but in reality, I wasn't. Even though

I built my own studio and I've done most of the things I've wanted to do, I still allowed other people to make me feel guilty and bad for doing it. I allowed that, and I won't allow that anymore.

**What did you like about working with Glen Ballard?**
The guy understood me. Not the rock star . . . the musician. He understood the depth of me. The passion. He understood me in a way no producer ever had, and we inspired each other.

**The three new songs have a new sophistication.**
Well, hopefully, over the years you get better at what you do. But like I've been saying, by taking control over the recording process, I was able to accurately capture what was given to me. I say "given to me" because I receive all my music in a completed form. I hear it before I play it. It's usually a matter of capturing what is in my head. I didn't allow anybody or anything to come between me and what was given to me. For the first time in my life, I felt comfortable doing what I do. And it's not about how many people like it; it's not preconceived or contrived. If one person is touched by it—like Matt, or you guys, or myself, or my son—then my mission is accomplished. I'm not motivated by money, fame, or ego.

**Your approach to playing rhythm guitar has also evolved. Instead of repeating your parts over the verses, on the last album and this one, your rhythm parts are more like a variation on a theme.**
I get easily bored playing the same thing, so I gave myself the freedom to change and play variations within the context of a song. Who made the rule that you have to play the same rhythm part under every verse? I'm not afraid to fall on my face. I think my ability has grown tenfold over what was on our early records, and it's because I care so much. I care so much that I don't care. It means so much to me that I allow myself to fail.

I'm very simple in my complication and very complicated in my simplicity. If I hear a sound in my head, I will stop at nothing to achieve it, because I feel there is nothing given to me that can't be achieved. It's a matter of letting go and being open to any possibility. I don't take prisoners 'cause I don't know where to store 'em. (*laughs*)

**What do you think of Pro Tools?**

If you ask me, the invention of Pro Tools—that's when the music business went down the tubes. Pro Tools tends to remove the life from music by making everything so asshole tight. I love slop. I love life. I love things that breathe. My dad called it "swing"; I call it a "groove." You want Velveeta or do you want something that is real?

**If you were creating your own Van Halen greatest hits album, what songs would you choose?**

I don't know, because I feel the best is yet to come.

**Depending on who sings the song, does your songwriting change?**

No, the music just comes to me. But I always give the singer, whoever they may be, the first right of refusal. If I have a different idea in mind, I will ask for them to try it, it's collaboration.

**Do you ever feel Van Halen's contribution to modern music is overlooked?**

Not really. That part of it is neither here nor there for me, and I don't look at music that way. Music is not a competitive sport; it's not about credit; it's just about the music.

**How much guitar have you played over the last six years?**

A lot, but I played more cello and piano. I only sleep about three or four hours a day, because there are so many things to deal with. I've learned to manage my time a little better.

Somebody recently turned me on to the classical cellist Yo-Yo Ma. I don't even know how to tune the instrument properly, but I can play whatever he does, because I just let it be. I'm not practicing, I'm just playing. I've never practiced a day in my life. Even if I have to relearn one of my old songs for a tour, I don't call it "practicing."

**Is it hard for you to remember how to play your old songs?**

Sometimes, but everything falls into place after I remember the first couple of chords. The truth is, I'd rather move forward. God put our eyes in the front of our head for a reason. When preparing for this tour, it took me a little time to relearn some of the older songs, because I don't sit around listening to my own shit; I'm always writing and moving forward. I only look back to remember what not to do.

**What Van Halen song is the most challenging song for you to play?**
Probably "Learning to See" because I have to replicate with one guitar what took six guitars to record. I have to make ten effects changes on the song to get it as close as I can, and most of the time I get pretty damn close to pulling it off.

**Do you have a large backlog of songs and ideas on tape?**
Yes, literally thousands. I write something almost every day. I have so much material that I never really have the time to sit down and listen to it all. I'd rather just write something new.

**What do you think of Howard Stern? He's always getting on your ass.**
Howard has never actually said a bad thing about me. He just sets the stage for other people to say things about me. He lets people embarrass themselves. That's how he makes his living, and I congratulate him on that. Howard is very clever, and I think he actually likes me, but I frustrate him because when he or one of his guys ask me a question, I turn it around on them and never answer anything. I think he's actually a huge fan of the band.

**You've had your share of disagreements with people in your band over the years. Do you think you are difficult to get along with?**
It's difficult to be in a relationship with me because I'm just like a cat, dog, or an animal who just eats, shits, fucks, and does whatever is needed. I don't enjoy eating all that much because every time I do, I have to shit, and I don't enjoy shitting. I have a fast metabolism, which means I have to shit five times a day and that's not fun. For one, it costs you a lot of toilet paper. (*laughs*)

**How was your hip surgery?**
The surgeon, Dr. John R. Moreland, was amazing, and I feel great. Beyond being a great surgeon, he actually designed the technology he uses. I have

one of the first prototype parts that they pound into your femur. It looks like a cheese grater—it's open so your bone goes into it. Because as young as I am and as active as I am, it has to be part of you. For older people, they just drill a hole and cement it in.

I was told I needed surgery around the time of the *Balance* tour [1995], but it was too late, and I couldn't back out of the tour. I went to the medical center and they said, "You're gonna go on tour like that?" I said, "Why not?" If you look at videos from that tour, you'll see I was heavier. I was in terrible pain, but Al told me just don't jump and run around, just play, so that's what I did. I started gaining weight, because I couldn't move around. Then my hip collapsed on me while playing soccer in the backyard with Wolfie.

**What was the operation like?**

It was a trip. I didn't want to be put under, I just want them to numb the area around it because I wanted to be wide awake and in control so I could call the shots in case something happened. The doctor told me that they would have to do a number of shots to numb the hip and that it would be painful. I said, How bad could it be? I knew the first shot would be the worst. But then you let it numb, then you get the second one and so on.

They said they wanted to have an anesthesiologist on hand in case I couldn't handle it, and I agreed to that. When the operation started, the anesthesiologist started giving me something anyway. As soon as I started feeling it, I pulled the oxygen mask off my face. After a discussion, Dr. Moreland agreed to let me stay conscious and told the anesthesiologist to leave the room.

I actually recorded the operation, too. Dr. Moreland spent twenty minutes with headphones to find the right place to put the microphone because he wanted to make it sound right. I wrote a song and had Alex play a drum pattern groove to match the noises, and it's all in Pro Tools.

**Not long after your hip surgery you were diagnosed with cancer. Do you feel comfortable talking about that experience?**

I haven't really talked about it much. I had my hip replaced on November 16, 1999, and two months later almost to the day, on my dad's birthday, January 18, 2000, I got diagnosed as having tongue cancer.

The hospital cut out a third of my tongue and told me to stop smoking and it won't come back. What was weird was there was no follow-up. They didn't say come back. But in April, I felt something wasn't right, so I went back. The first thing the doctor asked was, "Have you been smoking?" And I said, "What am I? A fucking idiot? You told me to stop and it wouldn't come back. But I'm telling you, something is going on, and it's very important to know what it is."

Mike Post, who produced *Van Halen III*, recommended I go to the MD Anderson Cancer Center in Houston, Texas, and the pathologist there said I still had a massive amount of cancer on my tongue, and they wanted to hack more of my tongue off.

What was really funny is that they used me. Somehow news leaked that I was going there because I came home and on the six o'clock news Dan Rather was saying, "Up next, Eddie Van Halen has cancer." When I went back, they give me an alias, which they should've done in the first place. But I think they got what they wanted out of me.

In the meantime, I was also exploring all this holistic stuff, but it wasn't really getting me anywhere. But through all these people, I ended up finding two great doctors—an ear, nose, and throat specialist named Dr. Salim Matar and a pathologist named Dr. Steve McClain. Dr. McClain helped save my life along with all the people that truly, unconditionally loved me.

**I couldn't help but notice that you're still smoking.**

I don't think cigarettes gave me cancer. I still smoke and drink red wine because I proved that's not how I got it. I got it from holding a pick in my mouth for years . . . a metal pick. For years doing this. (*puts a pick in his mouth*) I was a living EMF [electromagnetic field]. Walking around with a lightning rod in my mouth. I'm putting everything together. I have a theory that it came from electromagnetic energy. I used metal picks that I always held in my mouth when I tapped, and it's in the same exact place where I got the tongue cancer. I also spend so much time in a recording studio that's filled with electromagnetic energy. I mean, I was smoking and doing drugs, but at the same time, my lungs were clear.

**You played with a metal pick?**
Yeah, that was my bag. What do you think I made those sounds with?

**How did you beat cancer?**
When you beat cancer, you have to change your life. If you have your eyes wide open and can't see, well then close them and look inside if you want inner peace. That's how I kicked cancer's ass, I talked to it. You're one of the only people I've ever talked to about this—how I beat cancer. I attacked it multidimensionally—spiritually, how I thought, environmentally, nutritionally. It's a life-form of its own—it's just looking for a host. I wasn't about to drink Drano, because that's all chemotherapy is.

**Tell us more about Dr. McClain.**
He's starting his own pathology lab and I'm investing in it. He told me he wasn't supposed to get emotionally involved with his patients, and I said the fact that you said that proves you already are.

**What's the nature of your partnership with the doctor?**
I'm helping him, because he helped me. We inspire each other.

**Are you still in therapy?**
Yeah. My therapist always tells me to focus on myself. She told me that hundreds of times. If you're depending on someone else for your happiness, you've got it wrong. I'm there for people, and I'll help people and they'll help me, but you can't put your life in their hands. People will only do to you what you allow them to do. It's not their responsibility, either . . . they'll probably fuck it up.

**Have you been able to focus on music through all of this?**
(*aggressively*) It's got nothing to do with music. Music is something that comes from . . . I don't know where, but definitely a higher place. Somewhere else that is out of my control. I keep my chops up. It takes me about an hour to warm up. If you want me to come up onstage and jam, it'll take me three hours because I can't just come up and do that, but I can still play some wicked-ass shit.

Hagar came in recently, and I said, "See these?" (*points to a stack of CDs and tapes with studio music on them*) Take your pick—they all have music on them. I have so much stuff. I'm always writing. But I don't sit around listening to my old stuff.

**You're getting ready to go out on the road. You haven't played with Sammy for close to a decade. Do you remember how to play those older songs?**

Yeah! It took me forever to remember how to play the ending to "Dreams," which I guess proves I didn't write it—it came through me.

# MUSICAL INTERLUDE

*A conversation with Van Halen bassist*
**Michael Anthony**, *Part II*

---

Whenever things became contentious between the Van Halen brothers and their various lead singers, bassist Mike Anthony regularly found himself caught in the crossfire. Though he did his best to steer clear of any internal disputes, his neutrality was often met with some scorn from both sides, and eventually he was edged out of the band in 2004.

His dismissal had been in the air for some time. From the time Van Halen was formed, Mike had been a 20 percent member of all profits including merchandise. Then, midway through the band's 1984 tour, David Lee Roth and the Van Halen brothers suddenly insisted one night that he sign away all future songwriting credits and royalties, retroactive to their current *1984* album.

Although it is true that Anthony did not contribute much to the songwriting process, this must have stung. Nevertheless, Mike did a great job of masking his feelings and remained a staunch booster of the band throughout its many twists and turns.

Anthony was never officially let go from Van Halen, but when Ed and Al reunited with David Lee Roth in 2007, they announced that Eddie's son, Wolfgang, would be their bassist. If Mike was upset about it, he kept it to himself and stayed busy, mostly playing with Sammy Hagar in bands such as The Waboritas, the Circle, and Chickenfoot, a supergroup that also featured guitarist Joe Satriani and Red Hot Chili Peppers drummer Chad Smith.

In the following interview conducted for this book, the bassist talks about the band's post-1984 years. And though he was upbeat, he did toss out a few zingers that suggested that, beneath his good-natured veneer, he still feels hurt by the way his career with Van Halen came to an end.

*Starting with 1984, Van Halen pivoted to a more radio-friendly sound.*

None of that was really a conscious effort. We never said, "Hey, we need to write a hit song," or "We should try this formula." Ed just wrote what he felt, and we played along.

*The production became more polished.*

We would always laugh when we heard about bands that did all these elaborate overdubs in the studio. We were always in the mindset of, "If we can't play this live, then why should we record it?" Let's record it how it's going to sound when we play it live, because we don't want to have to hire musicians. On the second album we loosened up a little. We would add an extra little rhythm track here, whatever, but it wasn't anything that we couldn't cover live.

Playing with Sammy was completely different than Dave, so our sound changed. Sam had a greater understanding of songwriting from a guitar perspective, because he's a pretty solid player. Where Dave would go, "Hey, what if . . ." and sang something, Sammy would go "Hey, what if . . ." and pick up a guitar and play something. He had that musical sense and knowledge about how we could take an arrangement further. Maybe that's probably why a lot of the stuff started to sound more song-oriented and less of a jam.

Van Halen songs were always written around licks that Ed would come up with. If you took the vocal away from it, especially with Dave, you could still get away with just listening to the music because every song was almost written like an instrumental. A lot of times it would just be Ed, Alex, and myself jamming in the rehearsal room or whatever, and Ed would break into a rhythm and we would sort of figure out where the vocals would go. When we were done, we'd say, "Okay, Dave, put some words to it."

*When Dave was in the band, Van Halen almost reminded me of a jazz band—four guys bouncing off a groove. And when Sammy came in, there was structure, for better or worse.*

That's fair. Sammy knew more about song structure, because he'd been doing his thing. We felt he elevated the band.

**Could you give me a quick sketch of the different producers that worked with the band after Ted Templeman? How did Mick Jones impact the 5150 sessions?**

We needed—and *wanted*—that outside opinion. We would always say that if it was left to us, each of our songs would be about ten minutes long and it'd take us about three years to record an album. (*laughs*) You know, each song would have a five-minute guitar intro before the band would come in. Mick Jones really helped a lot as far as the song structure and stuff like that.

We really learned a lot from Ted, though. He was great at identifying parts that would work or seeing potential in cover material. For example, we used to play the song "You're No Good" in the clubs, and Ted would say, "Man, that could be a hit again." Or when Ted insisted on us doing "Dancing in the Street." None of us really were into doing it, but it was a hit for us.

**From what I understand, Andy Johns was a little wilder. He was more like a band member.**

Well, he was great for me on a personal level. I loved Donn Landee as an engineer, but he was used to working with people like Linda Ronstadt and the Doobie Brothers, who used a rounder, more subliminal bass sound. On most of his records, you could feel the bass, but the bass players didn't have their own sound. There was no identity.

I clicked with Andy almost instantly because for the first time we had a producer that cared about my sound. Suddenly, it was like, "Mike, have you ever tried re-amping your bass?" And I was like, "No, what's that?" The next thing I knew, it was like, "Oh, fuck. You can actually hear me." It was almost shocking. I loved Andy to death, man. We had the best time working with him on *For Unlawful Carnal Knowledge*, and I thought it was a great record and a great-*sounding* record. He helped us get our edge back.

**The album has a bit of that Led Zeppelin bite and grandeur.**

Alex was always a huge Zeppelin fan. He always loved John Bonham's snare sound, and he chased that tone forever. The biggest fight he would get into with our producers would be about his snare sound. He'd bring in a copy of "Stairway to Heaven" and say, "I want that!" So, he flipped when Andy brought in one of his snares that Bonzo had used. Most of our recording sessions would end with us sitting around Andy like little kids at a campfire while he would tell us Zeppelin stories.

**What did you think of Al's drum sound?**

Al had his own very identifiable sound. People take it for granted, but most other drummers sound like they are hitting a piece of paper compared to him—his sound always had body and tone. Sometimes it was a pain in the ass for me. Both Al and Eddie had such big sounds, it was difficult to fit the bass in.

**What did you think of Bruce Fairbairn?**

He didn't have the impact Andy did. We sorta knew what we wanted to sound like by *Balance*. Some of our producers were just babysitters, but we would always try new people because we'd be curious to see how different producers heard us.

**What did you think of Ed's relationship with engineer Donn Landee? It seemed like they took over for a while on 1984 and OU812.**

There were times where we'd record something and finish up for the day, then everybody would go home and then the next day you come in and everything would be different. Ed and Donn would just go into the studio all night and change everything around. It worried me a little bit when I'd leave for the day and go, "Man, this is sounding really good," while thinking, "Oh my God, I hope nothing gets erased by the time I come back in tomorrow afternoon." It used to really irk Sammy, too. It would've bothered anybody.

On some level, 5150 was great, because we had our own place, and we could do what we wanted and come and go as we pleased. Ed always left the gear on 24/7 so you could go and mess around anytime. But I lived about a good forty-five minutes away, so it's not like I would go, "Hey, yeah, I'm going to go up to the studio in the middle of the night." But Ed could just walk right up the driveway and be there.

After a while it became a bit of a curse, because Ed got too comfortable there. On occasion we wanted to go to another studio to record vocals just for a change of scenery, but that almost never happened. That's where some of the drama came in, but I don't want to rehash all of that.

*You were sort of the John Paul Jones of the band. His policy in Led Zeppelin was to simply stay clear when things got weird with substance abuse or personality issues.*

Yeah, Ed and Al would call me "Switzerland," because I'd try to stay neutral. When things would get heated, I would often think to myself, "Why is this argument even happening? It doesn't need to be happening."

My goal was to do the best job I could do. I didn't like the fighting. I tried to stay out of the fray because if I said anything, it would be just one more cook in the pot, which would make any given argument last even longer. It's been exaggerated how contentious the arguments were. Things could get heated, but most of the time we were able to take a step back and remember what it was we were trying to do before we started to overthink things.

*But eventually you and the Van Halen brothers parted ways. Was the fallout due to Ed's substance abuse or was there something deeper?*

Without really getting into it, there were times when somebody had to be blamed for something, and whether or not I had anything to do with it, they would blame me. And for the life of me, I wouldn't know why. But it was probably because of problems somebody else was having.

Towards the end, it wasn't even about music. I blame our manager Ray Danniels for Sammy leaving the band—or being kicked out—depending on who you talk to. I remember Sammy telling him, "Hey, you do what you do, and you let me do what I do."

Ray was the one that started the rift between Ed and Sammy. He created the bad blood. When you work with people and they keep saying the same things and keep drilling it and drilling it and drilling it, you start thinking, "Wow, maybe they're right." Or "We should be doing this or that." And that's as far as I'll go with that.

**What was the atmosphere like when Gary Cherone was in the band?**

It was a very tumultuous time. We actually did a couple group therapy sessions with Dallas Taylor, who used to play drums with Crosby, Stills, Nash and Young and became a counselor. We had heard bands like Aerosmith went through therapy and used it to air their problems. It was interesting.

But the most difficult period was the 2004 reunion tour with Sammy—that was like a trip to hell. It was a very dark time in Ed's life. I never thought that what I was doing could really be considered work, but that was *work*.

**Did you have any opportunities to resolve your conflicts with Ed before he died?**

Not really. There are still a few issues that I wish we could've talked about. A couple years ago [2018], our manager Irving Azoff called me about doing a reunion. I knew Ed was ill, but they told me that he was going through some treatments, and after he was finished, we'd be good to go.

I guess Ed got too ill. I don't know the whole story, but it would've been great to tour with the band again. All the money aside, I would've loved to have done it . . . just to have been able to jam with those guys and talk with them like we used to.

# 10

# THE WHOLE TRUTH

*After starting an entirely new chapter in Van Halen's
history with his son Wolfgang in the band and David
Lee Roth back in the fold, Ed finally embraces sobriety.*

---

" [Dave's] lyrics are hilarious ... I think he's brilliant. "

---

V AN HALEN'S 2004 tour might have been a success from a
financial perspective, grossing more than $50 million, but
from an interpersonal and psychological perspective, it
was a massive disaster. Before the tour even started, signs of tension had
already appeared. The Van Halen brothers did not want bassist Michael
Anthony to participate, and they only relented after Sammy Hagar issued
an ultimatum that he would not tour unless Anthony was included. An
agreement was finally reached after Anthony accepted terms to work
as a "hired gun," which involved accepting a significant pay cut from
the share he previously received as a band member, relinquishing his
rights to use of the Van Halen name and logo, and losing his share of
merchandise sales.

"What happened on that reunion tour was some of the most mis-
erable, back-stabbing, dark crap I've ever been involved with my whole

life," Hagar told journalist Sally Steele in 2012.[18] Ed's excessive drinking was a huge problem, and he was also infuriated with Hagar's refusal to stop the shameless promotion of the singer's Cabo Wabo tequila during shows. These issues drove a huge wedge between the Van Halen brothers on one side and Hagar and Anthony on the other to the point where the two factions stayed in different hotels and traveled on different buses. The only time the band spent together was while they were performing. Hagar tried to quit halfway through the tour and only stayed when he was threatened with a breach of contract lawsuit. By the end of the tour, Hagar and Ed were no longer on speaking terms.

As dismal as that tour was, there was one highlight for the guitarist that provided the first rays of hope for his eventual redemption. Ed's thirteen-year-old son Wolfgang joined his father onstage on numerous occasions to play rhythm guitar on the song "316," which was Ed's heartfelt tribute to his son. When Ed and Wolfgang performed together, it was one of the rare moments on tour when Ed's savage beast was soothed.

The tour wrapped up on November 19, 2004, in Tucson, Arizona, with a show Hagar later described as the "worst we'd ever done in our lives." As Ed returned home to his 5150 studio, he was faced with a future without a band for the first time in more than three decades. Around the time that the tour had begun, Ed had also severed his endorsement deal with Peavey, which had manufactured his 5150 amps since 1992 and his Wolfgang guitars since 1996. So many significant changes were taking place in Ed's life that it seemed like he was either starting anew or burning bridges in an attempt to reinvent himself.

During 2005, Ed secluded himself from the music world. His only press coverage during this period was in paparazzi photos in the tabloid media and in lurid reports that speculated about his declining health and new romantic partners. When Ed's mother, Eugenia, passed away on August 4 of that year, he withdrew even further from the public eye. Then on December 7, he was dealt a second heavy personal blow when Valerie Bertinelli officially filed for divorce after five years of separation.

"When he played," Bertinelli wrote in 2008, "he disappeared into a world that was his. There he was most comfortable, and whatever he shared was of his own choosing. This interior world would confound, anger, and frustrate me to no end later on, but early on it was seductive."[19]

Ed finally emerged during the summer of 2006 to announce that he had composed some new music, which turned out to be far different from what any of Van Halen's biggest fans could have imagined. On July 26, a press release revealed that he'd recorded two songs—"Catherine" and "Rise"—for the adult film *Sacred Sin* directed by Michael Ninn. In addition to writing the music, Ed also helped fund the production and allowed his house and property to be used for the filming of several sex scenes. This was one of only a handful of instances when a famous musician composed music for a pornographic film, and Ed's example was particularly unique because he was a bona fide A-list star who did it *after* he had achieved fame and he used his own name instead of a pseudonym.

The scenario of Ed making "boom chicka wow-wow" music and producing porn caused many of his fans to worry that he had gone off the deep end to the point of no return. The six-minute video he made for "Catherine" appeared to support signs of his descent into madness, as it showed the sweaty, shirtless guitarist alone in a darkened 5150, a bottle of wine on the mixing console and a cigarette dangling from his lips, violently molesting his Peavey Wolfgang guitar and angrily slamming it onto the studio floor at the video's end. The end result looked more like an act of rape than a passionate performance.

But the video did hint at a few big changes that were coming down the line. In the clip, behind Eddie were stacks of amps featuring the oval EVH logo (his own brand) that had first appeared on the 2004 Charvel Art Series guitars that led in part to Van Halen's departure from Peavey. Also, fans were relieved that Ed was still writing music, and the emergence of the two new instrumental tracks gave them hope that the guitarist might be working on a solo album.

But two even more important developments were taking place behind the scenes, both of which played significant roles in Ed's recovery. While working with Michael Ninn, the guitarist met Janie Liszewski, who was Ninn's publicist. Janie soon became Ed's publicist and girlfriend—his first truly serious relationship since his split from Valerie. Also, during the summer of 2006, Ed started jamming regularly with his drummer-guitarist son Wolfgang, who had recently started playing bass. Ed was blown away by his son's rapid progress on the instrument, as was Alex when he joined the two for their regular jam sessions.

Ed first revealed that Wolfgang had become the band's new bassist on the *Howard Stern Show* on Sirius satellite radio and confirmed that development in October 2006 during an interview with *Guitar World* magazine. "My son is only fifteen and has been playing bass for three months," Ed said. "It's spooky. He's locked tight and brings youthfulness to something that's inherently youthful. He breathes new life into what we're doing. I can't wait to see what he does onstage."

An even bigger surprise was Ed's announcement that he was launching his own musical instrument company, EVH. This was not the usual artist endorsement deal but a full-fledged brand directed and developed by the guitarist himself, with manufacturing and distribution to be handled by Fender's parent company FMIC (Fender Musical Instrument Corporation).

"Fender builds my stuff for me," said Van Halen, "but it's my own company. I started it because I want to do what I fuckin' want. What I'm doing now is like an extension of how I started. Nobody made what I need or want, so I made it myself. It's great to see my ideas become reality."

In 2007, EVH introduced its very first product—a limited-edition exact replica of Ed's red, white, and black Frankenstein guitar, with every ding, dent, and scratch meticulously duplicated. That was followed by the 5150 III amp in 2008 and an entirely new and redesigned Wolfgang model guitar a year later. The 5150 III and Wolfgang remain the company's best-selling products to this day, and over the years EVH has offered an impressive selection of guitar and amp models as well as accessories.

Then Ed dropped the biggest bombshell of all: "There's a possibility of doing something with [David Lee] Roth," he revealed. "I can't confirm or deny it right now, but the ball is in Dave's court. Whether he wants to rise to the occasion is up to him, but we're ready to go."

Roth accepted the Van Halens' offer, and on January 26, 2007, the band officially announced that Roth was back. Plans for a summer tour were released a few days later, but that turned out to be a false start; news of the tour's postponement leaked in late February. The reason? Ed's sudden admission into an undisclosed rehabilitation facility. Although he seemed fine by the time Van Halen held a press conference to announce the tour, the guitarist was still drinking heavily. It is speculated that Wolfgang, not wanting to see a repeat of the band's 2004 tour debacle, allegedly insisted that he would not be a part of it unless his father was sober.

After entering rehab, Ed issued the following statement: "I would like Van Halen fans to know how much I truly appreciate each and every one of you. Without you there is no Van Halen. I have always and will always feel a responsibility to give you my best. At the moment I do not feel that I can give you my best. That's why I have decided to enter a rehabilitation facility to work on myself, so that in the future I can deliver the 110 percent that I feel I owe you and want to give you. Some of the issues surrounding the 2007 Van Halen tour are within my ability to change and some are not. As far as my rehab is concerned, it is within my ability to change and change for the better. I want you to know that is exactly what I'm doing, so that I may continue to give you the very best I am capable of. I look forward to seeing you in the future better than ever and I thank you with all my heart."

Ed was still in rehab when the Rock and Roll Hall of Fame inducted Van Halen at its annual ceremony on March 12, 2007. Out of respect for him, his brother Alex and Roth decided to not attend, but Sammy Hagar and Michael Anthony showed up to represent the band. Ed had already made up his mind to continue without Hagar and Anthony after the duo toured in a band called the Other Half and performed Van Halen material without his approval or blessing. But their appearance at the Hall of Fame ceremony was especially damaging to their relationship. As a new chapter of Van Halen was about to start without Hagar and Anthony, seeing them at the induction was like watching a bride's ex-boyfriend crash her wedding and plant his meaty mitts on her butt during the reception.

In late May of 2007, Ed issued another statement announcing that he was out of rehab and expressing gratitude to his fans. "It was an intensely personal thing that I'm not really comfortable talking about right now," he said. "I want everyone to know that their support has and always will mean the world to me." Tour dates were officially announced around the same time, with the first of twenty-five shows scheduled to take place on September 27 in Charlotte, North Carolina. As the tour progressed and shows sold out, more dates extending into 2008 were added.

Van Halen's 2007–08 tour began well and received mostly positive reviews. Although Wolfgang was only sixteen years old and had a somewhat subdued stage presence, musically he fit right in like a seasoned pro, delivering powerful, punchy bass lines and expert harmony vocals. Ed performed well during the first month, but problems started to develop as the tour progressed. On November 3, 2007, during a show at the Meadowlands/Izod Center in East Rutherford, New Jersey, Ed became visibly upset at one point, violently throwing a stage monitor at a sound tech. Later, it was revealed that a blast of feedback had punctured the guitarist's eardrum. On several subsequent occasions, his solo segment was unusually sloppy, and rumors spread that Ed was drinking again.

The tour came to an abrupt halt after the February 20, 2008, show, and the next nineteen appearances were postponed. The only explanation for the stoppage that the band released was that Ed needed to undergo some urgent medical tests. The secrecy surrounding this news was baffling considering how forthcoming the guitarist had been about his physical ailments and substance abuse problems in the past, but now privacy had become the new norm.

All of the canceled dates were rescheduled, and the tour resumed as if nothing had happened on April 17, 2008, in Reno, Nevada. By the time the tour concluded on June 2, in Grand Rapids, Michigan, it had become the band's most profitable ever, grossing more than $93 million from seventy-six shows.

Ed became a legally free man when his divorce from Valerie was finalized on December 21, 2007. On August 4, 2008, he decided to get hitched once again—and proposed to Janie while they were on vacation in Hawaii. The two were married about eleven months later, in June 2009. The wedding took place at Ed's home in front of about a hundred guests, with Alex officiating the ceremony. Ed looked more fit and healthy than he had in decades, and more importantly, he was genuinely happy.

Ed had expressed his gratitude for his newfound sobriety and renewed positive outlook about a month earlier, when he accepted the Guitar God Award at the Spike TV Guy's Choice Awards. "I started drinking when I was twelve years old, when I started playing guitar," he said. "I quit a year ago—forty-two years later. That shows you anything is achievable. I want to thank my best friend and my son Wolfgang, my brother Alex, my friend Matthew Bruck, and most of all, my wife-to-be Janie. They have given me a reason to stop bullshitting myself, and that keeps me sober."

Later that summer after enjoying a honeymoon with his new bride, Ed traveled to Dusseldorf, Germany, to undergo surgery and arthritis treatment on his left hand, which he revealed during an interview with

# EDDIE'S ODDITIES

### GUITAR: EVH Wolfgang USA
### USED: On his final live performance

For Van Halen's 2015 tour, Ed initially planned on using the Wolfgang USA with a Stealth black finish and ebony fretboard with dot inlays that was his main guitar during Van Halen's entire 2012 tour as well as for the television appearances the band made in early 2015. However, shortly after rehearsals for the tour started, Ed took delivery of a Wolfgang USA guitar built by Chip Ellis featuring a heavily relic'd white finish, block fretboard inlays, and a custom kill switch, which Ed used to create stuttering staccato effects during "You Really Got Me" and his solo.

"I wanted a white guitar that was relic'd," Van Halen said. "Chip built that for me and did a wonderful job. I compared it to my trusty old Stealth, and the white guitar sounded better, so it immediately became my main guitar for rehearsals and the tour."

Although Ed loved the white Wolfgang USA, he found the neck a little thicker than he normally likes for his neck profiles. He sanded down the back of the neck until it was slim and comfortable enough for his preferences. "It's still a little fatter than the Stealth's neck, but I'm happy with it, so it stuck," he said.

The white Wolfgang also featured a custom-made BI Tech HPU low-friction volume pot designed to provide smooth, absolutely noise-free performance, which EVH also offered as an accessory that can be installed in any guitar. "We're testing it on this tour," Van Halen said. "It's the only volume pot I've found where I can play 'Cathedral' without any crackle or pop."

This was the very last guitar that Ed ever played onstage when he used it during Van Halen's final live performance on October 4, 2015, at the Hollywood Bowl. The concluding Db chord that Ed played on that guitar for the band's encore performance of "Jump" is still ringing out in the cosmos, as well as in the memories of Van Halen fans who witnessed what has now become a historic moment.

Tony Iommi on August 31. The specialist discovered a twisted tendon, and a bone spur and cyst in his thumb joint, which were the source of pain the guitarist felt during the 2007–08 tour. The surgery was successful, and after a few months of rehabilitation he was able to play better than he'd been able to for the previous ten years or so.

Ed expressed his reluctance to record new material during that interview with Iommi (see Musical Interlude, Chapter 3), but the following year, rumors that Van Halen was recording a new album emerged. In January of 2011, producer John Shanks, who had previously worked with Melissa Etheridge, Stevie Nicks, Joe Cocker, Santana, and many other artists, confirmed the rumors by tweeting a photo of an EVH amp logo and stating, "Here we go kids . . . VH." Details about the album and its progress remained scant during most of 2011, with only the message "Get ready" appearing on David Lee Roth's website in July.

As 2012 began, Van Halen announced that its forthcoming album would be called *A Different Kind of Truth*. A private preview show was held on January 5 in the cramped confines of the Greenwich Village nightclub Café Wha?, which was once owned by Roth's uncle Manny, who booked artists like Lenny Bruce, Bob Dylan, and Jimi Hendrix early in their careers before selling the club in 1968. Interscope Records released *A Different Kind of Truth* on February 7, 2012, and the album entered the Billboard 200 at number two.

Although Ed had never stopped writing new music during the fourteen years that passed between *Van Halen III* and *A Different Kind of Truth*, the new album consisted mostly of songs written before 1978. "We went through our archives of stuff we had already written," Ed explained. "Wolfgang picked out a bunch of tunes. The biggest trip is that I wrote some of those songs when I was still in high school and even junior high. When something is good, it's good."

Van Halen's tour in support of the album officially began on February 18, 2012, in Louisville, Kentucky, and continued through June 26 in New Orleans. But the third and fourth legs of their North American tour were postponed and subsequently canceled. An unfounded rumor that the band members were fighting made the rounds, but Roth squashed them by explaining that the band was getting along better than ever and that an overly ambitious schedule had simply left them feeling exhausted. During the hiatus, Ed underwent emergency surgery for diverticulitis in August, further putting tour plans on the backburner. A single-show appearance in Sydney, Australia, was added for April 2013, and a brief tour of Japan was rescheduled for June. Both would be the band's first appearances in those countries since 1998.

After performing at a pair of festivals in the United States in July 2013, Van Halen remained mostly silent for the next year and a half. During this period, Ed worked on new guitar products for EVH while Wolfgang started recording his first solo album, *Mammoth WVH*. He worked at 5150 with producer Michael "Elvis" Baskette (Alter Bridge/ Tremonti, Sevendust, Slash) and recorded all guitar, bass, drum, and vocal tracks by himself. Although most of the album was apparently completed by 2016, its release was delayed several times before it finally came out June 11, 2021.

In 2015, Van Halen activity started up once again, most notably with Ed's participation in "What It Means to Be American," a program hosted by the think tank Zócalo Public Square at the Smithsonian National Museum of American History on February 12. Before the event, Ed presented to the museum a replica of his black and white Frankenstein guitar along with one of his recent EVH Wolfgang USA stage guitars and an EVH 5150 III half stack. These instruments joined the replica of Ed's red, black, and white Frankenstein that the Smithsonian previously acquired for its collection in January 2011.

Next, Van Halen released its first live album featuring David Lee Roth as its lead singer, *Tokyo Dome Live in Concert*. The album, which featured an extended two-hour set, was recorded during the band's June 21, 2013, show. Shortly after the album's release on March 31, Van Halen made its first-ever television appearances, first on *Jimmy Kimmel Live!* on March 30 and 31, followed by *The Ellen DeGeneres Show* on April 2.

The Kimmel appearance was particularly noteworthy because the band appeared on a stage built on Hollywood Boulevard, which was shut down for the filming and packed with thousands of fans. The performance was cut short during the first song, "Hot For Teacher," after Roth whacked himself in the nose and started bleeding while twirling a steel baton. Roth returned later with a bandage across his swollen schnoz, joking, "How do I look? Like fucking Hiawatha, right?" Whereas this sort of mishap would in the past have led to arguments and fisticuffs, the entire band took the nationally televised setback in stride with shrugs and giggles.

That spirit of camaraderie continued as the band went on its last-ever tour, which started on July 5 in Auburn, Washington, and ended with a two-night stand at the Hollywood Bowl on October 2 and 4, 2015. In addition to being a triumphant homecoming for the band, the two Hollywood Bowl shows turned out to be Edward Van Halen's final public concert performances. He was in exceptionally fine form throughout the entire tour, playing with truly impressive intensity and precision. And his playing at the final show, particularly during his solo segment, was unusually transcendent and uplifting. The fans in attendance had no idea that they were witnessing history, but the divine powers of the universe certainly knew.

**In 2009, you said you weren't sure if you wanted to make a new Van Halen album, but here it's 2012 and you've released _A Different Kind of Truth_. What changed your mind?**

I think I was pissed off at the time. I didn't want to do something new because even if I did, the fans wouldn't like it anyway. We just snapped back and realized that, Hey, we're doing this for us, too. This is what we do. We make music for a living. Like I've always said, if you like what you're doing, you're halfway there. If someone else likes it, then that's even better. If they don't like it, at least you like it. Not to be selfish, but you kind of have to be. You can't second guess what the audience is going to like. If you make something that you think the fans are going to like but you don't, you're double fucked if they don't like it.

The other thing, which is very important with this band, is that it takes four people to decide. It wasn't really for me to say at the time, but it eventually became something that I wanted to do. Obviously, I wanted to make a record with Wolfgang, but I couldn't do that until Al and Dave were on board. I couldn't speak for them. What changed was that Al and Dave said, "Let's go!"

We went up to 5150 and started jamming. It felt like a comfortable old pair of shoes. Working with Dave was like we had never left each other. It was that comfortable. We've known each other since high school, so . . . When you have old friends, five or six years can go by when you don't see each other, but you just pick up where you left off. I have this friend, Mark Alexander, who lives out in Bora Bora, and I see him maybe once every ten years, but we just pick up where we left off. It's the same thing with Dave.

**What got the ball rolling on this album?**

Wolfgang's enthusiasm. He was going, "Come on, come on!" We started at the studio at my house with just Alex, Wolfgang, and me. Basically, it's the same way we start any record. "She's the Woman" was the first song Wolfgang picked. We started jamming on songs like "She's the Woman" and "Bullethead" and reworked them. Dave was onboard from the beginning, but he was the last to show up because I was already recording and engineering demos of "She's the Woman," "Bullethead," and "Let's Get Rockin'," which is now called "Outta Space." I sent Pro Tools files of recordings over to Dave, who was working over at Henson Studios where he likes to record, which got him totally excited. He said, "Let's get going!"

**How did you choose John Shanks?**

The most difficult part of the process was deciding whether or not we should use a producer and who we should use. We had a big list of producers. Ever since we did that interview together with Tony Iommi, I've been in contact with Tony a lot. Sabbath was doing their reunion, and they were working with Rick Rubin. I didn't think Rick was the right producer for the kind of band that Van Halen is, but his name was in the hat. So was Pat Leonard. Dave doesn't have a home studio, so he goes down to Henson to record, write, and keep his voice in shape. One day he told me that he ran into this guy named John Shanks. I thought he was an odd choice, but we were open to anything. The first meeting with him was a little odd, because we're really used to not working with a producer and we weren't sure what he was going to be doing. That was my big question. He asked what we had. I played him our three demos and he loved them.

The initial plan for this album, which was actually Wolf's idea, was to record three reworked songs, which would be new to our audience. The rest of the album was going to be a "greatest hits" collection of our B sides. Instead of the "Best Of" it would be the "B's Of," you know, songs like "Drop Dead Legs," "Girl Gone Bad"—a record of all the deep tracks, which I'd still like to do sometime in the future. It was supposed to be a record of our more hardcore songs and none of the pop stuff.

But the deeper we dug, the more we found. At the same time, I was writing new songs. Dave got very excited about that. We all did. We ended up recording demos for thirty-five songs. All of those songs were ready to go, and we were able to play them all. As we were getting ready to finally record the album, we called John again and asked, "Are you busy? Do you want to come up to 5150 and take a listen?" He was like, "Whoa! You've got a shitload of songs here!" We left it to John and Wolfgang to pick the songs, and it all went from there. Then we went to Henson and started recording.

It was a pleasant experience, although I missed working at home. I'm used to the monitors I have at 5150. After we went to Henson, we had to redo all of the guitars and all of the bass at 5150 because I couldn't hear them at Henson the way I'm used to. It was the same thing when Ross Hogarth did the mixing. He tried to do it at Henson, but he couldn't hear the guitars, so we mixed at 5150. The process of making the record was very simple. It took us maybe three weeks to lay down all the instrumental tracks. We played live and we were super rehearsed. We made a few nips and tucks here and there, but everything was pretty much there.

**How did it feel to make your first album with Wolfgang?**
The process itself was a lot of fun. It was great to watch Wolfgang work in an actual professional recording studio with a producer actually making a record, which was different than watching him work at 5150. He took the bull by the horns. He had a lot to say. I was shocked by all the great ideas he had, and he was very opinionated.

Wolfgang came up with the arrangement for "Stay Frosty." When Dave wrote it, it was just an acoustic thing like it is on the intro. Wolf turned it into what it is. It was interesting to watch, especially John's take on it. I think he was actually a bit intimidated by a twenty-year-old kid telling him how things should go. He was used to working with very young artists, which is why I initially thought he was an oddball choice. We already knew about song structure, so basically all we really needed was an outside opinion. I always think a producer should be an outside ear, whereas I think he's used to making records where he has to do pretty much everything for the young artists he produces.

I think Wolfie threw him a major curveball. It shocked him, so I think he tried to lean towards working with me, but I said, "He's a member of the band. You've got to deal with him, too." When I played my solos, I'd walk out of the room and leave Wolfie there to pick the best take. Sometimes I'd hear him arguing with John, which was funny. It was neat to watch Wolfgang stand up for what he believed in and thought was right. He'd tell John which part he thought was better and John would sit there and go, "Okay."

John is a great guy. We weren't there the whole time he was working with Dave, because Dave prefers to work at night and we like to start working at noon. Since my old life has kind of changed, I'm now waking up at six in the morning. If we start working at night I'm ready to hit the sack. We weren't there when a lot of the lead vocals were being recorded, but I think John did a great job.

**It must have been a relief for you to relinquish some control over the band to Wolfgang. In the past you were almost entirely responsible for that role.**

It was a relief in a lot of ways, especially since this was the first record that I've ever made being sober and I was nervous. I was glad Wolfgang wanted to do that. I said, "Go ahead!" I was as nervous as a motherfucker. Why? God only knows. I still get nervous every night before I go out onstage. It keeps you on your toes.

**It's interesting to compare your solos on the old original demos to the ones you recorded for the new album. Some of them are very different.**

You know me, I'm the kind of guy who likes to wing it. I don't plan out my solos. The one solo that I had to plan out was on "She's the Woman." I have to grab my guitar to show you it. (*opens case and pulls out a Wolfgang Custom*) The original breakdown of "She's the Woman" ended up being the breakdown in "Mean Street." Wolfgang came up with a new breakdown that had these crazy chord changes. (*plays chords to new breakdown*) The chord changes were so fuckin' weird, but I didn't even think about them until I had to solo over it. I couldn't just go—(*plays notes in a pentatonic scale*) It wouldn't be in key. Instead, I had to go like this: (*plays melodic line from solo*).

I never really worked out a solo like that before. It took me a couple of days to figure out what notes worked against those chords. If I don't hit these particular notes (*plays solo*), it wouldn't work. It flipped me out. When we did the demo, Matt [Bruck] punched me in and I just sat there going, "Goddamn. This doesn't work!" (*laughs*) You can't just noodle your way through those chord changes. You have to hit the right notes. The only thing I ever really planned before was the solo in "Runnin' with the Devil." Other than that, nothing else was planned or written out in advance.

**"Blood and Fire" used to be "Ripley," which you originally recorded with a Ripley stereo guitar. Did you break out the Ripley guitar again to record the new version?**

Oh yeah, but I had to send it back to Steve Ripley to have him go through it to fix a couple of the panning pots since I hadn't used it in quite a few years. But it was the same guitar. The Ripley guitar sounds different than a Strat. It's a hell of a sound.

**You, Al, and Wolf are incredibly tight, and the band sounds bigger than it ever has before. Sometimes all three of you sound like one big instrument because you're locked together so tightly. It's like you're all synchronized to the same psychic clock.**

I agree. It's definitely a family thing. You've got three Van Halens now. What can I say? We all know how we want our instruments to sound. When you put it all together, it seems to work. Wolfgang has a lot to do with the band's youthful energy. I've always said that I'm not that good of a player. I'm not a studio cat, so nothing I do comes out slick. Everything I do has a loose feel and a rawness that I can't get rid of no matter how hard I try. That element of my playing gives it an edge. It leaves you on the edge of your seat waiting for something to break. How ever old I live to be, that will always be part of the way that I play. I'm not reckless on purpose. It's just how I play. It's like a roller-coaster ride. It takes you all over the place, but it stays on track. It has a lot of g-force.

**Throughout Van Halen's history, you often recorded songs that were from the band's early days. It's cool how Wolfgang carried on that tradition.**

When we were digging around, I was amazed how fresh some of the songs sounded. I was going, Did I really write that way back then? We approached this record no differently than any other. When it first came out, some people were saying that we purposely did old songs to get the public to relate to our old sound. But this record wasn't planned that way. Whenever we make a record, the first thing we do is go over what we already have in the bag that we can pick from and we go over anything that is new.

**Even on *Fair Warning*, the band was still pulling material like "Mean Street"/ "Voodoo Queen" from the demos you recorded before the first album came out.**

We were doing things like that even later. "The Seventh Seal" [from *Balance*] was a song that I wrote before Mike was even in the band. A good idea is a good idea no matter when you do it. "Hang 'Em High" was written long before we put it on *Diver Down*. Same with [*1984's*] "House of Pain," which was also on those demos we recorded with Gene Simmons. The internet has changed everything. Now everyone knows where things came from. Before the internet, nobody would have known that these were old songs.

**The new material on the album fits seamlessly with the older songs. This is also an album that works well in its entirety. It really flows when you listen to it from beginning to end. It's not just a collection of disparate songs.**

That's how I've always liked to make records. Dave and I were surprised by the first reviews we got. A lot of people were saying it was heavier than they expected it to be. It just sounded like Van Halen to me.

**The album is also surprisingly aggressive for a band that's been around for nearly four decades. I think a lot of that has to do with the growl of Wolf's bass.**

That has a lot to do with it. He uses both a pick and his fingers. He played "Tattoo" with his fingers. It's all about what fits the song. But, man, that kid can pick! In the solo on "Chinatown" (*sings fast part at the end of the solo*), I can't even do that. I can fan pick, but he's really something else. A lot of bass players look down on players who use picks, but that's just because 99 percent of them can't play with a pick. I know many bass players like that. If you want it to cut through and have some balls, you need to use a pick. Jack Bruce used to use his fingernail as a pick.

Dave's guitar playing often gets overlooked. He's really good at fingerpicked, country-style blues like he plays on the intro to "Stay Frosty."

He played up until the band came in, and then I took over on acoustic. He played that on a nylon-string flamenco guitar. It's an interesting sound. But he can really fingerpick! Even on our first album, a lot of people thought that I played the intro to "Ice Cream Man," but that was Dave.

Dave's lyrics on the album are full of wit and personality. He's like a street poet. How did it feel to have that personality with your music again?

Some of his lyrics are hilarious. Dave's good. He's a very well-read person and it shows in his lyrics. I don't know of anybody else who can write lyrics that are so out there yet in. Some of the stuff is blatant, but a lot of it makes you think. It's tripped out and deep, but not so deep that you can't relate to it. I think he's brilliant. Sometimes on the first listen, I'll go, "What the fuck is he singing about?" and then I'll eventually get it.

On tour you played a lot of songs that the band hadn't performed for twenty-eight or more years. Did you have trouble remembering any of them?

That's why we did sound check every night. But Dave never did sound checks, so we didn't get to get together with him and go over some of the old songs we wanted to add to the set list. We played "Hang 'Em High" for the first time during sound check. That song is wicked. It has so many changes, there is so much shit going on, and it's fast. If you slip up once the whole song is fucked. After we did it, we were all looking at each other and going, "What do you think, guys? Should we take a chance?" And it was Dave of all people who said, "Fuck yeah! Let's go out there and do it." I thought he was going to say no. He said, "What's the worst thing that could happen?" and we played it great.

He's got an easier job than the rest of you guys. He's said "I forgot the fuckin' words" so many times now that people expect him to say that.

I've thought about that a few times. You know, there are a lot more notes in a song than words. . . . (laughs) I've got a lot of notes to remember. During sound check, Wolfgang would call out some songs for us to try.

Sometimes we'd argue a bit. I often dreaded playing the intro of "Girl Gone Bad" because the damn B string always sounds a tad flat on the chords that I play. I'd go, "Let's do 'Outta Love Again,'" and he'd say, "No. We're doing 'Girl Gone Bad.'" Wolfie usually won.

**Your tone onstage is very clear. Each note is very clean and precise.**

I dig in with both hands. That's why my thumb is like this. (*holds up right hand to show thumb, which is bent back at a 90-degree angle*) There was one gig where about twenty minutes before the show I was backstage and I went to sweep open a tapestry that was covering the door. I whacked my hand against the door jamb, and it swelled up really badly. I was able to make it through the show, but the next day I went to have an X-ray taken of my hand to make sure there were no hairline fractures or anything. The radiologist went, "Man! What's wrong with your thumb!" I said, "Nothing. It's this part of my hand that I hit." He said, "Your thumb is all fucked up. It's not supposed to bend back that far." It's from years of digging in with the pick. (*laughs*) It's an occupational hazard. My thumb won't bend the other way.

Before the operation on my hand, I wasn't able to stretch. I've never had very big hands, but I could do the splits with them. Eventually, I couldn't. I had a tendon in my little finger that was twisted that prevented me from being able to stretch. You can still feel the twist. When I flex the finger, the tendon feels like it's almost snapping. It would fucking hurt when I was playing. Now if it hurts, I just take a couple Advil instead of a couple shots of vodka.

**Did the surgery you had on your hand back in 2009 help improve your playing?**

That was done a long time ago. I forgot about that actually. I think it's just because my head is clearer. I'm aware of what I'm doing. It's amazing that I ever did it any other way, to tell you the truth. Looking back now, I don't see how I did it for all those years when I wasn't sober. I could not imagine going back. At the same time, I'm up there playing, so I can only go by what Matt tells me. "So how was that?" "It was good." "Okay." When I'm up there playing, I can't tell. I know that my playing is a lot more consistent. It's like all the little neurons are more connected.

**You've mentioned that a lot of your ideas and playing seem to come from somewhere else. Do you just let things flow or do you feel any anxiety about what comes out?**

The beauty of doing my solo now is that I get to sit down. I was just talking with Janie the other day about how the reviews mention that I sit down to do my solo like I'm sitting on my front porch or couch playing for people. Believe it or not, I can sit there and play like that all night long. It's harder for me to play when I'm standing up. When I sit down I can really play. It's a gas! I'm having fun.

Sometimes a solo goes by so quickly and the next thing I know it's over. I don't mix it up too much. I used to noodle so much, but now it's more mapped out. I know that people want to hear certain things, so I do the beginning and end of "Eruption," a bit of "Cathedral" and "Spanish Fly" in the middle, and a few transition parts to piece everything together. I don't remember what I did at the last gig, but Dave walked up to me afterwards and said, "Whatever you did in your solo tonight was different. It was great!" But it happened so fast with me that I don't know what I did that was different. I'll think that I played the same thing I always do.

**It's probably better not to think about what you did before and just let it happen.**

That's what I love about mistakes.

**As long as the tape is rolling.**

Exactly. I often listen back to something and go, "How the fuck did I do that?" When Wolf suggested doing "Light Up the Sky," for the life of me I couldn't figure out what I did on that song at all, especially on the breakdown where it goes (*sings guitar part at 1:42 when Roth sings, "Ooh Mama see the firelights"*). How did I play that? Where did I play that? And of course Wolfgang goes, "Right here, Dad!" He has a great ear and picks up everything.

**What was the motivation for releasing a live album at this point in Van Halen's career?**

I originally wanted to remix the original twenty-five-song demo that we recorded when we signed with Warner Bros. I thought it would be really cool to do that, but the tapes are lost so that was out the window. Then we started digging through bootlegs of our shows from the club days. We tried really hard to make those recordings sound good, but ultimately it just wasn't good enough to release. The sound quality was so bad. When we tried to enhance them, it sounded artificial, and you lost that live-sounding aspect.

After that we realized that we have never made a live album with Dave. Since we had already released a studio album with Wolfgang playing on it, it also made sense for us to do a live album with both Wolf and Dave. Another reason why we put out a live record was to give people the experience of hearing us play our classic songs live.

**Did you record any other shows or just the Tokyo show?**
We had a Pro Tools rig out by the front of the house and recorded every show since the beginning of the 2007 tour when Dave first got back in the band. But we never originally intended to put out a live record. We just recorded our shows to archive them. We had so much material that it was too overwhelming to listen to about 150 shows and pick the best one. I didn't even bother listening to any of the past shows, outside of a few jams here and there. We played pretty much the same set every night, although we changed a few songs here and there. We played the classics. That's what people want to hear.

Because the performances by Alex, Wolfgang, and myself were pretty consistent from one night to the next, we decided to leave it up to Dave to pick, and he happened to pick Tokyo. Performing live is a lot harder on a singer. Wolfgang and I sing backup vocals on the choruses, so we know how much the vocals can vary from one night to the next. When your voice is your instrument, it can be affected by a lot of different things. If you sleep with the air conditioner on or the bus ride is too long, you can wake up the next day with a fucked-up voice. That's the main reason we decided to let Dave pick.

**The sound quality is great, considering that the recordings were originally just archives of your shows.**
We didn't have any special engineers recording at our shows. That's also why there is no video of the Tokyo show—we didn't originally plan to release a live recording of that show. Making a video of a live concert is a whole other production. The way we did it was more impromptu and unexpected.

Although Bob Clearmountain wasn't at the Tokyo show and didn't have any say about how it was recorded, he did a great job mixing it. Alex and I listened at first to make sure that the basic instrument sounds were down, and then we let him go. Bob kept sending us mixes and we just said, "It sounds good to us!" As long as we could hear all the instruments it was good! (*laughs*)

**If you recorded video of the show, you'd probably feel a lot more pressure to get everything right.**

I already feel that pressure. Every time I get onstage, I want to give the people the best performance possible. Since we record every night, that doesn't make things any different from one night to the next. To film it would have been much more time consuming. Then we would have had to look at all of the footage and figure out what to use. The fact that we weren't planning it made it that much more special to us.

That's also why we decided to keep the recording completely live. There are mistakes. After it was mixed, I listened to a few parts and went, "Okay, I fucked *that* up." (*laughs*) But that's how it sounded that night, so we just left it. It's like a photograph of that evening, and we didn't photoshop it. We did nothing. When you fix parts or mistakes, it's not a real live experience anymore.

**The performances sound powerful, which is impressive for a band after more than forty years.**

Van Halen has been aggressive since day one. The rawness of the recording adds to the power. There's this uncontrolled energy that exists in us that spills over the edges. It's never really right or perfect, but it creates tension. It's like, Okay, who is going to blow it? (*laughs*) When you keep waiting for someone to fuck up but no one does, it keeps you on the edge of your seat. It's just raw. It's the real thing. If people are expecting a perfect live record, well, then it's not really live anymore.

I was really bummed when I heard from Andy Johns—rest in peace—that Cream's "Crossroads" [*Wheels of Fire*] was put together from different shows! That ruined it for me. I thought it was one performance, but it wasn't. I don't know if anybody else has ever put out a live album that is really, truly live. The only exception I can think of is the old Monterey Pop

Festival with The Who and Janis Joplin, where Hendrix burned his guitar. That was obviously not fixed. Woodstock was like that too. The only thing I hated about the Woodstock movie is that they had so many close-ups of things, but you never got to see the big picture of the bands performing. Like "I'm Going Home" by Ten Years After—all you saw was close-up shots of Alvin Lee, and you never saw the whole band. I didn't like the way it was filmed.

**What do you remember about the Tokyo show?**
I remember it was long! (*laughs*) I was beat at the end of that show. Japanese fans are always so over the top and animated, especially since they're now allowed to stand at shows. They used to be so controlled when they were forced to sit down, but now it's mosh pit craziness. We played at "The Big Egg"—the Tokyo Dome, which is a baseball stadium. There were more than fifty thousand people there, so it was loud.

**I didn't realize that Dave could speak Japanese.**
The funny thing is, we asked some Japanese people if they understood what he said, and they said, "No." (*laughs*) He has an apartment over there. Dave is always doing some tripped-out shit.

**It's really cool to hear Wolfgang's fills in detail on the record. Sometimes those details are easy to miss when watching a live show.**
He embellishes the classics in his own style. What blows my mind are some of the licks that he throws down during the breakdown in "Mean Street." He's hauling ass but still in the pocket and groovin'! It makes it exciting.

**There's a nice improv section during "You Really Got Me" that is longer and different from what the band did during the 2012 shows I saw.**
The little jam sections were the only parts that changed from night to night. Sometimes we'd play "Crossroads" or stray off wherever we felt like going that night. There might have been better ones, but that's what we played that night.

**At the end of "And the Cradle Will Rock," you played the "Smoke on the Water" riff.**

We always have to figure out how to end that song. Since we were in Japan, we decided to play "Smoke on the Water." Deep Purple's *Made in Japan* album blew that song out of the water, so we thought it would be fun to play that song there.

**Why didn't the band release a live album with Dave back in the seventies or early eighties?**

I don't know. We used to tour so much and were on the road constantly, but it never occurred to us that we should record our shows. Back then you didn't have Pro Tools, so it wasn't as easy to record shows. You had to hire a mobile truck.

People ask why we've never released the rest of the 1981 Oakland show that we recorded on video. The reason is because we only recorded three songs—"Unchained," "Hear About It Later," and "So This Is Love?" We actually filmed those three songs on two different nights. On "Unchained," I broke a string the first night, and if you watch the video, you can see my guitars change just for a few seconds, then switch back. We used the second night of audio, so you can't hear it, but we used video from both nights. The bottom line is we can't ever release the whole Oakland show because we didn't film or record the whole show.

**It seems like back then you were concentrating more on recording the next studio album.**

On the bus all I would do is write songs. As soon as we got home, people from the label would be asking me what new songs I've got. During our first tour in 1978, we were out for eleven months, but our contract stipulated that we owed our label our second record by the end of the year. We basically had three weeks left that year to finish our second record. We cranked out *Van Halen II* because that was what I had written.

**How did it feel to be honored by the Smithsonian National Museum of American History for your contributions as an inventor, musical innovator, and immigrant?**

It took me by surprise. To me, it's way beyond a Grammy or the usual music industry awards. To be acknowledged by the Smithsonian for my contributions to American music and pop culture is much bigger and more of an honor than any award I could think of. It's amazing to think that I've contributed something to the history of this country, especially since I came here from a different country. I think it's the highest honor you can get.

**One detail that really stood out to me from the event was your explanation of just how important your family has been to your music and motivation.**

The four of us—my mom, dad, Alex, and I—were very tight knit. When you come to a new country, you can't speak the language, and you have no money, you'd better be a team or else we wouldn't have made it. My mom was the one who basically wore the pants. She took care of the finances. We all worked, gave the money to her, and she took care of the rest. It forced us to be close. There was nothing else we could do but work and try to make it through our weekly payments.

I don't even know how to explain how it feels to have Wolfgang follow in the footsteps of my father and me. He's a third-generation Van Halen. When people ask me what it's like to play with my son, all I can say is that it's the greatest feeling you can imagine.

**What do you think of your son's album?**

It's like AC/DC meets Van Halen meets aggressive pop. The riffs are catchy. It's a little of everything and sounds like a freight train coming at you. I've never heard anything quite like it. It's so powerful that I'm jealous. Ah, to be young. I'm not saying that I've lost it, but as you get older you get so many more things to deal with in life. I just turned sixty, and my main priority now is to maintain my health. I've beaten cancer four times and dealt with other health issues. Now it's all about working out every day and doing Pilates. I used to spend all day playing guitar, but now some of that time is spent in the gym. I've lost ten pounds since people saw me at the Smithsonian and dropped a lot of body fat. You've only got one body. When I turned sixty, something clicked inside me, and I thought that I'd better get my shit together. Being sixty sounds old, but I don't feel any different in my head, which is scary in its own way, you know what I mean? (*laughs*) I feel like I should be smarter, but sometimes I feel like I'm still twelve. But music keeps you young.

I hadn't listened to any of Van Halen's early albums for years until we recently remastered them, and I was really surprised how well they still hold up. But I also realized that there is no music like that out there anymore. It's really sad. What happened to rock and roll? That's why I can't wait for the world to hear Wolf's record. I'll be bold and say that what Wolf and E-Rock [Baskette] are doing is important. It's like early AC/DC. It hits really hard. I think that people who hear it are either not going to believe it or they're going to go, "This kid is the real deal." When he plays drums, it's scary. When he plays bass to his own drums, it's even scarier. And then he's playing guitar on top of everything! He's a one-man band. E-Rock is very much involved, and I don't mean to belittle him at all as it's a team effort, but Wolfgang is playing three instruments that groove hard and are so locked in it's ridiculous.

**Does Van Halen have any long-term plans beyond the 2015 tour?**
We just take it as it comes. I'd love to do another studio record if everybody else is up for it. At the end of the tour, Wolf is going to finish his record. After that, we'll see. We don't ever plan that far ahead. That's how the live album came about. The best things aren't planned that far in advance. We like to keep it loose.

**Considering the reception to *A Different Kind of Truth*, how well the tour is going, and the fact that you recorded so many songs, it seems like there's good motivation to continue moving forward for a while.**

Oh yeah. We're working together better than ever. I see us doing this for a long, long time. It feels more like a family and a band than it ever has. When things feel right, why the hell not keep doing it? As far as I know, when we're done with this cycle we'll take a little break and make another record. That's what I hope to do. I'm pretty sure that's what our intention is. We truly are a band. It's not just a one-off thing. I don't want to say it's a rebuilding process. If anything, it's a continuation. We're truly a band now. It feels more like a band and a family than it ever has, and not just because three-quarters of it *is* family. Working with Dave has been very productive. We're all very opinionated about things, but it's all for the benefit of the music.

**I think being older and wiser you're no longer concerned with all of the distractions that take your focus away from the music.**

I was just thinking about that before you got here because I had the feeling that you'd ask me what's different now than it used to be. I think I finally put my finger on it. It wasn't really us. It was people around us. The guy in our crew who did the band's lights [Pete Angelus] would always talk in Dave's ear. "You don't need them. Blah, blah, blah." That kind of shit would go on. When you're doing drugs, drinking, and partying, you start believing shit. Those days are gone. We've gotten rid of people who don't belong here. Now it's truly just the band. We have no problems with each other at all. We're here to do a job, and we love doing our job.

**You seem to be genuinely happy now. You went through quite a dark period for a while, and we were worried about you.**

So was I. But I can't think of anyone on the planet who is luckier and more blessed than I am. Not only do I get to play with my brother, which I've done all of my life, but I also get to play with my son. Who else gets to do that? If my dad was still here now, that would really make things amazing. What more could I ask for? I have a wonderful wife, wonderful friends, a son who doesn't smoke, drink, or do drugs. I'm just a guitarist in a kick-ass rock and roll band, which is a lot of fun. What more could I ask for? I'm just glad to have an album out with my son and be doing what we do. How many people of our age can say that and be viable? I always laugh when people say, "Are Van Halen still viable?" Music is music. What's viable to teenagers today is not exactly viable to our audience. We're still viable to our audience. I'm just happy to be part of this band and team.

# MUSICAL INTERLUDE

*A conversation with*
*Edward and Wolfgang Van Halen*

---

Onstage during Van Halen's 2007 reunion tour with David Lee Roth, the singer often referred to the latest version of the band as being "three parts original, one part inevitable," with the latter part serving as the introduction of its new bassist, Edward's son Wolfgang. Whereas the singer's statements were often witty exaggerations, in this instance what he said was a different kind of truth—candid, honest, and accurate. Almost from the instant that Wolfgang emerged from the womb on March 16, 1991, Ed expressed that his biggest wish was to one day play music with his son and maintain the family tradition he enjoyed with his own father.

In interviews over the years that followed Wolfgang's birth, the guitarist discussed his son's musical progress as much as he talked about his own new music. "Wolfgang loves music," Ed said in 1994, when Wolfgang was just three and a half. "I'm really happy he's got good rhythm. We were in the studio playing the other day, and he was bopping along with a drumstick in his hand. He loves plinking on piano and beating on Al's drums. The other day he was up above the garage where I have a lot of my guitars. Valerie and I were looking for something and he looked at all the guitars and went, 'When I get big, I'm going to play the guitar!' The way he said it had conviction, like that's really what he was going to do. I thought it was so cool. I don't see how he won't somehow be into music, being exposed to it all the time."

While talking to the press during the early 2000s, Ed revealed how Wolfgang started playing drums at age nine after he showed his son how to play the basic beat behind AC/DC's "Back in Black." Shortly after Wolfgang started playing guitar at age eleven, Ed proudly went into great detail about his son's first public performance at elementary school and would show the home video to everyone to prove Wolfgang's talents. This was followed by Wolfgang's first musical performances onstage with Van Halen during the 2004 tour, where he would join his dad to play rhythm guitar on "316."

Ed's announcement during late 2006 that Wolfgang had become Van Halen's new bass player was a surprise only to the band's most casual fans. However, the fact that Ed's son had only been playing bass for three months at the time was shocking to even the most die-hard fans. The guitarist tried to downplay the situation by comparing it to when he and his brother performed gigs with their father during their preteen years, but there was a huge difference between Alex and Edward playing polka tunes for old geezers at the Continental Club and Wolfgang joining one of the world's biggest rock bands onstage at the Continental Arena. Nonetheless, the guitarist was insistent that Wolfgang could deliver the goods.

"Wolfie blows me away every day," Ed said. "He already sounds like Jack Bruce. I created an environment for him where music was always around. Bass is his third instrument. He's already a motherfucker on drums and guitar. He picked up the bass himself, and the spin he puts on shit is incredible. Everyone who comes up here and hears him play says he's really developing his own stamp. He's going to kick some major ass. It's a bummer that my dad never got to see him, but for all I know he may be my [reincarnated] dad. To have my son fall in my footsteps on his own, without me pushing him into it, is the greatest feeling in the world."

In January 2008, while Van Halen was on a brief break between the first and second legs of its 2007–08 tour, Edward and Wolfgang spoke to me in Wolfgang's very first press interview. The banter between the two definitively proved that Roth was 100 percent correct when he described Wolfgang's addition to Van Halen as "inevitable."

### How did Wolfgang join the band?

**EDWARD:** I just asked him.

**WOLFGANG:** Actually, there's a story behind that. It was in the summer of '06. My dad said, "Hey, do you want to jam?" and I said, "Sure. I'll draw up the playlist." I made up a playlist from the first six records. I don't know why. I just happened to do that.

**EDWARD:** Actually, we didn't have the playlist yet. We were just jamming on some stuff. I'll never forget it. You played the blond five-string bass with four strings on it. We were in the studio one day when Al came in to jam with me. He went straight to the drum room, which is in the back of the studio, so we couldn't see Al and Al couldn't see us.

**WOLFGANG:** When we play, we stand behind the console in the control room at 5150.

**EDWARD:** That way I can engineer and it's so much easier to monitor all the instruments. It's really fuckin' loud and crystal clear. It's like making a record. I have the ability to mix while we're playing.

Wolfgang picked up a bass and I put the bass in Al's headphones. It was the first time that you played bass, and Al had no idea that it was you. It was the first time in thirty years that Al had bass in his headphones. Al said, "Hey! How are you playing bass and guitar at the same time?" I got on the talkback and said, "Say hi, Wolfie!" and you went (*in high voice*), "Hi, Uncle Al!" Your voice was a lot higher then. When Al found out it was Wolfie on bass, it blew his mind.

**WOLFGANG:** Right, and it was after that, Al asked if I wanted to jam again. I said, "Yeah! I'll draw up a playlist." I came up with a playlist of about thirty Roth songs. There might have been a couple of Sammy songs in there too.

**EDWARD:** That's when I asked him if he'd like to be the bass player in Van Halen. He said, "Yeah, as long as I don't have to do a certain thing," which I won't mention. (*laughs*)

WOLFGANG: I can say that. I said, "Sure. I just don't want to do a bass solo." Then we just made it a religious thing on every Wednesday and Saturday to play. We kept playing relentlessly, and eventually we thought, "Hey, we're pretty damn good!"

*So, in the beginning everything happened organically?*

WOLFGANG: We didn't lay out a plan or anything. It just fell together. We played together a good four months without any vocals, and we just looked at each other and knew it was awesome.

EDWARD: It's like Dave says, "Three parts original, one part inevitable." And it was inevitable.

*Wolfgang, you play several instruments—guitar, drums, keyboards. What drove you toward the bass?*

WOLFGANG: Because it was the only open spot? (*everyone laughs*) And the people filling the other spots—drums and guitar—are the two greatest players of those instruments in the frickin' world. I find the bass safe. You don't have to go out on the line. I just like to be there to groove and keep the song going. I love being a bass player. It's just me and Al—a groove section. Just boom, boom, boom, and we're good.

EDWARD: Before we went on tour, a lot of people were saying that Wolfgang got the gig just because he's my son. But after that first gig, forget it. It's just hands down, hands up, hands sideways—he's a musician and a Van Halen.

*Was the time in between when the tour was announced and when you played the first show difficult?*

WOLFGANG: I just wanted to get it over with. I wanted to be where we are now. There was so much weight on my shoulders to fill the shoes and prove that I could do it. I *knew* I could do it, but I wanted to say, "Everybody, hey, I can do it!"

EDWARD: We rehearsed probably six months before Dave showed up. We were almost over-rehearsed. We got to the point where we were goofing around.

**WOLFGANG:** That's when we started playing "Little Dreamer" in double time.

**EDWARD:** When Dave walked in, it blew his freakin' mind.

**WOLFGANG:** That night was magical. That was the first time I heard vocals with everything.

*Wolf, you've gone directly from rehearsing with only your dad and uncle to playing in front of thousands of fans at some of the biggest venues in the world. Was it difficult for you to make that transition?*

**WOLFGANG:** Because we rehearsed so frickin' much, from spending six months in 5150, then at Center Staging and then for a few weeks at the LA Forum, I felt that we had done enough preparation for me to feel safe. Plus, when you're on the stage you're far enough away from people that you feel comfortable. With the lights and everything, sometimes I can just close my eyes and feel like we're in that room at 5150 again.

**EDWARD:** Playing on a big stage is a lot different than rehearsing in the studio here. It was probably more comfortable than being in the control room with a handful of people staring at you.

**WOLFGANG:** It was definitely a lot more open. That room is claustrophobic.

**EDWARD:** I've always said that the more people there are, the more chance there is that someone will like it.

**WOLFGANG:** When there are only ten people around, I can't really play. Then I get nervous. But when there are so many other people, it doesn't matter. Then it's just the four of us doing our thing.

**EDWARD:** If there's just one person and they don't like you, you're fucked. If you've got two people, at least there's a 50-50 chance one of the two people will like you. When there are twenty thousand people, at least half of them will like it, hopefully.

*Ed, how did you help Wolfgang prepare for the tour?*

**EDWARD:** The first thing I told him is look out for the bitches. (*laughs*)

**WOLFGANG:** He didn't really help me prepare. He just told me what not to do. His advice was just to do your thing.

**EDWARD:** I taught him what my dad taught me, which is you can learn from everyone. What to do and what not to do.

**WOLFGANG:** That, and practice.

**EDWARD:** Actually, he helped me more than I helped him.

**WOLFGANG:** I had to teach him how to play the songs again.

**EDWARD:** Because I couldn't remember the damn songs, and I don't know how to work a fuckin' iPod. He had one with all the songs on it. We hooked it up in the control room, and he'd go, "No, Dad, it goes like this!"

*Did you teach yourself how to play the songs?*

**WOLFGANG:** Yeah, I did. The night before we started practicing, I sat down in my music room and listened to every single song and played to them. I didn't do exactly everything that Michael Anthony did. I put my own spin on it, but not enough to make people go, "Whoa, what's wrong with the bass?" I kept it as close as possible but added just a little . . . *spice*. A little WVH flair.

*Ed, what is it like to be onstage with your son as a band member, not just as a special guest like he was on the previous tour?*

**EDWARD:** It's an amazing feeling. I'm just so truly blessed. I have pictures of me sitting in the racquetball court on our property in my pajamas with an acoustic guitar and Wolfgang is probably just two and a half feet tall. I'll never forget the day I saw his foot tapping along in beat! I knew then, I couldn't wait for the day I'd be able to make music with my son. I don't know what more I could ask for.

*Even after playing about forty shows together, do you still have noteworthy moments?*

**EDWARD:** Oh yeah. Every night. Sometimes we actually talk while we're playing. I'll go, "Hey! Are you all right?" because sometimes he'll look at me funny. When I give him a kiss or a high five or a low five, it's from the heart. It ain't all bullshit. It's just pure love.

WOLFGANG: That doesn't happen to me every night, but sometimes when I'm playing, I'll forget to sing or play a certain note, and I'll look up and go, "Whoa, this is crazy!" That feeling is always there, but I don't always have time to think about it because I have a job to do.

EDWARD: Believe it or not, I didn't know you'd be this good. He scares the shit out of me. He plays drums like a motherfucker. The first thing he does in the house is start playing "And the Cradle Will Rock" on the piano. Once Janie [Liszewski] walked by and said, "Oh! I thought that was you." But it was Wolfie. Drums, guitar, bass, keyboards . . . shit! And singing!

*Do you eventually see yourself having a solo segment onstage?*

WOLFGANG: I don't. I like having just my own moment for five seconds, like the "So This Is Love?" intro and doing the tapping part in "Romeo Delight." That's enough for me. It's like, "Hey! Watch me play! I can do it!" I'm more than fulfilled by being a team player.

*What's it like to be in a band with your dad and uncle?*

WOLFGANG: It feels right. I don't ever go, "This is weird. I'm with a bunch of older people." I feel like we're all the same age. It's just what we do.

EDWARD: I was going to say the same thing. Every now and then when we're onstage playing, I'll look at him and go, "God, that's my son! He's only sixteen, but he's not sixteen. He's an equal." Age doesn't matter.

WOLFGANG: There's nobody else my age on the tour, but I feel like I'm an equal. I hope that everybody thinks of me the same way.

EDWARD: I believe they do, but you wouldn't believe the legalities we had to go through to have him be the bass player in Van Halen.

WOLFGANG: I still have school.

*Why do you think you get along so well together?*

WOLFGANG: We're blood.

EDWARD: It's innately built in. The way Wolfgang plays bass is very similar to the way I play guitar. It's very unorthodox. His style is interesting. When other bands come by, like Green Day, I'll go, "Close your eyes and listen to him." People freak out. [Poison guitarist] C. C. DeVille left me a message and he didn't compliment me at all. He did say I was on top of my game, but my son really impressed him. Do you know how proud that makes me? I couldn't ask for more. Not only has he proven himself, but he also takes this stuff further. He does all the wicked shit on the bass that I do on guitar. It's fucking amazing.

WOLFGANG: It's like a genetic metronome. When we end every song, we don't even look at each other. We all feel it. It's all feel. It's good music and I love playing it.

EDWARD: If anything, I'm usually the one who is out of sync. On "Panama" I rarely start on the one, and Al hears what I'm playing backwards. I'll never forget when I wrote "Little Dreamer," which is one of the few songs where I do start on the one and he played backwards to that too. Al didn't hear it that way and it was like he was playing it backwards. Onstage, when we're playing . . .

WOLFGANG: Oh God, I have to watch you! At the end of "Unchained," we have to go eight or nine times before we freakin' end! Sometimes it's three. Sometimes it's five. It's always an odd number.

EDWARD: I can't count for some reason. It's always threes or fives for some reason. I only go by feel.

WOLFGANG: And sometimes that feeling is wrong! (*laughs*) But we always somehow manage to pull it together for the ending.

EDWARD: We fall down the stairs and land on our feet together. Onstage, I look at Wolfie because he can count! Actually, now I've got two people to help me—because both Al and Wolfie can count.

*Wolfgang, what music do you listen to?*

WOLFGANG: Mainly rock stuff—nothing too out of the ordinary. I really like Tool, which is one of my favorite bands, and I just started getting into Nine Inch Nails. They're really good. I love Primus and Sevendust, too.

EDWARD: You were totally into AC/DC for a while.

WOLFGANG: AC/DC is in all of our hearts because they rule.

EDWARD: You listen to us, too.

WOLFGANG: Not anymore. I haven't listened to us for a while.

EDWARD: That's because you're playing it now. I remember when I picked you up from school one day and there were boxes of records sitting in the shop at the studio. You looked at them and went, "Is this all you, Dad?"

WOLFGANG: Oh yeah. I probably was like five.

EDWARD: No, I think you were ten.

WOLFGANG: Whatever.

EDWARD: It blew my mind that I totally forgot to turn him on to all the music that I had written. All he knew was what he heard on the radio.

WOLFGANG: I only knew the Hagar songs and maybe, like, "Jump," and that was it.

EDWARD: I'll never forget when we were coming home from Castle Park [a family entertainment center]. "Hot For Teacher" came on the radio, and Wolf was going, "Who is that singing?" I said that's Dave.

WOLFGANG: I was going, "That's not Sammy!"

*What was your best personal moment so far on this tour?*

WOLFGANG: When we did the rehearsal show for our friends and family in LA, it was just the beginning and I didn't feel I had ripened yet. When we came back to LA and did the first Staples Center show, I felt a sense of accomplishment. I was a much better player. I felt like a member of the band.

EDWARD: For me, it's the fact that I get to play with my son, my brother, and Dave. Every night is special. Doing an interview with my son right now is special. It's all special.

# 11

# THE ART OF GUITAR

*How Edward Van Halen went from building a mongrel
guitar in his Pasadena garage to overseeing a successful
global empire responsible for manufacturing thousands
of high-quality instruments and amplifiers.*

---

" We never once said, 'Yeah, that will do.'
It has to be right because my name is on it. "

---

ONE OF EDWARD Van Halen's favorite leisure activities was
to poke around music and electronics stores to check out
gear and search for parts for his homemade guitars. Usually,
Ed found these visits soothing, a pleasant respite from the pressures of
being a rock star.

But in the late seventies, these visits began to leave him trembling
with rage. Guitars that were virtual clones of his Frankenstrat were
sprouting like mushrooms in all of his favorite shops. These copies,
featuring his configuration of one humbucker, one volume knob, and a
vibrato bar, ranged from cheap, garishly painted import models made
by overseas companies like Hondo to expensive instruments offered by
smaller American companies like Schecter.

He was particularly shocked and incensed when even his "friends" at Charvel jumped on the bandwagon. Without asking his permission, the manufacturer began selling reproductions of the black and yellow guitar he'd custom-ordered from them, brazenly calling it the "Van Halen" model.

Wasn't it enough that Ed featured the guitar on the cover of *Van Halen II* and generously mentioned Charvel in numerous guitar interviews? Fuck those guys, he thought.

It was bad enough that throngs of guitarists were stealing his licks, but this intellectual larceny was completely unacceptable to him. Guitar companies were making vast amounts of money by ripping off his revolutionary design, and none of them had offered him a dime. To make matters worse, they weren't even doing a good job of replicating his guitars. Most of the knockoffs looked like grotesque funhouse-mirror versions of the original, and it was enough to make him vomit.

But this dark turn of events also became the catalyst for one of Ed's greatest triumphs, and what might even become his most enduring legacy—the guitars and amps he designed and manufactured under his own name.

Though he was reluctant to do it at first, over the next three decades, working with four different guitar companies, he progressed from being a half-hearted shill to designing his own signature models and establishing his own major musical instrument company—EVH guitars, amps, and accessories.

The road Ed took from modifying a Les Paul in his garage to running a guitar empire was long and twisted. The journey began in earnest after Charvel's unapologetic exploitation of his name. Tired of seeing others profit from his work and genius, he decided to take a proactive approach and find a guitar company that would work with him and that was large enough to reward him handsomely for his efforts.

Fender and Gibson were the obvious choices, but during the early eighties they were too big, slow, and bloated with corporate bureaucracy to embrace someone as young and ambitious as Edward. Another option was calling one of the larger Japanese companies like Ibanez or Yamaha, but they were simply too foreign for him to relate to. That left a handful of up-and-coming American contenders: B.C. Rich, Dean, Hamer, and Kramer.

But before the guitarist could even reach for a phone, a fortuitous twist of fate led Kramer to Ed's door, literally. In early February 1982, Kramer Guitars cofounder Dennis Berardi was flying to Anaheim, California, to attend a musical instrument industry convention, and, by happenstance, he was seated next to Van Halen's tour manager. The two engaged in a friendly conversation about vibrato bar designs that inevitably led to a discussion about Ed himself, and the manager invited Berardi to meet Ed in LA.

"I didn't know that much about Eddie Van Halen at that point," Berardi said.[20] "I knew he was a great guitar player, but I didn't know anything about [the] guitars he played. He invited me into his house, and while I was sitting there, I saw his red, white, and black guitar. I took a closer look at it, and I was thinking, 'What a piece of shit!' We started talking, and I told him how Gibson and Fender's guitars were terrible, and they were ripping kids off. I told him that Kramer wanted to build really great guitars. Just like that he said, 'All right, let's do it. Let's make Kramer number one!' I asked if he wanted to endorse Kramer guitars and he agreed."

Edward's somewhat impulsive embrace of Kramer became official a few months later, in June, when the company announced the guitarist's endorsement deal. Kramer wasted no time touting "The Edward Van Halen Tremolo," a locking system developed by the German company Rockinger that was installed on a number of Kramer models. During his first meeting with Berardi, Ed agreed to endorse the Rockinger units, but he had second thoughts, because he personally preferred the Floyd Rose double-locking vibratos that he'd been using for a few years.

Kramer wanted to keep Ed happy and told him that they were open to licensing the Floyd Rose system for their guitars—but that there was one huge impediment: the unit was prohibitively expensive to produce. At that time, Rose was still making them by hand, and installation required extensive guitar modifications.

But Kramer realized that if they could produce an Eddie guitar with a Floyd Rose system, whose vibrato units had become something of a status symbol among discerning guitarists, their company would explode overnight. Quickly, they figured out a way to lower the cost of the hardware through mass production and factory installation, which made the once-exclusive Floyd Rose vibrato accessible to a much wider audience.

Edward's endorsement deal with Kramer was an instant success and soon the money came pouring in. By appearing in numerous Kramer ads, performing at guitar trade shows, and playing his homemade guitars with Kramer logos placed strategically on the headstock on tour and in music videos, Ed significantly boosted the company's image and sales, to the point where they became one of the leading guitar companies in the United States.

Though Ed praised the quality of Kramer guitars, observers wondered why the company didn't sell an official Eddie Van Halen signature model, or why Ed didn't play any of the company's off-the-shelf instruments. Instead of being a genuine endorsement artist, Ed was more like a salesman at a Chevy dealership who drove a hot rod to work every day while leaving the less sexy company car at home in his garage.

He liked the people at Kramer, the money, and the prestige, but when it came to guitars, he still preferred his home brew. The Kramer logo may have appeared on the headstocks of several guitars Ed played during the eighties—most notably the "5150" and "1984"—but none of them were really Kramer guitars. Those two instruments were built by Ed with his own two hands at the Kramer factory in Neptune, New Jersey. The others were custom made by Kramer employees for giveaways and as backups, were double-neck models for stage performance, or were specially modified instruments featuring nonstock innovations such as a Steinberger TransTrem or Fernandes Sustainer. Though the Kramer Baretta model introduced in 1984 was clearly based on the Frankenstein, Ed never played one, and he didn't even use the model's body or neck to build his custom instruments.

Ed's endorsement deal with Kramer lasted through the eighties, but the company didn't manage to survive much longer than that. Seduced by the high life that came with success and their close proximity to rock and roll royalty, Kramer's executives began conducting business in a reckless, wasteful fashion that made the Wolf of Wall Street look like the Wonder Pets. Berardi sunk a significant portion of the company's funds into an ill-advised band management side venture, and Kramer soon fell far behind on payments to endorsement artists, contractors, suppliers, and vendors. When, in 1990, Ed's accountant noticed that Kramer had failed for some time to make royalty payments for his 5150 brand strings—which were secretly manufactured by string titan Ernie Ball—the guitarist severed his relationship with the company for good.

Edward was suddenly without a guitar endorsement deal, but before that became public knowledge, he'd already signed on with Music Man, the guitar division of Ernie Ball. Company president Sterling Ball had carefully nurtured a relationship with Ed while the guitarist was still with Kramer and went in for the kill when Ed parted ways with them. Ernie Ball/Music Man began producing electric guitars and basses during the mid-eighties, and their exceptionally high-quality instruments had already attracted endorsements from "player's players" like Steve Morse and Albert Lee. And it was Sterling who convinced Ed to offer guitarists something that they wanted all along—a genuine Edward Van Halen signature model.

Truth was, Edward's interest in manufacturing had evolved during his time with Kramer. He definitely wanted to turn a profit, but his priorities shifted to offering instruments bearing his name that would make him truly feel proud. One of Ed's longtime heroes was guitar inventor and player Les Paul, and he yearned to make a guitar that would become the modern equivalent of the beloved Gibson Les Paul.

Instead of simply providing his image and public praise to sell a guitar, as he had done with Kramer, he decided to become fully immersed in the process of designing the Music Man Edward Van Halen signature model, collaborating closely with company designer Dudley Gimpel on an entirely new instrument that looked like a cross between a Fender Telecaster and Gibson Les Paul but that also had features of his own devising.

Edward's Music Man guitar was very different from the guitars he was known for playing. Although it still featured only a solitary volume knob—with no tone control—and a licensed Floyd Rose vibrato, this new model had two custom-designed, individually voiced neck and bridge DiMarzio humbucking pickups instead of just one and a basswood body with a figured flat maple top with a colorful hand-stained finish instead of his signature stripes. The guitar first appeared on the market in 1991.

"I'm not in this for the money," Edward insisted. "If I was, I wouldn't be limiting production to a thousand guitars a year. I just want people to pick up this guitar twenty years from now and say, 'Geez, that's a nice instrument!'"

"This guitar is much more versatile than my Frankenstein because of the front pickup, but the neck is exactly the same as my original guitar. They digitally measured every inch of it so they could duplicate it—it's [already] broken in. Basically, we copied a comfortable pair of old shoes. Like the ad says, I used to endorse the guitar I played, but I designed this one. It's a whole different ball game."

Throughout his career, Edward was very secretive about his personal gear. But his attitude shifted in the opposite direction when he began working with companies to provide guitarists with the exact same gear he used.

His next move was to develop a signature guitar amplifier. Sterling Ball suggested that Ed should contact Peavey, one of the largest audio manufacturers in the world. After a meeting with the company's CEO, Hartley Peavey, they struck a deal, and Ed collaborated with lead engineer James Brown on the 5150, a two-channel, high-gain, 120-watt amplifier head. He used the prototype and his new Music Man signature guitars to record Van Halen's *For Unlawful Carnal Knowledge*, and the amp became available to the public in 1992.

At first, limiting production of his Music Man signature guitar struck Ed as a good idea, but eventually he became frustrated when guitarists told him that they couldn't find the instruments in stores. Because Peavey also built guitars and was well-equipped to meet greater production demands, Ed left Music Man, jumping ship to Peavey in 1995.

Once there, Ed quickly designed a new guitar model he named after his son, Wolfgang. It was similar to his Music Man, the main differences being that the Peavey had a sharper upper cutaway horn, an arched maple top, and a tone control. The next nine years saw Peavey introduce several different Wolfgang guitars and 5150 amps, all of which enjoyed impressive success.

Peavey was able to keep up with customer demand, but eventually Ed felt that the Mississippi-based company was not quite prestigious enough for a guitarist of his stature. It was a substantial business, but its products' reputation was built on reliability and affordability, not greatness. Now that Ed understood the ins and outs of manufacturing, he wanted to reach for the stars and make guitars and amps that would stack up to the legendary likes of the Gibson Les Paul and the Marshall Super Lead. To do that, he felt he had to move on to an equally legendary maker.

By early 2004, the time was finally right for Ed to work with Fender Musical Instruments Corporation (FMIC), the largest guitar company in the world. Much had changed at Fender since the last time he took a look at them, back in the early eighties. In 1985, CBS sold Fender to a small group of employees and investors, and over the years the quality of the company's products improved dramatically. Most recently, FMIC had acquired several other major guitar companies, including Charvel, Gretsch, and Jackson, and had restored those brands' reputations, as well. FMIC had the unique advantage of being able to offer the quality control and attention to detail Ed enjoyed during his Music Man association, along with the higher production output provided by Peavey. FMIC's worldwide distribution advantages further sweetened the deal.

The arrangement between Van Halen and FMIC was an industry first. More than just an endorsement deal, Ed was given his own product brand called EVH—and free rein to create a comprehensive line of guitars, amps, and accessories, which would be built and sold by Fender but designed under his direction and subject to his approval.

It took three years before the first EVH brand products were launched. Ed had spent almost twenty years in the manufacturing trenches, and like his first guitar experiments, he learned things the hard way—through trial and error. But now he was determined to make a classic and he wasn't going to screw it up.

"The EVH brand is like an extension of how I started," Ed explained. "Nobody made what I need or want, so I made it myself. I started my own product line because I want to do what I fuckin' want. Fender builds my stuff for me, but it's my own company. Matt Bruck [Ed's business associate and former guitar tech] and I work on the company together and we're doing our own thing. It's great to see my ideas become reality. I come up with ideas for things and have them built. If people want what we're making, that's great, but I'm mainly doing this because no one makes what I want or need to do my job. And I've got a weird job!"

The first EVH product, introduced in 2007, was a detailed replica of Edward's original Frankenstein guitar. He entrusted it to the Jackson/Charvel Custom Shop, who were now part of Fender, and luthier Chip Ellis meticulously duplicated the guitar's every scratch, dent, and unique feature, from the 1971 quarter nailed to its top to the reflectors on the back. Production was limited to only three hundred guitars, each with a cost of $25,000. They sold out almost instantly.

Ed was so impressed by Ellis's work ethic and attention to detail that he enlisted him to collaborate on an entirely redesigned Wolfgang model guitar. At the same time, Ed worked with Fender amp engineer Mike Ulrich to create a new version of the 5150 amp, which featured independent channels for clean, overdrive, and high-gain tones. The new 5150 III, which hit stores in late 2007, was EVH's first regular production model, and it remains one of their most popular amplifiers.

The introduction of the first EVH Wolfgang guitar model took considerably longer, with the instrument benefiting from extensive testing on Van Halen's 2007–08 tour. Ed refused to compromise or cut corners in its manufacture, spending nine months alone working on choosing the right pickups and more than two years perfecting everything from the volume and tone control potentiometers to the screws that held the output jack in place. The EVH Wolfgang design has also remained a mainstay of the EVH product line, with the current Wolfgang USA Edward Van Halen Signature offering the same specs as the main guitar Ed played on Van Halen's last tour in 2015.

Edward recorded only two Van Halen albums during the last twenty-two years of his life, so in many ways the EVH brand became his primary avenue of creative expression. From instruments based on his iconic creations like the Ibanez "Shark" Destroyer to inexpensive products like the Wolfgang Standard that beginners could afford but also that pros like Ed himself could use onstage, he was closely involved with everything EVH offered. Since his passing, his business associate Matt Bruck and son Wolfgang have been running the company, so Ed's vision and the high standards he set for EVH are sure to continue.

IN THE FOLLOWING INTERVIEW, EDWARD discussed the hard work and dedication behind the development of the EVH Wolfgang guitars and 5150 III amps. When, as a teenager, Ed first picked up a hammer and chisel to hack a larger cavity in his 1969 Les Paul so he could install a full-size humbucking pickup, he couldn't possibly have imagined that he would one day have his own brand of guitars and amps. But that teenager's spirit of adventure and curiosity never left him, because he never stopped searching for ways to make his instruments sound and play better.

**You have decades of experience building your own guitars, and you developed two previous signature models. However, you still spent an unusually long time developing the EVH Wolfgang guitar—more than two years. Why did the process take so long?**

I'm constantly futzing with stuff and tone chasing—closing my eyes and playing guitar and getting a feel for it. The Wolfgang was a culmination of thirty-five years of experimenting with guitars. Everything that I've destroyed, everything that I've stumbled onto, everything that I know and have experienced in my journey to get to where we are now is in this guitar. And I'm sure that there's more to come.

A guitar is a very personal extension of the person playing it. It's kind of like a racecar driver. The racing team will ask the driver, "How does that feel?" as they adjust the camshaft. You have to be emotionally and spiritually connected to your instrument. I'm very brutal on my instruments, but not all the time. I'm not to the point where I'm like Pete Townshend and smashing the shit out of it after a gig. I wouldn't do that to an instrument that is a part of me.

I'm constantly searching. The only thing that the EVH Wolfgang has in common with the Peavey Wolfgang is the body shape, and even that's changed a little bit. Everything else is different—the way the neck bolts on, the frets, the tuning pegs, the binding, the pickups, the tailpiece, the pots. The cavity is developed to let the wood breathe and age better. Even the output jack is different. We tore apart and analyzed every little thing on the EVH Wolfgang. If someone didn't make something that was good enough for us, we found someone to make it. This is the Ferrari, Audi R8, or Porsche of guitars to me. I don't need to do this for financial reasons. It's just that people have always wanted to play what I use, so I decided to give that to them.

I've worked with a lot of companies, and this actually was my last attempt, sad enough to say. When you're working with a major company, it's not that easy for them to drop everything. They can't just stop making Strats and go to work on my guitar. Working with three-piece suiters and the BS I've got to go through to get through to these people . . . I could have just stayed at home and built this guitar for myself. It's a bit different to build a one-off guitar for myself, just like when I built my black and white Boogie Bodies "Frankenstein" guitar. All of a sudden every company on the planet started copying the one-pickup,

Strat-style-with-a-whammy-bar guitar, but none of them were anything like mine. They didn't get it. They just looked at it. They didn't play it or feel it or have any idea what went into that guitar.

If you hang the Wolfgang next to any other guitar in the store, people may not even notice it. It's kind of like chicks. They might look good dressed up, but take the clothes off, bitch, and let's see what you really look like. From the basics of the guitar to painstaking aspects like the binding and everything else, we left no stone unturned. We redid everything on this guitar. That's why it took so long. Thank God that Chip [Ellis, FMIC guitar designer] stuck it out because I was driving everybody nuts.

**What was the most painstaking process about making the EVH Wolfgang?**

Developing the pickups. We spent about nine months just working on the pickups. Nine months! Chip would show up with a new batch of pickups, and all I had to do was turn the new amp on and hit one note to tell if it was good or not. Chip would be looking at me confused, but I can really tell by one note. The funniest thing about me is that I know what I like and what I want to hear and feel. To explain sound to someone is like trying to explain color or like trying to explain what something looks like to a blind person. It's a very difficult thing. Over and over I would say, "It ain't hitting me in the gut!" It was either too shrill in the high end or too muddy.

Eventually anybody will hear it once they develop a good ear. But the feel is what's really important. The tonality has so much to do with how easy it is to play. It's the harmonic overtones that make the tone like butter. It's what feels right. It's either butter or it's fucking not. It's not this "I can't believe it's not butter" bullshit! (*laughs*) It's *got* to be butter. And it's not necessarily sustain. A lot of factors come into play with sustain—the pickup placement, coil windings, magnets.

A lot of people don't realize that there is a difference between a guitar's natural, organic sustain and forcing a guitar to sustain unnaturally using something like a distortion pedal. I've never used any distortion pedals. It was always just guitar cable straight to the amp. A lot of people don't realize this until they play my guitar through one of my amps. Then they go, "Holy shit!"

Billy Corgan interviewed me once, and we were up in my studio. My rig happened to be set up and I was playing when he walked in. He nervously asked me, "Can I try it?" I handed my guitar to him, he turned it up and it was uncontrollable for him. He was going, "Where's your distortion pedal?" I said, "There isn't one." Most guitarists who walk into a store think they need one. If you have a great-sounding guitar that's a quality instrument and a good amp, and you know how to make the guitar talk, that's the key. To me, anything you put in between that deviates from the pure tone. It starts with the guitar and knowing what it should sound and feel like. I don't care what a guitar looks like. Obviously, when you're trying to sell a guitar, its looks matter, because someone's not going to buy something that looks like a piece of shit. But it doesn't bother me. Do you think Ray Charles cared what color his piano was? I pick up the guitar, close my eyes, and go, "How does it feel?"

When I first picked up the first two Wolfgang production models, they felt better than the main Wolfgang prototype that I used on the whole 2007–08 tour. This guitar is the shit! In the beginning Chip was trying to feel me out and understand those little crazy things that I spew out when trying to establish a rapport and communication. It's a real supportive thing.

**There's something to be said for the team that you guys have formed. I think one of the smartest things that you did was to take this guitar out on the road on the biggest tour of the last two years and road test it. That's a very bold move.**

It had to be done. I don't let anything out unless I've dragged it around the block, taken it out on tour, and beaten the living shit out of it. It's like a Formula One race car. You don't want to go on the track with a wheel bearing that's going to go bad. I'm doing 275 mph onstage and I don't want the wheel bearing going out! And that happened! At the same time, the painstaking effort that we took starting from scratch alleviated a lot of problems, which gave me the confidence to take it on tour. The tweaks that we did on the road were very minor because of all the preparation that we did.

**What were some of the developments that came out of the road testing?**

The toggle switch, the improved jack plate, and certain parts of the tailpiece. The nut screws. The volume pot, because when I'm playing "Cathedral" most pots freeze up when I'm doing volume swells. This goes back to my Billy Corgan example. When he played my guitar, he would leave the volume control wide open and it would feed back uncontrollably. He said, "How do you control this thing?" I'm constantly turning down the volume between any breaks or pauses when I'm playing chords. The volume control is like my steering wheel. If it doesn't turn light, smooth, and easy, and if it isn't quality, I'm fucked. I have to turn that thing up and down in an instant.

The thing about guitars nowadays is that over the years the quality of parts declined. People are slacking. It's hard to find a toggle switch that clicks into place and doesn't wear out. Floyd Rose vibratos aren't as good as they used to be. The average person walks into a store and goes, "Oh, it's a Floyd," but it's garbage that will strip in a couple of weeks. All of a sudden you've got grooves in the nut. People don't know that, but for me that's unacceptable. Good enough isn't good enough for me, period.

**Why did you spend nine months just going through pickups?**

Even though pickups may look the same, they aren't always the same. We were getting so frustrated. We went through about eighty sets of pickups. We worked with two of the biggest pickup manufacturers out there, and they busted their asses, but the Wolfgang guitar is a whole different animal. The pickups were all great, but they weren't exactly what we were looking for. They were close, but no Tiparillo. Ultimately, we ended up saying, "Why don't we try to make our own pickup?"

**Why did that work?**

I think it's because we had a lot more control. We weren't on the phone trying to tell a guy, "Hey, warm it up. I want more sustain." I'm not saying the other companies couldn't have done it. It just happened a lot quicker when we started making the pickups here.

Before we made that decision, I said, "Let's try moving the pickup around." It was one of our last attempts to make things work. Chip wanted to take the guitar back to the shop to rout out a bigger pickup cavity. I said, "Let's just take out a screwdriver and chisel and make the cavity bigger. I don't care how it looks!" I didn't want to wait until the next day.

In the end, the pickup needed to be moved only one-thirty-second of an inch. The tolerance of things on this guitar was like NASA standards. It had to be tight and it had to be quality. It's not like a Toyota Celica or something. Le Mans is probably the most important race on the planet. It's twenty-four hours—a grueling, brutal race. There's a reason why an Audi R8 won that race three years in a row [2000–2002]. Those guys did what we did with this guitar. They paid attention to every damn detail. In that same race, Cadillac put in five cars, and within two hours the transmission blew in one, another one caught on fire, and I don't know what happened to the rest. If people focused on the details, that wouldn't have happened. You can't say, "Oh, that will do." No, it won't do.

That's like how I test-drive my equipment, whatever it may be—guitar, amp, you name it. I've never mentioned this before, but this is how I crash test my equipment. When we were designing the EVH 5150 III amp, we were at my studio and had one of the later prototypes. At the end of the day before we walked out of the studio, I took a six-string bass and plugged it into the amp. I laid the bass on the ground right in front of the speaker cabinet. Mike Ulrich, the amp engineer from FMIC who we were collaborating with, looked at me like, "What are you doing?"

I laid the bass down in front of the cabinet and positioned it properly so it would vibrate at a certain harmonic frequency. We walked out into the control room and I told Mike that's how I crash test my shit. I left that amp on with the bass feeding back for a month. I kid you not. We went through three phases of that, each amounting to a month to five weeks. The amp never blew.

Then I unplugged the speaker cable to see how long the amp would last with nothing plugged into it. Actually, I think I did that by accident. I had three or four heads in the control room where I prefer to play, and I was going "Shit! The amp's on, but I don't hear any sound!" Matt noticed that the speaker cable was unplugged. If you know anything about tube amp heads, they'll start smoking and blow up when you do that. Well, this amp would not blow! We don't recommend trying that, but it's good to know that if some idiot roadie goes behind your cabinets and accidentally unplugs them from the head, the amp will not blow.

We did a similar test with the Wolfgang guitar. I plugged it into a 5150 III half stack and left it feeding back, thinking that making the wood vibrate would make it age quicker. Maybe there's some truth to that, but after three weeks, it didn't make a damn bit of difference. The paint and other details had a bigger effect on the sound. I don't even know if many people can explain or hear the difference, especially if they use some type of device between the guitar and amp. Then it's not going to matter what type of pickup you use. But these pickups will even make that stomp box sound better.

It covers the whole dynamic range from every nuance and articulation of playing. It's easy to play, and it has the sustain, harmonics, and feedback that you want. That's how I can tell just by hitting one note. If it takes too long to feed back, it's not picking up the right frequencies from the string.

**It was obviously a lot more than just finding the right midrange frequency.**

It would blow your mind how many variables are involved, and not just with the pickup but also with the reaction between the pickup and the wood, and how it is wired. That's why I prefer to bolt the pickup directly to the wood. Everything needs to be connected. It starts with your fingers, the pickups take it from there, and then it goes through the cable to the amp. When I developed my first signature model with Music Man, that was the first time that the neck humbucking pickup was totally different from the bridge humbucker. I hooked up with some pickup companies and asked them to make me a different neck pickup. That helped. This guitar is the culmination of years of trial and error. We made a lot of errors, but they led to a lot of breakthroughs.

The instrument is the connection between you and the ears of the people that allows you to express every emotion that comes out in your playing. I don't want to say I'm pissed off all the time, because even when I'm happy I'm aggressive and I beat the shit out of my guitar. It has to hold up to every rage and happy moment.

**You've been through this process several times, so you know what you like.**

I need a totally resonant body. It just makes sense to me. It's common sense. What makes an acoustic guitar sound better than others? The wood and its resonance. It's the same with an electric guitar. The pickups are only there to amplify what the wood is doing. If you're amplifying a body made out of concrete it's not going to sound very good no matter how good the pickups are. If the guitar sounds great before you plug it in, it will sound great when you plug it in. But I guess that would put a lot of stomp box companies out of business.

**It seems like you did a lot of second guessing and you didn't let your own biases and tastes get in the way of your judgment.**

We never once said, "Yeah, that will do." It has to be right because my name is on it. I don't want anyone saying that my stuff sucks. A guitar is a very personal thing. This guitar might not be for everyone, but no one can say that it's not a good instrument. The funny thing is that with everything we do, whether it's an amp or guitar, I don't even check to see how other people do it. I wouldn't be doing it myself if I liked what they were doing.

I don't sit around and think about what other people would like. I think about things that I want and need. That's where everything starts. I'm not shoving it down anyone's throat. It's just there. If you want what I use, we've made it available. The stuff that I use onstage isn't modified. The modifications that I use are built into my guitars and amps when they come off the line.

**There are so many choices out there for guitar players today, literally hundreds of different models to choose from. What is the appeal of the EVH Wolfgang for someone who is in the market for a new guitar?**

The guitar is a very personal thing. If somebody walks into a store and goes a step further than just liking the look of an instrument and takes the time to play a Wolfgang, comparing it to other guitars while keeping his eyes closed, I guarantee you he'll take home a Wolfgang. It just feels better. Every component, everything that we put into this guitar is the best that it can be. We left no stone unturned. I want the best. I don't want to have parts wear out. The people have the best that I can give to them.

I never understood why, when a kid wants to play guitar and he goes into the store to buy a beginner guitar, they're set up like shit. A kid's fingers should not be bleeding when they're learning how to play. I've set up old Harmony guitars to play well. My son plays guitar and he walked into the house playing one of my old Harmonys, saying, "This thing plays great!" If you know what you're doing, you can set up any guitar to play great. Sometimes I wonder how many kids who want to play guitar say, "Fuck this! It hurts my fingers. It's too hard." Sometimes that even applies to world-class players. I won't mention any names, but I'll hear someone playing a solo and it sounds like they are wrestling with the instrument. It's not smooth. You don't have to have the most proficient dexterity to be able to play easily. I don't want to have to fight the guitar. I want to be able to speak through it and deliver my message. I want it to work with me. The easier it is to play, the better.

I don't know if there is such a thing as perfection. But this is the best of everything that we could find with these three minds making it happen. I'm always changing, so even the *best* is a tough word to define for me. It's like having three famous singers. Which one is the best? I love Joe Cocker, Janis Joplin, and Bon Scott. Which one is better? All three are different. But the Wolfgang guitar will do all three.

**Now that the EVH brand has officially launched, what's next?**
We're just continuing to push the envelope. It's wide open for anything. For Fender, the 5150 III amp project was definitely a shot in their ass because Fender didn't have a high-gain amp like this before. But with the EVH brand, they do now.

Everything I'm involved with has to outlive me. I'm brutal on everything that I use, so if it can survive me, it can survive anything. Microphone companies actually send me mics—very high-end ribbon mics—to see if they'll survive. They know if it will hold up to me, it will hold up to anyone. I have a reputation for being very brutal with my gear. I just beat the shit out of stuff.

The 5150 III amp and Wolfgang guitar were the culmination of years and years of tearing things apart. They represent my evolution as a player. Who knows what I'll come up with for the 5150 IV? Tomorrow is a brand-new day, and my needs may change completely. I've always been a tone chaser, but right now the 5150 III and Wolfgang are the tools I need to do my job. The reason why I've always been so flexible with my own shit is because no one else makes what I need. Why not make it myself? That's what I've done, and this is the latest version.

**It's very generous for you to share your knowledge with other guitarists and musicians. After all, you could have just turned this into a one-off custom guitar and amp for yourself.**

That is the key. We're not just shipping stuff out for the almighty buck. The Wolfgang had better outlive me and last forever. My name and my son's name is on it. It's not a Dixie Cup that you use once and throw away. It's not a fad. It's my thirty-five to forty years of knowledge of what makes a sweet, sexy, toney, quality, indestructible instrument. I'm very proud of it. And I'm proud to have this team that has stuck with me through all of this.

Initially, I was very worried about working with Fender because of all the bullshit you can go through with a huge company. But in a great way, they proved me wrong. They rose to every occasion and gave me the freedom to create and bring my vision to fruition. Fender is my home. It took me a long time to get here, but it's a good marriage.

# MUSICAL INTERLUDE

*The SoCal Guitar Triangle:* ***Edward, Les, and Leo***

---

When journalists asked Eddie who his biggest influence was, he often puzzled them by responding with a name from the distant past: Les Paul. But anyone who knows about guitar history understands exactly why he would cite Lester William Polsfuss, the imaginative American pop guitarist, luthier, inventor, and inspiration for the legendary Gibson Les Paul solid body guitar. Acknowledged virtuoso, legendary technical innovator, and all-around sunny presence, Les was the smiling Van Halen of the 1950s.

Despite their age difference—Paul was born in 1915, Van Halen in 1955—the two had become extremely close friends before Les passed away in 2009. Eddie often chuckled at the memory of Les calling him at three a.m. to discuss some esoteric guitar-related concept, or else simply to bullshit. He also recalled with pride how, at the end of those late-night chats, Les often signed off by saying, "There's only been three great electric guitar makers: me, you, and Leo [Fender]."

It was an unimaginably huge compliment—one that Eddie cherished perhaps above all others. But Paul, Fender, and Van Halen had at least one other thing in common: all were part of an unofficial fraternity of guitar innovators who lived, worked, and congregated—albeit at different times—within thirty miles of each other in Southern California. Also from that same area were Adolph Rickenbacker, whose distinctive guitars were played by the likes of the Beatles, John Fogerty, and Tom Petty, and Paul A. Bigsby, best known for developing the iconic vibrato bars used by companies like Gretsch and Gibson and for designing one of the earliest Spanish solid body electric guitars.

This geographical phenomenon, however, goes back even further, to the 1920s, when two young guitar-playing brothers,

George and Alton Beauchamp (pronounced "Bee-chum"), left their home in rural Texas for booming Hollywood, then solidifying its status as the film capital of the world and glamorous entertainment hot spot. The duo quickly found steady work playing parties and nightclubs, but when performing at any venues larger than a small club, they had to deal with a problem that plagued many guitarists of that age: the need for greater volume. Without guitar amplification—which did not yet exist—George and Alton were often drowned out when playing with other musicians or even by the inevitable noise made by audiences.

Frustrated, George decided to do something about it. In the early 1930s, he not only invented the first fully functional guitar pickup but also designed the world's first successful commercially produced electric guitar—nicknamed the "Frying Pan" because of the resemblance of the lap steel guitar's round, metallic body and long neck to the kitchen tool.

Anxious to mass produce his invention, Beauchamp enlisted his friend Adolph Rickenbacker, an engineer and manufacturer with a fascination for electrifying musical instruments, to help. Adolph became president and George secretary-treasurer of their new Electro String Instrument Corporation, and they agreed to call their "Frying Pan" the Rickenbacker Model A-22, because *Rickenbacker* was easier to pronounce than *Beauchamp*.

Production of this early electric guitar began in 1932, in a small rented shop at 6071 South Western Avenue in Los Angeles, which was approximately just twenty miles from Eddie Van Halen's childhood home in Pasadena, where the Frankenstrat was born. Although the initial response to Beauchamp's instrument was hardly promising—Electro String sold only twenty-eight guitars during its first year in business—by 1935, the number of sales had increased to a total of 1,288.

The Model A-22 was the Big Bang of the electric guitar, and soon several other companies jumped into the fray, but because of the double whammy of the Great Depression and World War II, further development of the electric six-string slowed to a crawl.

Ten years later, at least one guitarist was dissatisfied with the sound of the electric guitars manufactured by companies like Gibson, Vega, and Electro String. Guitarist Les Paul, working in a garage in Hollywood only ten miles from the Rickenbacker plant, made it his personal crusade to radically improve the sound and design of amplified guitars. Most manufacturers favored placing pickups on the hollow body archtop guitars favored by jazz musicians, but at high volume levels, they were prone to feedback—the "howling" sound that results when the pickups interact with the amplifier's speakers. So, Les decided to push forward with the concept he'd been exploring for almost a decade—an electric Spanish guitar with a partially or completely solid body.

Born in Waukesha, Wisconsin, in 1915, by age thirteen Paul was performing semiprofessionally as a singer and guitarist. After making a name for himself in Chicago and New York with his jazzy Les Paul Trio, he and the band relocated to Los Angeles, and Les settled in a house at 1514 North Curson Avenue, in West Hollywood, just around the corner from a section of Sunset Boulevard known today as "Guitar Row."

While in LA, he was hired to back Bing Crosby, one of the first true pop stars of the modern era. Bing loved the sound of the guitar, and the Les Paul Trio's first recording with Crosby, "It's Been a Long, Long Time," became a number one single for Decca Records in 1945.

From there, Les quickly established himself as one of America's most popular guitarists through frequent radio appearances, live performances, and recordings with his own three-piece group. Though he enjoyed being in the spotlight, at heart he was more of a guitar nerd and inventor than a performer. "Looking back over my life," Les once said, "I think I probably spent a little more time tinkering with electronics than I did playing music."

In addition to building early solid body guitar prototypes on Curson Avenue, it was also where he began conducting some of the earliest-known experiments with multitrack recording and slapback echo. Les would sometimes play host to two other tinkerers, Leo Fender and Paul A. Bigsby, who shared his obsession with refining the electric guitar. But unlike him, they weren't famous guitarists, just humble instrument makers from Fullerton and Downey, respectively, located about forty-five minutes to an hour's drive from Hollywood.

Fender was a quiet, bespectacled man who, in 1946, transformed his radio repair business into the tiny Fender Electric Instrument Company, which manufactured lap steel guitars and amplifiers. Bigsby, a far wilder figure who was once a motorcycle racing champion, built custom pedal steel guitars for western swing instrumental stars like Speedy West and Noel Boggs.

Bigsby, Fender, and Les enjoyed "sharing our likes and dislikes in life," Les recalled. "We'd sit in the backyard on the patio by the fire for hours and discuss sound."

All three men had been working separately on creating a solid body electric guitar, and in the late 1940s and early 1950s, each came up with his own unique version, all of which would change the sound of rock and pop music for years to come.

Les Paul's solid body, which he called "the Log," served as an inspiration for the iconic Gibson Les Paul, first issued in 1952. Leo Fender went on to develop the first mass-produced solid bodies, the Esquire and Telecaster (originally named the Broadcaster) in 1950, followed by the Stratocaster in 1954. And Paul Bigsby designed custom solid body electric guitars for great country musicians like Merle Travis (built in 1948) and Grady Martin. Perhaps more significantly, he also devised the Bigsby vibrato tailpiece, which later inspired Fender to engineer his own improved version introduced on the Stratocaster.

Anyone who knows Ed's guitars is of course familiar with the foregoing guitar pioneers, as all had an incalculable impact on Ed's designs. As Ed told Les when they were interviewed together by *Guitar World* magazine in 1986, "With my guitars, I guess I'm trying to bring together what you and Leo did. There are things I've always liked about Gibsons and things I've always liked about Fenders, but neither one did everything that I wanted, so I've created a combination of the two. My guitar is essentially a Strat body with Gibson humbucking pickups."

Ed further acknowledged that the shape of his 1991 Music Man signature model guitar was a mashup of a Gibson Les Paul and a Fender Telecaster.

Although it isn't shocking that Eddie would have been influenced by Rickenbacker, Paul, Fender, et al.—most electric guitar makers are, in one way or another—there's also that geographical quirk to consider: What are the odds that Van Halen, in the 1970s, would live within thirty miles of where the electric guitar was invented in the 1920s and where, in the 1940s, his two favorite guitar models were conceived?

One thing is for sure, as Les confirmed, Ed deserves a seat at the table with these giant visionaries of the electric guitar. And if there was any doubt about the lasting significance of Van Halen's guitar innovations, in 2011 the Smithsonian National Museum of American History in Washington, DC, came knocking on Ed's door to ask if they could add his Frankenstrat to its hallowed collection. Eddie did not want to part with the original, but, recognizing the great honor the request represented, handed over the "Frank 2," an exact duplicate made by master guitar builder Chip Ellis at Fender and played by Ed during Van Halen's 2007–08 North American tour.

Smithsonian director Brent D. Glass said at the time, "The museum collects objects that are multidimensional, and this guitar reflects innovation, talent, and influence." Ed would no doubt agree with that assessment, though in his earthy, self-deprecating fashion would add that it was the product of "a whole lotta dickin' around."

llll

# 12

# CAN'T GET
# THIS STUFF NO MORE

❖

*Edward Van Halen is excited to take an extended victory lap with all the people who made his band legendary—his brother, Michael Anthony, David Lee Roth, Sammy Hagar, and Gary Cherone. But in the end, he could not outrun his own mortality.*

---

*"* Those truly magical fingers opened
a door to a new kind of playing.*"*

---

LTHOUGH HE WAS pushing sixty years old, slowing down was the last thing on Ed Van Halen's mind. In interviews conducted before Van Halen's 2015 tour, he said that he hoped to record another album of new material and was looking forward to more tours in the years ahead. At the same time, he expressed the caveat that he was not the sole arbiter of Van Halen's future and that the other three members of the band had to agree about what they would do going forward.

After the 2015 tour ended in October, the immediate plan was to take an extended break, just as the band had done after its 2007–08 and 2012–13 tours. With his bank account generously replenished after three successful tours, David Lee Roth vanished in Tokyo. Wolfgang Van Halen continued to work on his solo album, and Ed and Alex were content to relax and enjoy some private time with their families.

For most of 2016 and 2017, Ed stayed out of public view, spending quality time with his wife, Janie. He kept up a healthy exercise regimen, rode motorcycles, and occasionally played golf with his good friend, actor-comedian George Lopez. With no tour or new album to promote, Ed's name was absent from music publications and online outlets. But he did consent to a handful of interviews with guitar and musician magazines in Europe to promote his EVH brand there, as well as a brief question and answer session with *Car and Driver* magazine to discuss his passion for exotic supercars and track racing. Ed also kept busy working on a handful of new product projects with EVH, including the limited-edition Wolfgang USA Tour Relic Replica and EVH Striped Series 5150 guitars, and the expansion of the 5150 III amp line.

In late 2017, Ed's relatively idyllic life was upended by an aggressive recurrence of his cancer. Unbeknownst to the public, he began traveling regularly to Germany to receive a noninvasive radiotherapy treatment that wasn't approved for use in the United States.

At the time Ed was first diagnosed with cancer in the early 2000s, he was basically on his own after his separation from his first wife, Valerie. But this time around he had a much stronger support base, thanks to Janie and Wolfgang, better equipped to deal with the situation this time around as an adult. In 2008 Janie had played a crucial role in helping Ed overcome his addictions, including his alcoholism, but now the pair faced the even bigger challenge of battling cancer.

"At the end of 2017, [my dad] was diagnosed with stage-four lung cancer," Wolfgang told Howard Stern in November 2020.[21] "The doctors were like, 'You have six weeks.' And then he went to Germany. Whatever the fuck they do over there, it's amazing, because I got three more years with him."

Ed's cancer and treatments were a closely guarded secret kept from all but his family and most devoted friends. Interestingly, in May 2018— six months after receiving his dire prognosis—Ed, in an interview with the authors of this book, revealed that preparations were being made for a 2019 Van Halen reunion tour with all four members of the band's original lineup: Edward and Alex Van Halen, David Lee Roth, and Michael Anthony. It was clear that after three decades, he was finally ready to put past grievances behind him and give Van Halen's fans what so many of them wanted most. The plan was for the tour to be held in stadiums across the country, with supporting acts including heavy hitters like Metallica and the Foo Fighters.

In his interview with Howard Stern, Wolfgang confirmed that Ed did hope to have the reunion tour, adding that he eventually decided that all three of the singers he worked with in Van Halen would appear. "After [my dad] was okay with that arrangement [reuniting with Michael Anthony], it was like, 'Fuck, then let's get Dave and Hagar and even Cherone. Let's do a giant, awesome thing.' We talked to [Van Halen manager] Irving Azoff about it and how cool it would be. Irving got it ready and reached out to Mike . . . but by that time Dad wasn't able to."

In a 2019 interview with SiriusXM Radio host Eddie Trunk, Anthony confirmed that Azoff had discussed the tour with him.[22] "I spoke with [Azoff] last October [2018]," he said. "That's when I first heard from him. He asked if I would be interested in any kind of a reunion, and I said, 'Yeah. I'd be interested to hear what you guys have going on.' I never got a call back. For whatever reason they never got in touch with me about any kind of a contract or meeting. The next thing I knew, the plug got pulled on it."

"We had lots of stops and starts," Azoff told *Pollstar* magazine, "but there was every intention of doing a summer stadium tour [in 2019]. As the cancer moved around, [Eddie] was unable to do it. There is no doubt in my mind that it would have been massive."[23]

Although Ed's condition prevented the tour from taking place as scheduled, hope remained that he would recover and it would still happen. In fact, soon he felt well enough to start talking to the press again. He conducted a brief interview for the February 2019 issue of *Golf* magazine, answering a few questions before cutting the interview short, saying, "I gotta go. There's a coyote in my backyard. Big fucker."

It appears these are the last words the public would hear from him. Bizarre? Absolutely, yet somehow appropriate coming from a man who had spent his entire life as an artist who confounded people and their expectations of him.

In March 2019, Ed agreed to do a detailed interview with *Guitar World* about the recording of the *Van Halen II* album. He also scheduled a trip to New York City to attend the April 1 preview of a major exhibit at the New York Metropolitan Museum of Art: *Play It Loud: Instruments of Rock & Roll*, which included among its displays of iconic rock gear Ed's original Frankenstein guitar and a re-creation of his 1978 touring rig. Unfortunately, both plans were canceled abruptly, without explanation.

Turns out that the explanation was that Ed had had a motorcycle accident. "Things started getting really bad at the beginning of 2019," Wolfgang told Stern. "[My father] had the accident, and he had a brain tumor. We took care of it. He got this crazy procedure, and he was okay. But as time went on, shit kept stacking up and stacking up. It just never let up."

Apparently, the brain tumor was discovered on the X-rays for internal injuries Ed underwent following the accident. (Ironically, "motorcycle" and "accident" were two of the first words Ed learned to say in English after he and his family arrived in the United States from Holland.) His cancer had spread far more than was previously known, and from that point on Ed decided to spend his precious remaining time with his family and friends. Wolfgang delayed the release of his first album and its supporting tour so he could spend as much time as possible with his dad.

Van Halen fans were mostly in the dark about Ed's declining health, although a few reports about his cancer treatments appeared in media outlets like TMZ in late 2019. He was rarely seen in public, but those who did see him often noted that he looked healthy and happy. On October 21 he and his son attended a Tool concert at the Staples Center in Los Angeles, and both were amused when a Tool fan, who did not recognize Ed, asked the guitarist to take a picture—not a picture with Ed, but a picture of himself, with the stage in the background.

Rumors of the Van Halen reunion tour eventually reached the public, but before fans could get their hopes up, David Lee Roth pretty much crushed the dream when, in July 2020, he told the *New York Times*, "I don't know that Eddie is ever really going to rally for the rigors of the road again . . . he's down now for enough time that I don't know that he's going to be coming back out on the road. You want to hear the classics? You're talking to him."

In so many words, Roth confirmed the worst fears of everyone who loved Eddie: He wasn't doing well. It was unlikely he'd recover. Roth also admitted something that every member of the band knew but few acknowledged: without Eddie Van Halen, there is no Van Halen.

Ed appeared to accept that his time was nearly over. Perhaps the greatest evidence of this is that he resolved his differences with Sammy Hagar. "Eddie and I had our problems for so many years," Hagar told podcaster Kyle Meredith.[24] "[We] reconnected right before Covid. Our texts and conversations were plain and simple: 'Hey, man, how are you doing?' He started opening up to me about how sick he was. 'Dude, I just had this tumor on the side of my neck.' I was just always checking on him to see how he was doing. We were trying to be friends and let each other know that we were okay and there for each other."

In early October 2020 Ed was admitted to Saint John's Health Center in Santa Monica, and on October 6 he passed away, with Janie, Valerie, Wolfgang, and Alex by his side. After his long, courageous battle, Ed finally succumbed to the cancer that riddled his body. He was only sixty-five years old. He had often remarked that he didn't want to die at sixty-six like his father, but sadly he didn't survive even that long.

Wolfgang announced the terrible news on Twitter: "I can't believe I'm having to write this, but my father, Edward Lodewijk Van Halen, has lost his long and arduous battle with cancer this morning. He was the best father I could ever ask for. Every moment I've shared with him on, and off stage was a gift. My heart is broken, and I don't think I'll ever fully recover from this loss. I love you so much, Pop."

Janie Van Halen expressed her sorrow on Twitter the following day: "My husband, my love, my Peep. My heart and soul have been shattered into a million pieces. I never knew it was possible to cry so many tears or feel such incredible sadness. Our journey together has not always been an easy one, but in the end and always we have a connection and love that will always be. Saying goodbye is the hardest thing I have ever had to do, so instead I say so long."

Tributes soon flooded in from every corner of the music world, including dozens from his guitar-playing peers, who appreciated him best. "He was the real deal," said Led Zeppelin's Jimmy Page. "He pioneered a dazzling technique on guitar with taste and panache that I felt always placed him above his imitators."

Ed's good friend Brian May wrote, "What a talent. What a legacy. Probably the most original and dazzling rock guitarist in history. Those truly magical fingers opened a door to a new kind of playing."

Pete Townshend expressed similar sentiments to *Rolling Stone* magazine: "He was not just an innovative and stylish player with great taste, he was also a laidback virtuoso showman who just blew us all away every time. Every shredder today has lost their master teacher and guide."[25]

"Eddie was a guitar wonder, his playing pure wizardry," wrote AC/DC's Angus Young. "To the world of music, he was a special gift."

New generations of guitar players born after 1978, when Van Halen had released their debut album, might not fully comprehend just how revolutionary Edward's playing actually was because his licks, techniques, and gear innovations have all become common standards of the rock guitarist's repertoire. Although many guitarists have emerged over the years who could play faster or who were more technically advanced, none have resonated with the masses the way Eddie did. He wrote songs filled with joy and excitement. He made his virtuoso displays of musicianship fun instead of intellectual. He was truly one of a kind, a player that comes along only once in a generation.

Edward Van Halen the man, the guitarist, is no longer with us, but his immense contributions to music will live on long after most pop stars of his generation have been forgotten. To fellow guitarists, he will always be a legend. In the larger music world, he will always be a giant.

# THANK YOU

F
IRST AND FOREMOST, the authors would like to thank the late, great Edward Van Halen for the time, energy, and enthusiasm he bestowed upon us over the last three decades. The idea behind this book was to provide his words and ideas with the proper historical context, and it is our sincerest wish that we have accomplished that goal.

We would also like to thank (alphabetically) Michael Anthony, Gary Cherone, Ray Danniels, Chip Ellis, Tony Iommi, Steve Lukather, Steve Vai, and Wolfgang Van Halen for their candid insights, which punctuate this book. Their reflections on Ed as an artist and human being significantly elevate the narrative. We would also like to extend our appreciation to Rob Hoffman, Steve Karas, and Bradley Starks for their aid in arranging many of the above interviews.

While most of the material in this book comes from our hours of conversations with Eddie, interviews conducted by other journalists supplement the story. Noted music writer and Van Halen authority Steven Rosen generously allowed us to use quotes he had gathered during the time period covered in Chapter 4. We also dipped into his archives for some of the material used in other chapters, all of which has been cited. We would also like to thank Vic Garbarini, whose remarkable interview with Edward in the March 1998 issue of *Guitar World* provided much of the backbone for the dialogue in Chapter 8. All of the material was given to us with the express permission of the writers, and for that we are grateful.

We would like to thank both Matt Bruck and Janie Van Halen, who often arranged and managed our interviews with Ed. While they did not contribute directly to this book, much of it would not have been possible without their assistance.

Brad Tolinski would like to express his gratitude to Harold Steinblatt for his counsel, and to Tom Beaujour and Richard Bienstock, authors of the magnificent *Nothin' but a Good Time: The Uncensored History of the '80s Hard Rock Explosion* (St. Martin's), for sharing their thoughts and resources. He would also like to give a shout-out to the former publisher of *Guitar World* magazine, Greg DiBenedetto, who often accompanied him to 5150 and contributed to his conversations with Van Halen.

Though they are often overlooked, we'd like to salute the photographers who provided some of the stunning images in these pages, particularly Ross Halfin, who allowed us to use his iconic image of Ed on the cover of this book, and Kevin Scanlon, whose 2013 shoot for *Guitar Aficionado* magazine furnished us with spectacular images of Ed and his guitar collection. Gratitude also goes out to Larry DiMarzio, Mark Weiss, and Kevin Estrada for their invaluable historic shots of Van Halen.

We also would like to acknowledge *Guitar World*, *Guitar Player*, and *Guitar Aficionado* magazines, places both of us writers considered home for many years. It was through these publications that we became acquainted with Van Halen.

Finally, the authors would like to extend our appreciation to our editor, Ben Schafer, for his excitement and commitment to *Eruption: Conversations with Eddie Van Halen*, and to our literary agent, David Dunton at Harvey Klinger, for his dedication.

Thank you, one and all, for runnin' with us devils.

—BRAD TOLINSKI & CHRIS GILL

# NOTES

1. Craig Marks and Rob Tannenbaum, *I Want My MTV: The Uncensored Story of the Music Video Revolution* (Boston: Dutton, 2011).

2. VHND, "Van Halen's Early Days at Gazzarri's," Van Halen News Desk, April 11, 2014, https://www.vhnd.com/2014/04/11/van-halens-early-days-at-gazzarris/.

3. Neil Zlowzower, *Eddie Van Halen* (San Francisco: Chronicle Books, 2012).

4. Ted Templeman as told to Greg Renoff, *Ted Templeman: A Platinum Producer's Life in Music* (Toronto, Ontario: ECW Press, 2021).

5. Noel Monk and Joe Layden, *Runnin' with the Devil: A Backstage Pass to the Wild Times, Loud Rock, and the Down and Dirty Truth Behind the Making of Van Halen* (New York: Dey Street Books, 2017).

6. Jas Obrecht, *Guitar Player*, December 1982.

7. MDuffy, "Ask Eddie: Have You Played with Allan Holdsworth?" EVH, September 13, 2013, https://blog.evhgear.com/2013/09/ask-eddie-have-you-played-with-allan-holdsworth/.

8. Justin Beckner, "Steve Vai Explains Why He Left Zappa's Band, Recalls How Frank Reacted to Eddie Van Halen," UltimateGuitar.com, June 3, 2020, https://www.ultimate-guitar.com/news/interviews/steve_vai_explains_why_he_left_zappas_band_recalls_how_frank_reacted_to_eddie_van_halen.html.

9. David Lee Roth, *Crazy from the Heat* (Westport, CT: Hyperion, 1997).

10. Ted Templeman as told to Greg Renoff, *Ted Templeman: A Platinum Producer's Life in Music* (Toronto, Ontario: ECW Press, 2020).

11. Charles M. Young, "The Oddest Couple: Can It Last?" *Musician*, June 1984.

12. Steven Hyden, "Set List with Sammy Hagar," *A.V. Club*, April 5, 2011.

13. Roy Trakin Entertainment News Wire, "Difficult Years Give 'Balance' to Van Halen's Newest Efforts," *Spokesman Review* (Spokane, WA), January 24, 1995, https://www.spokesman.com/stories/1995/jan/24/difficult-years-give-balance-to-van-halens-newest/.

14. David Wild, "Eddie Van Halen: Balancing Act," *Rolling Stone*, April 6, 1995.

15. David Huff, "Ain't Talkin' 'Bout Love," *Guitar World*, April 1997.

16. Steven Rosen, "Eruptions," *Guitar World*, December 1996.

17. Sammy Hagar, *RED: My Uncensored Life in Rock* (New York: It Books, 2011).

18. Sammy Hagar, interview by Sally Steele, Vegas Rocks! TV, June 4, 2012, http://vegasrockstv.com/?p=77.

19. Valerie Bertinelli, *Losing It: And Gaining My Life Back One Pound at a Time* (New York: Atria Books, 2008).

20. Dennis Berardi, interview by Dave Nardelli and Mike Wolverton, Vintage Kramer, June 2003, http://www.vintagekramer.com/sounds/Berardi4.mp3.

21. "Wolfgang Van Halen Speaks Out for First Time After Death of His Father, Rock Legend Eddie Van Halen," *Howard Stern Show*, SiriusXM Radio, November 16, 2020, https://www.howardstern.com/news/2020/11/16/wolfgang-van-halen-speaks-out-for-first-time-after-death-of-his-father-rock-legend-eddie-van-halen/.

22. "Michael Anthony on Van Halen," *TrunkNation*, SiriusXM Radio, June 19, 2019, https://music.mxdwn.com/2019/06/21/news/michael-anthony-confirms-plug-got-pulled-on-plans-for-van-halen-reunion-tour/.

23. Ray Waddell, "Irving Azoff on Eddie Van Halen: 'Unqualified Genius, Loving Soul,'" *Pollstar*, October 8, 2020, https://www.pollstar.com/article/irving-azoff-on-eddie-van-halen-unqualified-genius-loving-soul-146599.

24. Spencer Kaufman, "Sammy Hagar: I Would Cancel My Own Show for an Eddie Van Halen Tribute," *Kyle Meredith With* (podcast), Consequence Podcast Network, February 24, 2021, https://consequence.net/2021/02/sammy-hagar-eddie-van-halen-tribute-show-discusses-final-texts/.

25. Angie Martoccio, "Pete Townshend Honors Eddie Van Halen: 'I Was Hoping He Might Be President One Day,'" *Rolling Stone*, October 6, 2020, https://www.rollingstone.com/music/music-news/pete-townshend-eddie-van-halen-tribute-1071811/.

# INDEX